Juliet Ash is Tutor in Dress/Textiles Design History at the Royal College of Art. She is co-editor with Elizabeth Wilson of *Chic Thrills: A Fashion Reader* and has written a number of articles on the history and theory of dress.

DRESS BEHIND BARS
Prison Clothing as Criminality

Juliet Ash

I.B. TAURIS

LONDON · NEW YORK

Published in 2010 by I.B.Tauris & Co Ltd
6 Salem Road, London W2 4BU
175 Fifth Avenue, New York NY 10010
www.ibtauris.com

Distributed in the United States and Canada Exclusively by Palgrave Macmillan
175 Fifth Avenue, New York NY 10010

ISBN: 978 1 85043 893 9 (HB)
       978 1 85043 894 6 (PB)

A full CIP record for this book is available from the British Library
A full CIP record is available from the Library of Congress

Library of Congress Catalog Card Number: available

FSC
Mixed Sources
Product group from well-managed
forests and other controlled sources
Cert no. SGS-COC-2953
www.fsc.org
© 1996 Forest Stewardship Council

Printed and bound in Great Britain by
CPI Antony Rowe, Chippenham, Wiltshire

For Annie and Jesse

contents

figures

acknowledgements

The Arts and Humanities Research Leave Scheme that provided a matching term to study leave granted by the Royal College of Art supported the writing of this book. I would like to thank the academic team at Oslo University College, Norway, for inviting me to present this research at a conference entitled, 'Dressing Rooms: Current Perspectives on Fashion and Textiles' and Liudmila Aliabieva for commissioning an article based on my research for *Russian Fashion Theory Journal*, 'Dress behind Bars: Consumption as Redemption', Issue 7, Spring 2008, pp. 35–50. Thanks are also due to Fashion and Textiles and History of Design MA and research students at the Royal College of Art who contributed insightfully to aspects of the research when it was introduced into my teaching.

I am indebted to Phillipa Brewster for believing in this project from the start and providing support and professional editorial suggestions. I would also like to thank those who have read drafts, helped with historical detail and checked various elements of the book, particularly Elizabeth Wilson, Nigel Fountain, Charlotte Brunsdon and Hermione Harris. This book would not have been possible without criminological discussions with Jock Young in particular and Jayne Moonee, John Lea, Roger Matthews and Larry Sullivan; historical discussions with Juliet Gardiner, Sheila Rowbotham and Ros Baxandall; and general discussions with Dave Morley, Ellana Dallas, Melanie McFadyean, Michelle Ryan, Yve Lomax and Pennina Barnett.

Nor would the research have been possible without the detailed experiences of prisoners and ex-prisoners in interview and e-mail correspondence, particularly Erwin James and Ronan Bennett and men and women in British prisons in the 1970s and 2000s and in American prisons in the 2000s.

I am eternally grateful to Bev Baker, Curator at the Galleries of Justice photographic and prison clothing archives in Nottingham who was painstakingly knowledgeable and patient with research that spanned a number of years. I am also grateful to curators and individuals who provided access to information about prisoners' clothing internationally. These include the library staff at the Royal College of Art and John Jay College of Criminal Justice at City University New York, Dave Brotherton, Thomas McCarthy, Bruce Olsen, Eileen McHugh, Michelle Brown, Marc Fisher, Mick Carter, Kim Simpson, Lola Chatterji, Lucila Fernandez, Catherine Prade, Jill Heine, Jennifer Wolfenden, Anja Cronberg, Maggie Wykes, Keith Hayward, Carol Tulloch, Hugh Brody, Joseph Piasek, Sumi Tonooka.

For cultural, history of design and dress ideas I would like to thank colleagues at the Royal College of Art and the Victoria and Albert Museum, numerous dress historians, fashion designers, friends and acquaintances who sent me information about prison clothing historically and contemporaneously throughout the duration of the project.

I would like to thank my father, Bill, for inspiring this project with his experiences of prisoner of war camp in the Second World War and his wife Ranjana for her interest in the project. I was inspired by the writing and politics of my partner David Widgery and memories of living through the trials and tribulations of his writing books spurred me on when I despaired. Above all I want to thank my daughter and son, Annie and Jesse, without whose humour and insightful encouragement this book would never have been completed.

introduction:
unravelling prison clothing

When you are in the nick you become something of a monk...You live the best you can and wear very uncomfortable cloths [*sic.*] which are very corse [*sic.*].

Frank Norman, *Bang to Rights: An Account of Prison Life* (London, 1958)

The guard handed me a dress...It looked like a light blue sack made of cotton. It was tight under the arms but too large everywhere else...It had obviously had previous incarnations and owners...and had obviously seen much misery.

Sunny Jacobs, *Stolen Time* (London, 2007)

A man and a woman in different times and countries – England and America – voice concerns about clothing as punishment. This book is about what it has been like during the past two hundred years to experience prison dress and how the institution of prison has changed.

I am a former prison teacher, prison visitor and latterly an academic researcher. Through my acquaintance with prisons, archives, ex-prisoners, staff and prison clothing providers, this book travels inside and outside the walls, balancing the experience of prison clothing inside and the vision of the clothed inmate from the outside. It weaves the inmate's awareness of the cloth and cut of garments with the history and politics of changes in prison conditions: to study dress as punishment must address how clothing is worn.

visible/invisible criminality

One day in 1972 I walked from outside inside, through the prison gate from the winter street wrapped in the raiment of the times: flared jeans, tight top, dishevelled bohemianism, collective living and alternative politics. Hatches opened, eyes prodded and hands searched. I was inside. A female prison officer in military black jacket, straight skirt, sensible shoes and jangling keys marched me to a bare classroom. I was a literacy teacher at a women's jail in London and I was protected by my garb.

Two girls of my age, Jackie and Sandy, strutted into the room in dungarees, denim jackets and plimsolls. Two older women, Eva and Isabelle, sat in long cardigans and wrinkled dresses. Yvonne, a black British girl in tight jeans and sloppy jumper walked in. Diane, Phyllis and Mary came in hitching up over-sized straight skirts and loose-fitting tunic tops. The prison officer checked us, left the room and locked us in.

By the 1970s women did not wear prison uniforms, but restricted clothing divided inside from outside. And in restriction there was difference. Some wore their dungarees with bravado. Others revealed suffering from under their sleeves: gashes and cuts, flesh growing over inserted pins in their arms. They were Hungarian refugees, young prostitutes, mothers who had shoplifted and had babies in the maternity wing. Crimes were petty, induced by poverty, marked out by a system and labelled by indifference, class and neglect. In a play performed by women for outsiders, personal stories were acted out. Women sang 'The Streets of London' as they enacted childhoods with abuse and tears in front of officials dressed in authority suits and chewing cucumber sandwiches. Only Jackie, Sandy and Yvonne really performed, whereas others remained locked up in long cardigans and wrinkled dresses criminalised, forgotten and invisible to the world.

Outside had entered in, and inside occupied me until I started work on this project.

A year later, in 1973, I was in the north of England teaching current affairs to top security male prisoners. An officious prison officer in immaculate military style clothing met me. He talked conspiratorially of the control of inmates. His jangling keys punctuated my classes from the back of the room. His eyes surveilled me and the content of my classes as they did the men. In his eyes I was subversive in my unprofessional dress.

Gender and dress did indeed separate the men and myself. In 1973 men still wore prison uniforms. My students – Bob, John and Doug – conformed in blue-and-white-striped prison shirts roughly made of coarse fabric. Younger men, Taffy, Billy and Danny wore loose functional workwear, dark blue dungarees and grey utility jackets. Some wore their prison shirts smarter than others, asked questions and gave opinions. Others – Michael, Andrew and Ron – looked grey and shifted in tight clothing or lost themselves in overalls that slipped from the shoulder.

Formal political and cultural debates between outside groups and inmates were a weekly occurrence. Articulate students communicated on their own terms with the outside world. They dressed for the occasion in clean and ironed prison clothing, while the keys kept us in check. Passion, politics and knowledge – born of doing time – informed these debates, not witnessed in discussions outside.

But others remained locked away, uncomfortably hidden from the eyes of the world. Their sartorial histories, like those of women prisoners such as Mary, are difficult to unravel. For this is an uncharted area of study.

Why over the centuries was there a gendered disparity between prison clothing rules? What sort of a solution to criminality was it to force people to 'wear weird clothes'[1] or 'degrade us and strip us of our identity'[2]? Why, when and how did prisoners' uniforms change? How do inmates see themselves or humanise embodiments of punishment?

This book is about the way perception and knowledge of 'self' have been formed and concealed in prison garb as, in historical time, they travel through impenetrable walls and wires.

At times we have been allowed glimpses of images of clothed inmates at politically expedient moments. But the pages of the newspaper are turned, the film ends, the book is closed and criminals are returned to oblivion, labelled and guilty. Clothes are used as signifiers of the power of the penal establishment to bodily punish miscreants. Prison dress is defined by the power of political systems that dominate networks of criminal justice and stigmatise in order to reduce inmates to interchangeable identities. They are 'othered' in their culpability and excluded from society by clothing that regulates and incarnates the punishment of the wearer.

There are a minority who infringe moral codes in any society. But there have always been a multitude of prisoners who are there for largely socio-economic reasons. That is not, however, a distinction that prison systems make. Clothing provision is, thus, inextricably part of levelling all to the status of common criminality, both as self-knowledge and in the eyes of the world. Thus, the word 'as' in the subtitle of this book is not used lightly.

Penal institutions, under the authority of particular States, use dress strategically to diminish the imprisoned. Prison clothing takes many forms, whether as uniforms or in the neglect of the maintenance and distribution of clothing. Yet, while clothing is an embodiment of punishment, it cannot take away either personal histories or the small signs of resistance to institutional labelling. This book traces the history of visible sartorial punishment and the previously invisible political and cultural collective and individual resistance to it.

mythologies

There are a lot of half-truths and myths about prison clothing. The book attempts to uncover, as far as is possible, what prison clothing was really like. Just how was clothing transformed into this embodiment of punishment – the iconic prison uniform? Did broad arrow clothing actually exist? Why are stripes redolent of prison dress? How did the material changes in prison clothing converge with historical and political shifts in crime control? How did clothing as the embodiment of crime react to waves of reform and right-wing backlashes? Why did iconic prison uniforms, in the form of the orange jumpsuit, return between 2001 and the end of 2008?

There isn't a chronological progression towards more relaxed forms of dress. Prison regimes modernised the architecture and culture of the prison[3] in the nineteenth century and replaced eighteenth-century chaos with the vision of tidied-up, incarcerated bodies in publicly humiliating uniforms. Yet, the standardised practices of hooding and broad arrows, black-and-white stripes and the lock step[4] might have blurred the idea of the rehabilitative purpose of those nineteenth-century reforms in the public eye. So a mythology grew around the nature of prison uniform, a mythology symbolically exaggerated in images in the printed media and film. In exposing the complex history of prison clothing, this book traces the way individuals and collectives resisted these prescriptive conditions.[5]

In Western democracies, eras of reform – for example, between the two world wars – led to the abolition of iconic clothing, but prison regimes did not relinquish the regulation of the imprisoned body in everyday uniforms; prisoners were still stripped of their identity and self-esteem. Meanwhile the mythology of the iconic uniform – the balck-and-white stripes and broad arrow – lingered on into the 1960s. As for penal reformers, they rarely addressed such issues. But in debates about imprisonment the issue of dress polarises between those who ask why society should worry about what criminals wear when they have infringed the law and reformers who focused on the implausibility of expecting people to be rehabilitated when fundamental rights such as a 'clean change of underwear'[6] are denied them. Yet, such small reforms in prison culture, important in affecting the self-esteem of prisoners, have been sidelined in comparison to larger issues, such as the need to relieve overcrowding in prisons, the need for more stringent 'law and order' policies or new programmes of prison building.

Post-9/11, 2001 until 2008, at Guantánamo, iconic prison clothing returned to the global gaze, modernised in the form of the orange jumpsuit that had been introduced in to the US prison system in the early 1990s[7] for American male and female prisoners. The term 'iconic' is used in this book to differentiate between a prison uniform that was publicly held up as the embodiment of punishment in the 'War Against Terror' and everyday prison uniforms. Its use conformed to type as in the black-and-white stripes and broad arrow – in a form of dress that visually replaced the body of the prisoner as criminal in the public imagination. Transmitted to the world, the orange jumpsuit was offered by the Bush regime as proof of 'normal' American punishment procedures in, what was put across by politicians as, a justifiably 'exceptional' situation.[8] The uniform proclaimed success in the 'War Against Terror' and provided associations with the captured body that were politically central to the promotion of the cause.[9] The intention was not to reform prisoners; and there was no traditional prison space either. Instead there were hidden prisons scattered around the globe and one at Guantánamo, a camp geographically outside national and international law.[10] Clothing of the punished was part of the punishment and the jumpsuit, a reliable sign of embodied discipline, was very much an updated version of the nineteenth-century prison uniform. Illegality became familiar in the eyes of the world. The contradictions of power were visually evident in one item of clothing once again and myths pertained. Who were those captured? What happened to them for years on end in Guantánamo Bay? What crimes had they committed as 'enemy combatants' now in prison clothing?

Iconic prison clothing had been abolished since the 1920s. Yet, in the early twenty-first-century, we were led to believe we saw the inmate, but we didn't. We saw only the garb of the imprisoned. How did inmates cope with the labelling as

criminal that was inscribed in the apparel of the powerless? Only when the imprisoned open their mouths is the visibility of clothed invisibility revealed.[11] Thus wher-
ever possible I refer to the words of prisoners.

Additionally, the myth of the modernisation of imprisonment is a phenomenon
of the Western world. Half the incarcerated world still lives in eighteenth-century
conditions of 'malign neglect',[12] in rags and inadequate clothing, sentenced or not
convicted, criminalised in the raiment of impoverishment and locked from sight.

My examination of the history of prison clothing brings us to the late modern
present. Although we live in a globalised homogenised world, it is still one where
prison systems continue to fragment people's lives in archaic formulations of the
embodiment of punishment – like the iconic prison uniform.

This book traces the origins of these myths in the history of prison clothing and
the experience of the incarcerated.

approaches

The study of dress interprets the fashion system as the establishment of the design
of cloth and clothing – the social and commercial relations of its production and
consumption – integral to the political conditions in which it operates. Fashion history has broadened as access to the sensuality, frivolity and mass production of
clothing spreads to all corners of the world. Fashion is now a global commodity
mediated by ever-expanding printed, electronic and commercial technologies. Its
history spans class, race and gender in the construction of identity in clothing. Yet,
prisoners' clothing has been largely omitted from this process.[13]

Perhaps this is because prison clothing is one of the few forms of dress that is
not determined by design and consumption within the mainstream system of commodity production. Nor is fashionability a characteristic of prisoners' clothing. It is
also set apart from other forms of institutional clothing such as uniforms of authority[14] or school uniforms.[15] These forms of standardised clothing operate within the
ideological parameters of formality in the social world. Prison clothing does not.

Yet, its manufacture is historically connected to the outside world of industrialisation. Prisoners were and are used as cheap labour in the manufacture of prison
clothing as well as clothing for outside markets (see Chapters 5 and 6). Prison clothing is thus both excluded from the mainstream fashion system and yet tied into the
industrial relations of any one historical or geographical mode of production. With
the increase in global mass production and consumption of clothing in the twentieth and twenty-first centuries, people of all classes and regional localities have
had increased access to branded fashionability. This has transformed the way people make meaning of clothing within local communities and cultures.[16] The global
expansion of the transmission of fashion images has also increased the awareness
of inequalities inherent in the fashion system. Our identities are fragmented in the
potential transformative nature of clothing that is restricted by poverty.

These contradictions become apparent within penal systems, and crossover with them. Prisoners are forced to work in the cheap production of clothing and are encouraged, in many parts of the world, to consume clothing when prison issue dress is not provided. Yet, they are discouraged from the expression of identity in clothes.

At best prison clothing is part of a complex internal prison system of regulated consumption, provision, distribution and maintenance. At worst it is about embodied punishment to the extent of neglect, torture and death. The fundamental nature of clothing that crosses class, race and gender lies in the sensuality and comfort of cut and cloth against skin. Sartorial punishment denies these basic rights. It diminishes self-esteem and it is a characteristic of all prison systems.

However, poverty and institutional regulations do not prevent people from constructing identity in clothing. Dress traverses prison walls in both directions. Throughout prison history, and no more so than in the contemporary world, inmates are aware of fashions outside. Prison clothing is creatively customised in the construction of identity, and inmate styles are proclaimed 'cool' – the fashion of resistance. Thus, the fashion of low-slung jeans and 'bum-cheek' status amongst youth on the streets originated from the denial of belts in prisons, ostensibly as prevention of self-harm.

The history of dress parallels the history of prisons in that they are both integral to capitalist development. But whereas the history of dress has been celebrated, the history of the raiment of the convicted is shrouded in secrecy. It is as though the exposure of prison clothing undermines, and threatens, the prevention of crime.

Maybe this is because the history of prison clothing is the history of mechanisms of the embodiment of law and order. At times the design of clothing is deliberate, at times seemingly arbitrary. But the neglect of prison clothing reveals as much about the politics of penalty and retribution as its intentional design and construction. This characteristic seems to have deterred design and dress historians from unravelling its specific history.

When we look at the cross-overs between conventional dress history and that of penal clothing, it becomes clear that ideological constructs of modernity, intrinsic to the regulation of the body in the social relations of the production and consumption of dress in the outside world, brush fleetingly with the history of dress as punishment. Yet, the shifts in the form and function of prison clothing rely more on penal processes, according to the politics of the time, than on changes in fashion.

At times, the modernisation of the prison does converge with dress history as fashions affect improvements in prison clothing. Yet, prison dress history diverges from the history of fashion when the focus is on the quality of design as increased social inclusion, for example, during the inter-war years of European modernist design. Prison dress only becomes modernist by default, in the paring down of decoration for the purpose of functionality.

In the period of post and late modernity, after 1945, there are more cross-overs between prison dress history, design and fashion history, and contemporary prison history and criminology. For, the fragmentation of the 'self' in the supposedly homogenous contemporary world fits with a diversity of types of inmate dress within late twentieth/early twenty-first-century global prison expansion.[17] The power of the fashion and prison industrial complexes are stacked against the individual inmate locked in the contradictions of the raiment of shame.

Prison literature and inmates' accounts are packed with references to bodily punishment in dress and in this book, prisoners' perceptions juggle with archival information. Where possible, interviews, questionnaires and correspondence were conducted with ex-prisoners and present prison inhabitants in order to clarify their experience of prison clothing.[18] Prison histories[19] and criminological histories[20] sit alongside reform documents and parliamentary debates on criminal justice.

The history of the prison brings together social and political history, criminology and architecture, the culture of surveillance, the visualisation of the restriction of space and the history of the punishment of social groups, particularly in relation to class. The history of prison clothing draws on all these approaches. Yet, there are slippages in the implementation of dress reforms conveyed in the words of inmates. The history of dress personalises the history of the social power relations of the prison space.

The way in which prison regimes visually represent the inmate in the mediation of power to the public gaze has to be compared with the words of the prisoner. The photographic and documentary imagery of the dress of the prisoner that were produced by prison regimes accelerated from the late nineteenth century. But so too did prison literature, diaries and autobiographies, providing alternative testimony to officialdom. This prison literature traces the class, gender and racial nature of imprisonment. Nineteenth-century prison writing was largely middle class and for the most part male. Yet, these writers reveal everyday class hierarchies as well as political and personal resistance in the regulation of the imprisoned in dress. In the twentieth century, literacy rates improved as the rate of imprisonment increased. Global mobility revealed conditions of sartorial imprisonment from the perspective of the inmate across class, gender and race.

Throughout, the book depends on this literature for accounts of the touch, cut and regulated denial of the incarcerated 'self' in dress. It provides us with graphic evidence of the maintenance, provision and distribution of prison clothing systems, as well as the design and neglect of dress. The prison culture of tattoos has a literature of its own[21] and is therefore omitted. Distinctions between prison staff uniforms and inmate clothing are considered comparatively within the regulated space of the prison.

As my research progressed, I realised that the only way to understand how fashion and prison histories converged was to approach the subject chronologically. The book spans 1800 to the present, from the rise of American reforms, the modernisation of the prison and Jeremy Bentham's 'model prison' to the present and the birth of private and titan/supermax prisons. Prison dress moves in and out of grades of embodied stigmatisation, from iconic humiliation to neglect, according to waves of reform and reaction. My study focuses on America, Europe and Australasia, but in Chapter 6 the contemporary context of imprisonment takes in the developments in Asia, Africa and South America.

The last chapter looks at the way in which inmate dress is appropriated in the outside world as fashionable 'cool'. Prison film, television series and photography dramatise and make sartorial prison dress visible and new mythologies are formulated. But in the end, we return to the invisible voices of Ron in Wakefield and Mary in London three decades ago and the words and images of more celebrated inmates who represent themselves in prison clothing, in literature and in art. They contribute to public knowledge and demystification of the historical journey of prison clothing. Yet, inmates' sartorial identities remain invisible behind the prison bars.

from near naked to uniforms, pre-1800 to 1830s

The prison was covered with half-naked women.

Mary Sanderson, *Journal* (1817)

A woman prisoner came in to Newgate in silence, no covering, no stockings and a thin gown. We provided for her when she came in. And we provided clothes for her child.

Elizabeth Fry, *Observations on Visiting, Superintending and Government of Female Prisons* (London, 1827)

The same commitment to regimentation...dictated that inmates wear uniforms...ones made of crude and simple design, with stripes.

David J. Rothman, 'Perfecting the Prison: United States, 1789–1865', in Norval Morris and David. J. Rothman (eds.), *The Oxford History of the Prison: The Practice of Punishment in Western Society* (Oxford, 1998)

introduction

Clothing is not merely a reflection of broader developments in the history of penal reform. It is part of the culture just as much as prison architecture, public and hidden executions, enforced prison labour (as part of the industrial system) and differences of treatment across class and gender. Although included in penal literature and debates, clothing is rarely, if ever, their focus even when the 'body' is discussed as an aspect of the vacillations in penal policy between the overtly oppressive and the rehabilitative in line with current political thinking.

This chapter about clothing conditions in prisons in the late eighteenth and early nineteenth centuries focuses not only on England but also on Scotland, Wales, the USA, Australia and Europe. The differences in how the more, or less, favoured prisoners were dressed in the eighteenth century comprise a caricature reflection of the class differences, and anarchy, of the society outside.

This chapter traces prison clothing as a series of political reform advances and retreats between 1760 and 1830. As early as 1779, John Howard (1726–1790) proposed the introduction of a prison uniform. There were a few practical attempts at instigating uniforms in English prisons, such as at Gloucester Gaol in 1791, but they came to nothing. With little or no provision for prisoners' needs, clothing came low on the list of priorities as the Quaker Mary Sanderson could still note in her journal in 1817 quoted above. Her friend and fellow Quaker Elizabeth Fry (1780–1845), one of the early female penal reformers, regarded clothing as just as crucial to prisoners' morale and health as the broader reforms advocated by John Howard.

prison dress and reform movements

In official prison literature of the first half of the nineteenth century dress is occasionally mentioned specifically or appears amongst other prison conditions in reform documents, reports of prison visits and accounts by the prisoners themselves. But, at this time, it is only the more literate prisoners' voices that are heard filtered through the religious, moral and political leanings of the reformers. The majority of penal reformers were male – so of course the literature also presents a gendered approach particularly to women's prison dress. As is evident in the quotes above, the ethos of the time prevails in the writings of the reformers. When Elizabeth Fry, for example, argues for an improvement in women's prison clothing, she does so in the name of 'decency' and philanthropic concern for morality as much as the comfort of women convicts. One of the objectives of the organisation she started, The Ladies Association for the Improvement of Female Prisoners in Newgate, was 'to provide for the clothing, the instruction and the employment of the women ... which may render them docile and peaceable when in prison and respectable when they leave it.'[1]

In the early nineteenth century, creating order out of disorder was of primary importance in attempts to convert, rehabilitate and control the criminal population, with dress occupying a central role. Prisoners were less enthusiastic. Far from 'falling at their feet in penitent gratitude', as Fry's lady visitors expected, 'they simply derided their efforts'.[2]

Enlightenment, Quakerism, the French Revolution and the Napoleonic Wars aside, it was the conditions experienced by the mass of England's population that helped trigger prison reform. Indeed that reform can be seen as a counter-revolutionary response to the disturbances of the early nineteenth century.

The period was characterised by an unequalled diminishment of rights for the labouring and dispossessed poor owing to 'commercial expansion, the enclosure movement, the early years of the Industrial Revolution', writes E.P. Thompson and adds, 'all took place within the shadow of the gallows ... It is not a pleasant picture'.[3]

The result was prisons filled with the poor and potential or actual revolutionaries. Criminological and prison historians talk of the authorities' 'malign neglect' and historians comment on how prisons were 'evil, disease ridden places, managed by corrupt officers',[4] where the provision of clothing was negligible. This laissez-faire state of the jails persisted well into the nineteenth century and although historians have been tempted to describe 'it as benign neglect…malign neglect is more accurate'.[5]

Not, of course, that all prisoners lived in rags and absolute squalor. Alongside the destitute were those with money that bought them access to clothing, food, bedding and books. So some prisoners could live in reasonable comfort. But they were the minority.

Penal reformers were shocked by what they saw and elements of the upper classes, mindful of what had happened after the French Revolution, began to think that their own safety from revolutionaries who had been imprisoned might come through reform.

John Howard and penal dress conditions in England

According to penal reform literature in the late eighteenth century, the conditions in English prisons needed improvement and clothing was recognised as contributing to a situation of neglect of prisoners' moral and physical welfare.

In 1773, John Howard, the philanthropist and newly appointed Sheriff of Bedfordshire, began an exhaustive survey of prisons which was to occupy him till his death. The work was to take him to the Low Countries, Germany, Scotland, Spain, Portugal, Ireland, France, Scandinavia and to assess, by reading the literature, conditions in the USA. By 1781, he calculated he had travelled more than 40,000 miles in his work, and he was still at work on the survey when he died in Southern Russia in 1790.

The first publication of his work was called 'The State of the Prisons in England and Wales' (1777). Prisons, he pointed out, were run by regimes that often broke existing laws. Amongst other iniquities was the disregard for clothing and other material and nutritional needs of prisoners. He called for purpose-built institutions, the abolition of prisoners' fees and separation of different categories of prisoners. There had to be very basic changes if prisoners were to lead relatively healthy and sanitary lives.

In 1779 the Penitentiary Act, inspired by his research, went through Parliament. It aimed to regulate and control prisoners' conditions via justices of the peace and magistrates 'also with respect to the keeping, dieting, *cloathing* [sic.] [emphasis mine], employing, and providing for such Prisoners, and for the better regulating and governing the said Gaols and Houses of Correction, and to lay such Fines and Penalties for the Non-observance or Non-performance of the same, as the said Justices in their Quarter Session assembled'.[6]

This was a beginning. Not only were prisons to be reformed in order to provide prisoners with the rudiments with which to conduct their lives in a more sanitary and ordered manner, but the authorities were also to have the power to carry out the reforms rather than exact fees from prisoners. For the first time the regulation of clothing and a proposal for prison uniforms were mooted.

Howard published a series of tracts on prisons in 1784, amongst which was a pamphlet that was translated into English outlining the conditions of prisons in France. In his introduction to the pamphlet, Howard mentioned that there were lessons to be drawn for English reformers from the examination of inequalities in other countries. In the Bastille prison, Howard discovered that similar clothing conditions prevailed as in England. Distinctions existed between staff who 'are clothed, provided with linen, shoes, salt, candle and firewood and have 10 sous a day' and prisoners who were stripped of everything they possessed on entry. They could only acquire clothing, shaving equipment, toiletries and bed linen 'as privileges to be bought if [they] can afford it'.[7]

The Marquis de Sade, for example, who was incarcerated in the Bastille in the years prior to its fall in 1789, 'bought in...a full complement of shirts, silk breeches; *frac* coats in camel-brown, dressing gowns, several pairs of boots and shoes; a selection of hats; three fragrances – rose water, orange water and eau-de-cologne – with which to anoint himself'.[8]

Howard was aware that the wealthy continued to live in luxury while the poor were in rags in both French and English prisons. 'Malign neglect' in terms of the unavailability of clothing for the poor was to continue in many European prisons until well into the nineteenth century. This was despite attempts by Howard and others to reform these conditions and the advent of broader changes in society brought about by revolutionary movements such as occurred in France in 1789.

Howard's review of English prisons (1789)

It was partially the recognition of the iniquity of prison conditions throughout Europe that fuelled Howard's determination to review whether the regulations he had earlier proposed for English prisons were carried out.

Additionally, in comparison to French and English prisons, he noted that the number of prisoners of all kinds in Holland, Switzerland and Scotland '[was] very small'.[9] This was due to, he said, 'the care which is taken in those countries to bring up children in habits of industry, and to give even the poorest a moral and religious background'.[10]

For Howard, decency, industry, order, moral and religious education were considered vital in order to improve the likelihood that prisoners would not re-offend. Institutions should provide nutritional food, washing facilities and improved living conditions, including adequate clothing across gender and class lines.

It was this attitude which contextualised many of the reforms, amongst them prison clothing, throughout Europe and America during the first half of the nineteenth century.

Howard wrote in 1784, 'That all prisoners, except debtors, be clothed on their admission with a prison uniform, and that their own clothes be returned them when they are brought to trial, or are dismissed.'[11]

Additionally, he proposed the separation of classes of prisoners from each other.

Twelve years later Howard published a review in which he investigated how far his proposals had been implemented. His review of 1789 covered not just prisons but also schools, hospitals and workhouses and both local jails that housed convicted prisoners and houses of correction that were the equivalent of the earlier – and still existing in places – Bridewell Prisons. These, largely, housed vagrants who were incarcerated in order to be reformed into industrious contributors to society. There were many cross-overs between workhouses and Houses of Correction and, in some instances, issues of clothing the poor in workhouses coincided with the reforms proposed regarding clothing and uniforms for prisoners.

Howard's work anticipated debates that countered prison as rehabilitative against prison as a form of continued privation after sentencing. Later Jeremy Bentham (1748–1832) and his Utilitarian secular disciples took Howard's arguments for reform and channelled them into more regimented nineteenth-century penal regimes. Bentham saw punishment as 'an impartial act of social necessity'[12] but people like Howard and later Fry were informed by piety and a charitable concern with the improvement of prisoners' souls through the everyday structuring of time, space and employment. The rehabilitation of prisoners through a more ordered environment and employment, thought Howard, was 'in their [offenders'] own interests'.[13]

Despite Howard's efforts, improvements in the provision of clothing were haphazard. Despite the acts passed between the 1790s and 1830s, referring to the introduction of uniforms, there is no evidence of the arrival of a universal uniform until the late 1840s.

The chasm between the reforms Howard wanted and their implementation in his lifetime underlined just how dramatic the change in prison culture was for which he argued. Similar problems have dogged reformers and rulers ever since. Uniforms in the mid-nineteenth century were discussed for years before they were put into practice, and subsequently often revised or reversed, as other ways of thinking about crime and criminals came to the fore.

Back in the 1780s, the gaps were huge. In Oxford, when prisoners were not employed in building the new prison, they were fettered. Despite this, Howard wrote, 'the encouragements here given with respect to their diet, *clothes* [emphasis mine], and terms of confinement have been the means of recovering many from their bad habits and of rendering them useful members of society'.[14]

Meanwhile at Dorchester County Gaol, prisoners were kept in irons for long periods of time. Even worse off were the 32 men chained in dungeons in Warwick County Gaol and where 'some of the felons complained of having been forced to pay 4/2d for garnish [a drink which was not beer] or be stripped of their clothes'.[15]

Although some prisons carried out the reform to provide men and women with separate cleaning facilities, others had not carried out any reforms at all as to white-washing walls or providing separate accommodation and washing facilities. During the period of Howard's review in the 1780s, women were seen wearing 'irons' at Derby County Gaol although at the Town Gaol and the Bridewell, it was reported that felons were provided with bedsteads, straw and blankets and baths. It was much improved said Howard.

At London's Newgate Prison conditions had got worse:

> On the men's side there were many boys of 12 or 14 years of age; some almost naked. In the men's infirmary there were only seven bedsteads; and there being twenty sick, some of them naked and with sores, in a miserable condition, lay on the floor with only a rug...Unless a reform be made in the prisons, an audacious spirit of profaneness and wickedness will continue to prevail in the lower class of the people in London.[16]

In the New Prison in Clerkenwell, 'some pawn their scanty clothing to obtain a discharge. Of 167 prisoners only ten could pay for a bed which was a fee of 3/6d a week' and in the Clerkenwell Bridewell, 'prisoners were very dirty and some almost naked'.[17]

The County Gaol of Horsham was 'well conducted'. However, at Southwark, 'fifty of the felons in 1787 who were convicts for transportation' had for 4 years been languishing in prison, and 'these poor wretches lay almost perishing in the gaol. Many had worn out their shoes, stockings and shirts and had hardly clothes to cover them...such dreadful nurseries have been a principal cause of the increased number of crimes'.[18]

Howard's arguments around reforms provide the first debates concerning how the impoverished prison population should be dressed. It was middle-class reformers and critics, in response to authorities' policies of 'malign neglect', who mainly initiated reform. Both sides shared a class background that shaped their ideas of how dress, in their view, conformed to working class respectability and uniformity. This was tinged by a moralism that asserted that prisoners would only recant their crimes if stripped of their former identity. Whether enforced or provided, under the guise of improving the appearance of an ordered prison population, these attitudes towards clothing underlie much of the history of prison dress.

dress inside and outside prison in the early nineteenth century

Despite the forward thinking of Howard's work, many of the conditions of 'malign neglect' that he had suggested should be eradicated continued on a national level. The authorities still retained the power to mete out punishment through depriving prisoners of adequate clothing. This meant that male prisoners were often reported wearing ragged breeches or 'trowsers' and no top while women's dresses were ill-fitting, unwashed, slipping off shoulders exposing parts of the body to the cold and damp. Many poorer prisoners went without shoes and washing facilities were rare.

Thus, Mary Sanderson talked of 'half-naked' women in her journal in 1817. Many early nineteenth-century social commentators as well as penal reformers wrote of the poor as 'half-naked'. Clothing in prisons tended to be worse than for many of the poor outside but often mirrored the conditions of some of those who were worst off owing to specific economic hardship. The perception of many middle-class commentators with regard to the clothing of the poor was often that it was a permanent condition. For example, in an article in the Liverpool Courier reporting on the effects of the 1826 cotton depression, the reporter states, '*many of the sufferers are almost naked* [emphasis in the original] it would be a great kindness if old clothing or bedding could be obtained for them'.[19]

This might have been the situation for the poor at a time of crisis but may not have been a perpetual condition. Poverty fluctuated considerably according to social and economic conditions, personal situations and employment. There is no doubt that 'by the nineteenth century at least 70 per cent of all people would experience part of their lives in relative or absolute poverty'. But 'in practice, only perhaps one-fifth of the labouring classes might be actually poverty stricken (in the sense of being dependent upon community or charity or on the margins of being in such a position) at any point in time in even the most pauperised of counties of the early nineteenth century'.[20]

The stereotype of the poor in the early nineteenth century, whether inside or outside prison, was perceived by the propertied classes relative to their own increasing consumption of clothing. As a result, the poor were often characterised as 'dressed in rags' rather than as living in hard times in which their appearance might change according to social, economic and regional fluctuations.

Variations in clothing conditions existed from one prison to another even within the same county as Howard had pointed out in his review of prisons in the 1780s.

The observations of middle-class reformers, then, often tended to ignore specific fluctuations and instead typified the labouring classes and the impoverished as ill-dressed whether imprisoned or not. It was a perception partially, if not entirely, based on actuality. This stereotype of the poor is represented in both the writings about prisoners and the paintings at the time and has been termed 'the ragged Picturesque'. Contained within images as much as the penal reform documents is the idea of both 'what the poor actually wore and the preconceptions and moral positions underlying attitudes to their clothing on the part of the elite'.[21]

When looking at the way prisoners and their clothing are talked about and represented, it is, therefore, important to keep these class attitudes in mind.

the gendering of prison dress

When Elizabeth Fry visited Newgate in 1813, her description of conditions echoes those of Howard three decades earlier. The women there had been reduced to 'riot, licentiousness and filth'.[22] It was still a private prison and everything had to be paid for, including clothing. This meant that the disparity between those who could and those who could not afford clothing that Howard had witnessed earlier persisted. In 1817, Fry's visit was painted (see Fig. 1.1). The women prisoners are represented as a mix of working class 'types' familiar from contemporary paintings. They include those who might have been servants such as the woman, head in her hands at the bottom right-hand corner and a woman sitting beside her, one in a mob cap and the other with an apron. Both items of clothing were part of respectable servant dress.[23] By mid-century they were part of official female prison uniform (see Chapter 2). Older women in the right-hand corner wear mob caps, not dissimilar to that worn by Fry herself, and are indeed clothed rather than half-naked. The woman prisoner in the centre of the picture, on whom all eyes are focused, wears a dress that is slipping off her shoulders. Her hair, however, is neatly pinned up. Under the lowered gaze of the middle class, bonneted visitors to the left of Fry, the prisoners in the centre of the picture cast their eyes down in humiliation. In contrast to the fashionability of the women visitors and the buttoned Quaker attire of Fry, the key woman prisoner is a romanticised working class type. Her lack of morals is implied by her

Figure 1.1 'Elizabeth Fry visiting Newgate Prison'. Engraving by T. Oldham-Barlow from original painting by Jerry Barrett (1840s).

failure to pull the sleeve up on to her shoulder. She does not have shoes and is there to be pitied rather than considered 'licentious'.

The painting's gendered image of prison dress raises issues about the representation of prisoners historically and in modern times, painted or photographed. Photographs of prisoners later in the nineteenth century demonstrate similar traits as this painting in 1817. In the nineteenth century, middle-class 'domains of expertise' – urban planning, criminology, public health – informed discourses surrounding the representation of 'the working classes, colonised peoples, the criminal, poor, ill-housed, sick or insane [who] were constituted as the passive objects of knowledge. Subjected to a scrutinising gaze, forced to emit signs, yet cut off from command of meaning, such groups were represented as, and wishfully rendered, *incapable of speaking, acting or organising for themselves*' (emphasis mine).[24]

The painting of Elizabeth Fry does not present the same 'rhetoric...of documentation' as the photography of prisoners at the end of the nineteenth century as it explicitly provides 'emotional appeal and dramatisation.'[25] But the characterisation of the visual control of the less fortunate 'other' is pertinent in discussing how early nineteenth-century reformers both talked about prisoners and painted them.

Fry's main concern was not only to provide women and children with clothing but also a belief that by dressing in a less conspicuously exposed manner, women who had been convicted of prostitution, for example, would mend their ways. Early nineteenth-century morality set great stock on the idea that women of all classes should be demure and pious. Later in the nineteenth century, the writer on prison conditions, Henry Mayhew (1812–1887) commented favourably on how women prisoners looked 'picturesque' in their prison-supplied uniforms of mob caps, aprons and dresses.

The painting of Elizabeth Fry's visit romanticises poverty. It also provides a moral framework for looking at working class women that both feminises and infantilises them. Such a representation portrays women as unable to help themselves and thus in need of Fry's philanthropic reforms in order to become domesticated women. The ladies who became prison visitors, meanwhile, were role models for 'fallen women'. Indeed Fry not only provided clothing but also started sewing classes for the prisoners. In this way, Fry became, on canvas at least, a saintly person, gazed upon by an admiring painter and middle-class spectators.

prison dress as a class issue

In the early nineteenth century, alongside a mass of poor prisoners were a minority of more wealthy individuals and debtors whose conditions were separate from the local or convict prisons.[26] More affluent individuals could buy themselves out of starvation or near nakedness or petition through the visiting magistrate of the county gaol to be provided with clothing. Thus, in 1801, magistrate Sir Charles

Marsh wrote to the Duke of Portland asking that the State prisoners Robert Oliphant and Bartholomew de Boisson should have bills paid for their clothing amounting to £39 and 6 pence. 'Therefore, as visiting magistrate, I informed the Keeper he could not be doing wrong in supplying them with what appeared to be absolutely necessary, I have no doubt but your Grace will order the said bill to be paid.'[27]

Two decades later, Robert Adams, one of the Cato Street conspirators, convicted in 1820 of attempting to murder members of the Tory Cabinet, wrote a letter to the local magistrate, a Mr. Hobhouse. He pleaded his innocence and asked for clothing:

> I have been very unwell...and the clothing that I now have are not fit for the season of the year they are so threadbare and so light that when I goe out I am rapt up with the cold had it not been for the kindness of Mr. Adkins I must have bin naked long ago.
>
> What I really want is as follow:
>
> A suite of close, a hat, one flannel weastcoat and drawers, a pair of short legans.'[28]

Both instances highlight the way that access to clothing was a matter of individual privilege, as in broader society. Adams' letter prefigures later struggles as some prisoners sought to define a political as opposed to a criminal identity. This conflict continued once the uniformity of convict clothing was imposed as a disciplinary measure alongside the more stringent penal policies of the later nineteenth century.

Robert Adams' letter also points to a changing political environment in England. The aftermath of the Battle of Waterloo and the end of the Napoleonic Wars in 1815 saw an increase in poverty, harsh Government repression and a rise in political agitation that led not only to Cato Street, but the Peterloo Massacre in 1818.

prison dress as uniform

Early nineteenth-century attempts to implement Howard's ideas and introduce uniformity of dress had mixed results and the issue was still alive beyond the 1850s.

One early experiment came at the time of the protracted construction of Millbank Prison in London. In 1799, land at Millbank had been bought for the building of a prison and 2 years later the building was finally started.[29] In 1819, Parliament enacted what were to be significant 'Rules and Regulations to be Observed and Enforced for the Government of the General Penitentiary, Millbank'. These included a section on clothing that anticipated later reforms. Prison dress was to be 'made of cheap and coarse materials, with such marks or peculiarities, as may tend to facilitate discovery in case of escape. The two classes of prisoners shall be distinguished by different clothing'.

Markings on prison clothing that identified potential escapees were initially specifically for male prisoners since women rarely attempted escape. It is worth noting
that the introduction of prison uniforms in the main targeted the male offender.
Partly this was because the criminal population mostly comprised men.

The 1819 'Rules and Regulations' additionally stated under 'Cleanliness'
that 'prisoners shall put on clean linen every Sunday...The hair shall be kept
short'[30]

The 1819 Rules raised issues that have continued to resonate in different countries into this century. That the fabric of clothing was to be cheap was unsurprising,
that it was to be coarse and uncomfortable indicates how bodily punishment was
to be maintained as part of the humiliation of prison life. These forms of clothing
for the prevention of escape varied from 'parti-coloured' clothing – with sections or
patches coloured differently – to 'broad arrows' – where large arrows were painted
or roughly stamped all over the clothing. These were a feature of 1830s Australian
prison gangs as well as English chain gangs in Dartmoor and Wakefield prisons later
in the nineteenth century. The Rules also heralded the start of the 'political technology of the body',[31] the categorisation of prisoners through marks on their clothing.
This labelled them on the basis of their level of industry and co-operation.

In 1823, the Tory Home Secretary Sir John Peel introduced the Gaol Act.
Clothing was mentioned but only within the overall framework of the introduction
of the separation of men and women and the segregation of prisoners one from
another. Along with the introduction of the 'silent' system – whereby prisoners were
not permitted to talk to each other since redemption was only considered possible
through the silent contemplation of their sins – came reforms such as the abolition
of fettering prisoners in irons. The assumption behind the Act was that convicted
prisoners would wear a prison dress and that it was clean:

> The wearing apparel of every Prisoner shall be fumigated and purified, if
> requisite, after which the same shall be returned to him or her, or in case of
> the Insufficiency of such Clothing shall be furnished according to the Rules
> and Regulations of the Prison; but no Prisoner before Trial shall be compelled
> to wear a Prison Dress, unless his or her own Clothes be deemed insufficient
> or improper.[32]

There had been an attempt to introduce a prison uniform as early as 1779, and then
again in 1823. But even 11 years later, regulated prison dress remained a rarity.
A surgeon asked by Parliamentarians about prison conditions in Newgate in 1834
explained that male prisoners did not wear prison dress. When asked whether prisoners were sufficiently clothed, he replied that indeed they were. 'On this Principle,'
said the surgeon, 'that the Governor orders them Clothes the moment we see any
one deficiently clad; but they cut their Trowsers [*sic.*] up to make Straps to protect
their Legs from the Chains, or they dispose of them by means of their Friends out
of Prison'.[33]

Irons were supposed to have been abolished by the 1823 Act. Clearly they were not. But another use had been found for the clothing that prisoners had. Indeed what Newgate prisoners were doing was using their clothes and their own alterations of clothes as a way of establishing and maintaining their identity in order to survive.

Many historians of the period have suggested that prisoners were entirely subjugated to a passive life of the 'docile body' at the indiscriminate behest of prison and governmental authorities, however harsh, regimented and disciplinarian the regime. Yet, prisoners did operate a type of social agency in order to both alleviate and enhance their bodily condition. They did this despite the prison authorities' attempts to eradicate prisoners' individual identities.[34] Prisons became increasingly disciplinary institutions from the mid-nineteenth century. However, even in the 1830s, despite the oppression of the individual, bodily and mentally, there is evidence to show that prisoners sought to express their identity in some way and that this was a survival mechanism. Inmates experience prison clothing and restrictions not merely as victims of penal systems but as active agents. 'Prison clothing is anonymous. One's possessions are limited . . . the urge to collect possessions is carried to preposterous extents . . . anything made by man and forbidden in man's institution – anything – a red comb, a different kind of toothbrush, a belt – these things are assiduously gathered, jealously hidden or triumphantly displayed.'[35]

Clothing, then, permits the expression of identity whatever the privations of the incarcerating institution. Whether for the purpose of alleviating the pain of irons or in the retention of personal possessions, prisoners act in altering clothing conditions in innumerable ways. This was particularly the case as prisons became both more regimented and tougher from the mid- to later nineteenth century. This aspect of prison dress is an important consideration throughout this book.

British transportation and the Broad Arrow

Britain's colonies in the late eighteenth and early nineteenth centuries were extensive and penal policies introduced domestically during this period were reflected abroad. Prison uniforms were introduced in the colonies in a piecemeal fashion, as they were in England, as a way of controlling transportees and convicts whether in Australia and Tasmania between 1787 and 1868 or in Southeast Asia in the nineteenth century.[36]

It was around Australian convict policy that many of the piecemeal experiments with clothing as a disciplinarian practice developed. Not until the 1850s and 1860s did uniform codes come to English prisons.[37] The transfer of the direct control of local prisons to Central Government came with the 1877 Prison Act, 9 years after the end of transportation to Australia and Tasmania.

In Australia, as in England, in the first half of the nineteenth century, there was a lack of uniformity in convict clothing.[38]

Yet, while the diversified dress of British working people distinguished them from convicts – who were, anyway, mainly inside prison – in Australia, convicts were put to labour outside the prison. It was 'for the most part difficult to distinguish the appearance of convicts from free working settlers'. Thus, 'in Australia an almost inadvertent dichotomy existed until the 1830s between the self-appointed elite and the lower social grouping of tradespeople, convicts, farmers and poor settlers'.[39]

As for transported women convicts, it was even more difficult to distinguish between them and free immigrants since they were mostly destined for domestic service, and their clothing was the same as normal working class dress.[40]

This was partly because of the lack of provision by the British Government of clothing of any sort, let alone convict uniforms, to the colonies. Unlike Europe – where throughout the eighteenth century conspicuous consumption[41] of fashion had denoted wealth – Australia was not then a society where class differentiation in dress was clear.

This would surely have spurred on the introduction of uniforms for prisoners and there are extant examples of rough, coarsely made Australian convict clothing,[42] mostly from the 1840s – as new prison regimes became established – to the 1870s. Harsh styles of female convict dress were also introduced from the 1840s and were regularly met with resistance.[43]

Changes in convict clothing for women were also tainted with the moralism of reformers such as Elizabeth Fry who was involved in the development of women's convict clothing in Australia and wanted to encourage a 'modest, domestic demeanor in women prisoners'.[44]

Similar issues are raised through the examination of colonial penal clothing practices in Australia in the early nineteenth century as took place in 'the Indian convict diaspora'.[45] Although attempts were made to standardise convict clothing, these were tempered by local conditions in the 'penal settlements in Southeast Asia and the Indian Ocean,'[46] where Britain transported mainland Indian convicts. Male convicts mainly wore white dhotis[47] everyday and there are few records of women convicts until later in the nineteenth century. 'Until at least the 1840s there were no sanctions preventing convicts from wearing other clothes.'[48]

The conditions of transportees in the colonies were, however, universally harsh. In Australia and Tasmania, visual depictions and written accounts show the use of chains on convict gangs from the late eighteenth century to mid-nineteenth century.[49]

Although Thomas Watling, who was transported for forgery, was reporting in the 1790s, he described conditions of neglect that were to continue throughout the early nineteenth century:

> Instances of oppression, and mean-souled despotism, are so glaring and frequent, as to banish every hope of generosity and urbanity from such as I am: – for unless we can flatter and cajole the vices of and follies of our superiors, with the

most abominable servility, nothing is to be expected – and even this conduct, very often…meets with its just reward – neglect and contempt.[50]

Parti-dress[51] for male convicts – consisting of variations of large white and later yellow and black blocks of colour on clothing – occasionally feature in early nineteenth-century English prisons but were not uniformly adopted until later in the century. It was introduced as convict clothing in New South Wales and Tasmania as early as 1814 not only to prevent escape but also as a symbol of humiliation instead of 'the administering of corporal punishment'.[52]

But there was also the issue of the broad arrow mark on prison dress in England and in the colonies (see Fig. 1.2). This was to represent the beginning of the move towards humiliating prison uniforms. One of the first visual depictions of the broad arrow is an image of a convict jail gang in Sydney drawn by Augustus Earle in the 1830s. Convict uniforms with broad arrows, dated 1830–1850, are also to be found in clothing archives in Australia and Tasmania.[53] The broad arrow appeared on Australian and Tasmanian convict clothing earlier than it did in English prisons.

The broad arrow indicated not only that the clothing was the property of the prison authorities – and thus the Government – but also that the convict's body was similarly owned. The mark was taken from the head of the pheon – or mace-like

Figure 1.2   'A Government Jail Gang, Sydney, New South Wales', by Augustus Earle, c. 1830.

javelin – carried before Royalty that denoted Crown property. In fourteenth-century England, items such as wine were stamped with a mark showing they were the property of the King, and by 1330, the King's butler, Richard de la Pole, was carrying the broad arrow on his own coat of arms.

Two centuries later, the Thrale family, who reputedly harboured Queen Elizabeth 1 between 1556 and 1558 when she was fleeing from her sister Queen Mary, were honoured with the broad arrow for their coat of arms.[54] Indeed the Thrales stamped the broad arrow on their sheep as a mark of ownership. The mark had become a common heraldic device, and the Sidney family, who coincidentally had the same name as the Home Secretary, also carried it.

The broad arrow, then, initially marked objects or animals as the property of someone with authority, power and wealth. Once imprinted on the clothing of convicts, the arrow became a mark of humiliation. The arrow was not the only such mark. There were also the less visible letters 'BO' (The Board of Ordnance) and 'WD' (War Department) in nineteenth-century Australia[55] and later, in England, 'HMP' (Her Majesty's Prison). But they lacked the power of humiliation that came with the all-over broad arrow mark painted or stamped on the fabric as the symbol of the embodiment of prison property. One of the reasons the broad arrow persisted in the typography of criminality in film and cartoon representations is the immediacy of its visible identification with convict status and public humiliation.

The broad arrow was transported from England to Australia and Tasmania along with thousands of convicts. It appeared on male convict attire in Australia and Tasmania since it was used principally as a mark to deter escape from chain gangs. The mark was first used here as the stigmatisation of the convict body as colonised property in servitude to British authorities. Only later in the nineteenth century was this mark of humiliation to become fully implemented as prison uniform in English prisons for both men and women.

black-and-white striped prison dress in America

Changes in prison clothing in the US penal system during the early nineteenth century were of equal significance to the convict clothing in English prisons and the colonies.

The US penal system had been much the same as in England until the ratification of the American Constitution at the end of the War of Independence in 1789. Up until this point it had been 'a colonial system...which vacillated between comparatively lenient and harsh punishments', including execution and was considered by signatories of the Constitution, such as Benjamin Rush (1745–1813), as 'the natural offspring of monarchical governments'.[56]

A penal system based on privileges operated until the 1780s in America and prison clothing was one of the items that prisoners could either obtain by paying a fee or barter for. At Chester County Jail, Pennsylvania, 'the English custom of charging for various ... services was also in force, for example fees for food, heat, clothing and for attaching and removing irons incident to a court appearance'. Alternatively, in the new prison on Walnut Street in Philadelphia, 'prisoners awaiting trial might barter their clothes for liquor or be forcibly stripped upon entering by other inmates seeking funds for the bar. The result was great suffering when the weather turned cold.'[57]

It was as a result of these conditions in jails in Pennsylvania that the Philadelphia Society for Alleviating the Miseries of Public Prisons was founded. It recommended 'solitary confinement at hard labor as a remedy and reformative strategy'.[58]

In 1790, an Act was passed that introduced, initially, a more lenient system of incarceration. It would later be seen as the precursor to the regimentation of prisoners and inhumanitarian measures that prevailed in the 1820s in the notorious Auburn and Pennsylvanian institutions.

In an account of a visit to a Philadelphia jail written by Robert J. Turnbull of South Carolina in February 1796, the conditions of the prisoners' dress were outlined in some detail:

> The clothing of the convicts is altogether manufactured in the prison and adapted to the climate and season. In winter the men are dressed in jackets, waistcoats and trowsers of woollen, and in summer, with coarse linen shirts and trowsers. The women in plain gowns of the same. The stuff for the whole is woven by the males and made up by the females.[59]

The account goes on to show how the aim of the 1790 Act, proposed by Quakers, was to replace the corruption that had previously prevailed under the colonial system with an ordered prison. The prison community was 'a small industrious community.' The Act also legislated that there was to be total segregation of the prisoners. There was to be 'no intercourse between the males and females; they cannot even see each other'.[60]

These rehabilitative reforms were similar to those suggested by John Howard. In fact, the account finishes by announcing: 'What a feast would this have been for an Howard's heart'.[61]

Turnbull's article demonstrated a knowledge of the disorder prevailing in French and English prisons and pointed out that reforms provided for in the 1790 Act and implemented in Philadelphia heralded an improvement in prison conditions.

The clothing was not dissimilar to the plain dress worn by Quaker communities outside prison walls, particularly in Philadelphia. Production of clothing took place within the prison based on the cheap labour of prisoners and gender division in the workforce. The reformers of the organisation of prison labour in these American prisons took, as their model, the factory system in industrial Britain. But it was only later in the nineteenth century that prison clothing manufacture in England was to reproduce these conditions.[62]

The comparative leniency of the 1790 Prison Reform Act was interpreted differently at Newgate Prison in New York, following a law passed by the State legislature in 1796.

This new penal code took the Philadelphia model of convicts producing clothing and being paid for their labour but they were charged out of their earnings for the replacement uniform clothing: 'On reception at Newgate, the new prisoner was stripped of his clothing, washed and given the prison uniform: shoes and stockings, flannel shirt, and brown jacket and trousers for a first offender, with second offenders distinguished by a "dress one half red and the other half blue" '.[63]

This clown-type clothing that was introduced in Newgate Prison in 1796 was already in use by American chain gangs at this time. It was similar to the parti-coloured clothing of transportees in Australia in the early nineteenth century and parti-coloured clothing worn by convicts in London prisons later in the 1850s.

It is no coincidence that the convict uniforms first implemented inside prisons resembled costumes worn by court jesters in the mediaeval period. Not only were prison uniforms designed to prevent escape but they were also fashioned to humiliate the wearer. As prisoners have indicated in their writings,[64] prison clothing marked out convicts as risible or to be pitied in the eyes of the public. This first uniform that embodied punishment was an integral part of an increasingly surveillant prison culture in America in the first half of the nineteenth century.

Not only was the clothing a visible reminder to the prisoner, prison staff and visitors of the convict status of inmates, but the conditions in Newgate prefigured later nineteenth-century categorisations of prisoners, their increasing segregation and punishment through different forms of enforced prison clothing.

But Newgate was not as harsh a prison as the later Auburn regime that replaced Newgate in 1817 after it was burnt down. For example, although the 'silent' system – whereby prisoners would be punished if they so much as uttered a word to other prisoners – was in place at meals, as in Philadelphia, prisoners at Newgate could speak in the workshops. This gap between legislation and the actuality of the prison experience extended to the supposed segregation between males and females. Owing to overcrowding in the prison, they had to co-exist.

By 1815, the regime at Newgate had disintegrated into chaos not dissimilar to the conditions Howard had found in English prisons in 1789. Harsh measures were taken to counter this. Amongst them was the introduction of a new uniform 'of clownish striped suits for first termers'.[65] This uniform heralded America's iconic black-and-white striped uniform. It was in 1815 that the emergence of the striped uniform took place in Newgate Prison. The reason for its adoption was primarily the cheapness of the production of simple black-and-white striped cloth. Additionally the black-and-white horizontal stripes symbolically represented prison bars that not only surrounded the inmate but were also imprinted on the convict's body and thus became an embodiment of imprisonment. The American use of horizontal stripes meant that when the arm was raised, the stripes were changed into vertical stripes on the arms that crossed with the horizontal stripes on the body forming a grid pattern in which the body was enclosed.[66]

Auburn prison continued to clothe convicts in this uniform and it was to become the standard practice of American state penitentiaries.

Women convicts in the early nineteenth century were not regimented in the same way. The comments of a Swedish visitor to Newgate in New York in 1819 were similar to the moralising tone of Elizabeth Fry when talking about women prisoners in London's Newgate. They were in a state of 'bestial salacity...agonizing to every fibre of delicacy and virtue'.[67]

The introduction of prison uniforms in America was less piecemeal than in Australia and England. It nonetheless represented historical slippage in so far as changes in prison dress emerged alongside previous prison uniform strictures and categorisations. The implementation of uniforms depended on contemporary clothing production technologies, gender and cultural differences that existed outside the prison walls. Social influences as well as penal policies affected the way in which clothing was subsequently adapted to prison conditions.

The black-and-white striped iconic prison dress was associated with male criminality and was specific to the American situation in the early 1800s. Men comprised the majority of the prison population and were, for example, uniformed as punishment for causing the riot of 1819 in Newgate, later to become Auburn prison.

The striped uniform was deliberately humiliating and particularly so when worn by prisoners who were forced to march in 'the lockstep' formation (see Fig. 1.3). This enforced movement of lines of prisoners who were tightly packed together first took place in Auburn prison.[68] The uniform was part of the wider embodiment of punishment implemented at Auburn prison and cannot be divorced from other oppressive conditions that prevailed in the 1820s. These included the rigorously implemented 'silent system' and the factory working conditions of prisoners where 'time' was scrupulously divided between working and sleeping and where prisoners were unable to have any educational or leisure time. Sing Sing prison was also built in New York in the 1820s and was finished in 1828 and modelled on the same principles as Auburn.

The striped uniform and the conditions in New York prisons had their opponents and proponents. Proponents of this method of embodied punishment – through the imposition of visibly humiliating uniforms and prisoners regimented by the 'lockstep' – considered that this was the only way to control prisoners if the previous disorder in prisons was to be prevented. Redemption from criminality was to be enforced by stripping prisoners of their identities, reducing them to numbers and stripes and forcing them to reflect on their evil ways in silence, cut off from the world around them. Uniforms were part of the process of making prisoners into 'docile bodies.'[69]

However, reformers, such as Gustave de Beaumont (1802–1865) and the French political historian, Alexis de Tocqueville (1805–1859) who visited New York in 1831,

Figure 1.3 'Prisoners in black-and-white striped uniform in the lockstep formation in Auburn Prison, America'.

were appalled by a system where they felt 'that they traversed catacombs'.[70] They saw the uniforms as counter-productive to inmate reformation and that the clothing was integral to the harshness of the system. Above all the uniforms and 'lockstep' formation undermined inmate self-esteem.

By the time the English novelist Charles Dickens (1812–1865) visited Philadelphia in 1842, the prison had changed from the earlier Quaker-run system to the Auburn model, as had many prisons in America. He condemned its silence and regimented work ethic and considered it 'an unnatural solitude'. He commented on the evil of keeping prisoners in 'a black hood. This dark shroud is an emblem of the curtain dropped between him [the prisoner] and the living world'.[71]

conclusion

The piecemeal introduction of prison uniforms in this period in England, Australia and Tasmania and its more deliberate implementation in American prisons have been shown to be not merely the policy of one particular prison system. Rather, it was convergent with ideological and penal prerequisites and historically specific.

Reformers in late eighteenth and early nineteenth-century America and England positioned themselves in favour of rehabilitative measures and the building up of prisoners' self-respect through the improvement of everyday prison conditions. Among these was prison dress.

Although prison uniforms were proposed as early as the 1770s, they were only introduced as a piecemeal measure in English prisons in the early nineteenth century. British colonialist experiments comprising the imposition of parti-coloured clothing and the broad arrow in Australia and Tasmania were, however, more wide-spread amongst male convicts. Meanwhile, in early nineteenth-century American prisons, black-and-white striped uniforms were implemented as an embodiment of penal discipline, humiliation and the stripping away of male prisoners' identities.

By the 1840s, the iconic broad arrow in British colonies and black-and-white striped prison clothing in the USA had been established for men.

Female prison or convict dress changed less visibly. Women were either inad-equately dressed or reformed through the donning of domestic servant attire. This was partly because of the relative paucity of female prisoners or convicts in com-parison to men. Partly it was because at this time women who had infringed the law were regarded by religious reformers as pitiable rather than punishable.

As the nineteenth century progressed, prison uniforms as an embodiment of punishment were more widely reinforced. Although prison clothing was integral to penal policies introduced by reformers such as John Howard, Elizabeth Fry and Utilitarians such as Jeremy Bentham (1748–1832), it was rarely the focus of penal debates. Nevertheless, Bentham's work on prisons – written in the 1790s – had influenced disciplinary measures put in place in Auburn prison in the USA. But it was not until 1842, when a new prison was built at Pentonville in London, that his ideas were to have an impact on prison clothing in England.

When Henry Mayhew was researching the Criminal Prisons of London in 1862, he discovered that the provision of clothing, while varying from prison to prison, was moving towards uniformity of production and distribution. This brought imme-diate improvements in health – yet it intensified problems in terms of the severity and regimentation of prisoners' lives. In an era subsequently seen as the high tide of laissez-faire political policies, clothing was to become part of a newly centralised distribution of punishment and enforced labour. It is these issues, particularly in relation to the development of prison dress in England in the mid- to late nineteenth century, that will be examined in the next chapter.

uniforms: stripes, broad arrows and aprons, 1830s to 1900

Then, again, we manufacture about 10,000 yards of shirting for the prisoners... Yes, sir, everything made for the convicts has a red stripe in it – sheets, stockings, towels, flannels, and all.

Their dress consisted of a loose, dark, claret-brown robe or gown, with a blue check apron and neckerchief, while the cap they wore was a small, close, white muslin one, made after the fashion of a French *bonne's.*

H. Mayhew and J. Binney, *Criminal Prisons of London and Scenes of Prison Life* (London, 1862)

introduction

In Britain, in the latter half of the nineteenth century, increasingly harsh measures for controlling prisoners were established, alongside the uneven implementation of a uniform. Prison dress innovations in this period were commensurate with Utilitarian values rooted in the belief that the order and control of prisoners' lives would lead to self-evaluation and subsequently rehabilitation. This meant the increasing segregation of prisoners according to the crimes they had committed, their financial status and their behaviour within the prison and that they should be involved in productive labour. Capitalist imperatives were also behind the re-organisation of prisons. Utilitarians, such as Jeremy Bentham, considered that the conditions necessary for creating a disciplined community should be established and enforced through the physical control of prisoners and their labour.

The latter half of the nineteenth century was thus demarcated by both a continuity of reforming ambitions and an increasingly reductive approach to prisoners' lives. It was an approach that resulted in the imposition of punitive measures such as the masking of prisoners or their regimentation in silent rows and employed, for example, in the task of picking the frayed ends of old rope.

The Auburn system in America – whereby prisoners were permitted to associate with others in workshops during the day – was established in British prisons from the mid-nineteenth century. Prisoners were often masked when they moved around the prison, when visitors were present or as punishment for talking to others. Hoods, masks, striped clothing and uniforms were introduced. These disciplinary reforms that included dress were mirrored in broader society where industrial and factory regulations were increasingly being employed in order to control the workforce.

The advent of the mass production of clothing during the nineteenth century, particularly in Britain, meant that vast systems for the provision, distribution and maintenance of clothing were established on an industrial scale. Production of clothing in prisons replicated factory conditions outside the prison walls. Prison authorities justified the employment of prisoners in the cheap production of clothing as a rehabilitative measure in their acquisition of skills in order to enter the workforce on release.

The introduction of Jeremy Bentham's 'model prison' in Britain, although never fully implemented, had an effect on clothing in prisons. The 'model prison' was an architectural prototype in which the prisoner could be observed at all times of day and night. Inseparable from the design of the prison were the rules and regulations that reinforced the physical control of prisoners.

There was categorisation of prisoners – whereby prisoners' crimes outside the prison walls, their status within the prison and their behaviour either as potential 'escapees' or as 'co-operative' were bodily identified. This took the form of labels on clothing or different types of uniform that represented rewards or punishments. The labelling of 'types' of 'criminal' was, later in the nineteenth century, reinforced by the work of early Italian criminologist Cesare Lombroso (1835–1909). This approach was later taken up in the early work of the British reformer Havelock Ellis (1859–1939). Lombroso's thinking informed the politics of social engineering, or eugenics, that suggested criminality could be eliminated once 'types' had been effectively identified physically. Throughout Europe, these early criminological positions triggered the increasingly prevalent physical categorisation of prisoners.

Categorisations in prisons were part of a more general nineteenth-century classificatory mania for appeasing disorder diagnostically in institutions such as the army and police force, hospitals, factories, schools and local government offices.[1]

Striped cloth and the broad arrow marking were introduced to the fabric of prison clothing as signifiers of criminal identity. The use of a specific cloth in the design of prison clothing demonstrates the 'classifying function of clothing [which] overshadows its Utilitarian function'.[2] Thus, standardised dress and cloth became internal penal regulatory devices integral to the classificatory system.

The obviousness of nineteenth-century prison clothing was intended to 'emphasize that those who wear such a uniform are excluded from the social order and subject to a separate regime'.[3] Thus, prisoners' uniforms were visibly distinctive from those of prison guards and those in authority.[4]

Gender segregation continued through the nineteenth century in relation to the physical and sartorial divisions between men and women prisoners. Women prisoners' clothing was markedly less regulated than that of men. But bodily punishment occurred as physical restraint, labelling and numbering as well as the use of cheap, coarse cloth and the ill-fitting nature of prison dress.

The universal principle of denying prisoners their previous identity outside the prison was applied throughout the prison system in Britain, Europe and America. In America severe prison systems of silence and total segregation were modified from the 1830s. Yet, they were still harsh. In America and Europe, the nineteenth century saw a complex progression of penal developments that were characterised by increasing centralisation. At the same time, inconsistencies and contradictions persisted in the management and implementation of these systems.

This chapter explores the ways in which specific clothing practices emerged parallel and integral to the concept of the 'model prison' in the mid-nineteenth century with reference to the theoretical, historical and criminological work that contributed to the penal debates of the period. This chapter ends by examining political resistance to the visible embodiment of criminality in dress that took place in Ireland and Russia in the late nineteenth century.

Bentham and the model prison

Jeremy Bentham wrote his Utilitarian tracts on prisons in the 1780s and 1790s, yet, they did not significantly influence prison reform and prison clothing until the mid-nineteenth century in Britain. His ideas were influenced by observations of the organisation of military cadets in a French military school in Paris that had been constructed in 1751 and a factory at Arc-et-Senans.

Each pupil in the school lived in an individual cell made of glass so that they could be seen at all times of the day and night. They were not allowed contact with other pupils. Additionally, there was no bodily contact with staff.[5]

The factory was constructed along the same lines as the military school but with an additional feature. It had a central observation point from which the workers could be supervised.

Bentham's proposals for the design of the 'model prison' were based on these observations and he named the all-seeing eye construction, 'a panopticon'. The design of the prison centred on a tower in the middle of a circular building. Cells were built around the periphery walls with inner and outer windows. A guard would be able to see prisoners from this central observation post and prisoners would be seen backlit from the outer windows. The guard was invisible to the prisoners, although they were aware that they were being watched. Observant that they were overseen, prisoners would learn to control their own behaviour.

Additionally, complicated ventilation devices and machinery were invented to prevent prisoners from communicating with each other. Above all the building construction was one where prisoners were at all times visible to the unseen controlling 'eye' of the prison guards and the public view of visitors. Prison dress became intricately linked with the concept of the 'panopticon'. In the same way as the architecture of the prison enabled the surveillance of the prisoner in order to exert power over the individual, so too would prison clothing provide the guards with constant visible knowledge about the prisoner's behaviour and identity.

Bentham considered this a reform because instead of guards chaining prisoners and instead of using violence to exert power over them, the system was designed to openly control prisoners through observation. In a broader political sense, the original concept of the panoptic prison was linked with the idea whereby the workings of any institution would be transparent to all those who entered it. Although based on ideas taken from institutions that had existed under a monarchical system in France in the mid-eighteenth century, the practical application of Bentham's ideas in Europe after the advent of the French Revolution was no coincidence. Bentham was aware of the ideas of Jean Jacques Rousseau (1712–1778) who had advocated the 'dream of a transparent society'[6] in place of a hierarchical society dominated by the excesses of an absolute monarch. Bentham's original concept of the panopticon welded technical design ideas with the visibility of a transference of power to those in authority who were in possession of knowledge about the people under their control. Bentham's design of the prison exemplified Utilitarian values in so far as it represented a self-contained vision of a society where individuals who had erred from their preordained place in society were to be suppressed for the benefit of the greater happiness of the wider community. Thus, the techniques employed for this end would include 'each individual, under the weight of the gaze ... interiorizing to the point that he is his own overseer ... each individual thus exercising this surveillance over and against himself ... There is no need for arms, physical violence, material constraints'.[7]

In practice Bentham's ideas were rarely fully implemented and when they were adopted it was in tandem with the harsh disciplinary measures that they were meant to eradicate. These often amounted to physical violence and material restraints alongside a 'silent system' introduced for punishment rather than rehabilitative ends.

There was thus a disjuncture between Bentham's Utilitarian conception of the 'registering of knowledge' of prisoners in order that their potential for reform could be monitored and the surveillant Benthamite notion whereby the continual observation of prisoners led to ever-increasing disciplinary procedures.

Clothing featured little in Bentham's original plans. Although the visible body was central to the idea of the panopticon and dress uniformity, markings on the body and badges were integral to the visibility and identification of prisoners, clothing was given little detailed mention.

Prison clothing was implicit, however, in the conceptualisation of the 'panopticon' structure. In order to work it required the prisoners to be physically ordered, even mechanised in order that they could benefit from a system that promulgated the 'production of a progressive self'.[8] But the system did not just require prisoners to wear specific clothing. They were also inducted in the production of clothing as hard labour within the prison walls in order to provide the economic underpinning of Utilitarian reforms and capitalism with cheap labour.

Prison dress in the 'model prison' was thus both integral to Bentham's overall concept and peripheral to this concept in its documented design details. Prison uniforms in Britain in the nineteenth century, and in many other countries in the West, both diverged from or complied with the values intrinsic to the 'model prison' regime.

Although Bentham's 'panopticon' prison was never fully realised in British prisons, his notions of bodily surveillance techniques as reform effected the implementation of prison clothing.

There had been short-lived Benthamite experiments in Gloucester prison in the 1790s and in Millbank in 1822. Both of these ultimately failed. Gloucester prison's implementation of strict solitary confinement came to an end in 1808 as a result partly of radical campaigns against the iniquity of a system where prisoners were prevented from any contact with others. There were also practical problems associated with a prison building that was not purpose built with individual cells for the implementation of total separation.[9]

Similarly at Millbank the experiment had proved costly and unmanageable and had resulted in prisoners rioting against the conditions. Both experiments proved to the authorities that the Benthamite scheme could only be fully implemented if the design of the entire prison was along the lines set out by Bentham as 'the panopticon'.

In terms of dress, Gloucester prison not only implemented a uniform but also, in line with cutting off prisoners from their previous criminal identity, they were 'stripped, examined, bathed'[10] and their clothes were taken away from them. The uniform prisoners wore consisted of 'alternate panels of bright blue and yellow material'.[11] This was remarkably similar to the way condemned prisoners were dressed as early as the fourteenth century in London. A condemned man had been paraded to the public on his way to hanging, 'wearing a striped coat and white shoes, his head covered by a hood' and 'the convicted man was drawn upon a horse, facing the tail, and wore a fool's cap'.[12]

This blue-and-yellow pattern was also reminiscent of jesters' apparel in the mediaeval period in Britain. The provenance of the mask, an adapted form of the 'hood', that was introduced in the 1840s in Britain alongside 'model prison' reforms also dated back to this period.[13]

Thus, prison uniform design, whether striped or not, was inspired by archaic systems of humiliation that had little to do with the emergence of the modern prison. Clothing practices based on the visible exclusion of prisoners from outside society and their public spectacle as risible persisted well into the nineteenth century and beyond, despite attempts to reform prison conditions. Bentham would have considered this uniform inadequate in terms of his overall desire to 'control' the prisoner within the designed environment of the prison. Although it addressed the issue of prison clothing as indicative of 'the humiliation of the wearer…and the prevention of escape',[14] it could also be discarded. Bentham suggested a more indelible method with which prisoners might be labelled; that 'most effective of all would be a painless semi-permanent dying of the skin.'[15]

He considered the possibility of chemical dyeing procedures that, although not adopted, were consistent with the bodily techniques of surveillance integral to his designs for the model prison. In 1863 in England some members of a Committee on Prison Discipline were in favour of marking prisoners with India ink. Governor Shepherd of Huntingdon prison suggested that this mark should be inscribed 'under the arm'.[16] Bodily markings and prison uniforms were thus integral to his ideas about the control of prisoners' lives and identities and yet arbitrary in their application.

Throughout the nineteenth century, prison clothing developed in a variety of ways. It harked back to previous more archaic systems, was intended by prison authorities to provide regulatory bodily surveillant techniques and looked forward to clothing and bodily restraints that were to be more about continuing punishment than rehabilitation.

local and centralised prison clothing in Britain

Local prisons operated a multitude of clothing practices. Debtors prisons, for example, were exempt from any type of prison uniform well into the mid nineteenth century. Dickens' *Little Dorrit* was located in the Marshalsea Debtors Prison in the 1820s. Although fiction, the book was based on visits to his father who was imprisoned in Marshalsea in this period. The 'Rag Fair' Dickens describes inside the prison walls applied to conditions in many local prisons:

> Such threadbare coats and trowsers, such fusty gowns and shawls, such squashed hats and bonnets, such boots and shoes, such umbrellas and walking sticks never were seen in Rag Fair. All of them were the cast-off clothes of other men and women, were made up of patches and pieces of other people's individuality, and had no sartorial existence of their own proper.[17]

This image of the prison provides the novel with a metaphor for the whole world imprisoned by appearances dominated by the gap between the rich and the poor. The conditions in Marshalsea were much as Elizabeth Fry had described those in Newgate and the clothing of the poor outside the prison walls was replicated within them. The hierarchical domination of fashionability excluded the poor from participating in its artifice.[18]

The implementation of uniforms in prisons, then, developed unevenly through the nineteenth century. It was intended to rid prisons of the impoverished conditions that Dickens described and yet, in practice, the introduction of the prison uniform set up another form of hierarchy. Centralised convict prisons such as Millbank

(1816) and Pentonville (rebuilt 1842) provided uniforms while local prison clothing and that of debtors were, for the most part, neglected.

centralised prison dress: Britain, America and Europe

Pentonville prison was not entirely rebuilt according to Bentham's design as it was not circular. Instead cells were constructed off corridors emanating in a star shape from a central apex from where the prison guards observed the comings and goings of the prison. But many of Bentham's principles such as the regimentation and constant visibility of the disciplined prisoner effected prison clothing. This took the form in America of labels, numbers, iconic black-and-white stripes and more discrete stripes in Britain and later in the century the broad arrow. The introduction of the American 'silent' and 'separate' system in British and European prisons took place at the same time as the implementation of Bentham's ideas. Prison authorities introduced masks (see Fig. 2.1) specifically in order to separate prisoners from each other so that they reflected on their crimes in silence and felt humiliated in the eyes of the outside world.

The 'silent' and 'separate' system that had been introduced in Philadelphia and Auburn prisons in the 1820s was transported to British prisons in the 1840s. Pentonville prison was the most perfected example, in Britain, of this convergence of the 'silent' system and Benthamite philosophy. The clothing embodied many of the model prison's objectives as becomes evident in representations of prisoners in the mid- to late nineteenth century.

One of the techniques developed in this period for the visible identification of criminals was the implementation of a permanent register of police photographs. These were kept in individual prison files[19] from the 1840s in Europe and America and contributed to the increase in the knowledge of inmates held by the institution.[20] These mug shots showed just the prisoners' faces. The engraved image in Fig. 2.1, however, shows a Pentonville prisoner in his entirety, in a mask-like contraption and with a prison number hanging on his jacket. These engraved images, rather than police portraiture, are of value in the critical examination of prison dress in the period.

The skill of the engraver was to interpret the photographic image through the use of a variety of tonal qualities[21] rather than to reproduce it exactly. Thus, the image of the clothed prisoner resembles the original and is not an exact copy. However, since the image is taken from a photograph rather than a drawing, there is less likelihood of exaggeration than was the case in earlier engravings.

There are similarities between the police mug shot and the engraving in the position of the incarcerated body for public scrutiny. The focus of the image emphasises the 'disciplinary method' of the clothing of the incarcerated subject. The mask that obliterates the prisoner's identity catches our attention. Thus, clothing cannot

CONVICTS.

(From Photographs by Herbert Watkins, 179, Regent Street.)

MALE CONVICT AT PENTONVILLE PRISON. | FEMALE CONVICT AT MILLBANK PRISON.

Figure 2.1 Male convict at Pentonville prison/female convict at Millbank prison, 1850s. Mayhew and Binney, *Criminal Prisons of London* (1971/1867), Frank Cass & Co. Ltd.

be separated from the method by which it is visually represented as 'the body made object...enclosed in a cellular structure of space'.[22]

Clothing as a form of control is also evident in the prominent position of the prisoner's number engraved on the brass badge that hangs on a chain from the jacket. The mark inscribed on the brass badge identified the convict as his cell number and the position of the cell on the landing. The marking shows the number '1' separated from the '9' by a full stop. The prisoner's identity was reduced to an anonymous number and became an embodiment of part of the building construction itself. The body as sign merged with the apparel as signifier of the ideological and actual construct of the prison. Prisoners were thus literally overseen by the unseen 'eye' of the prison warder. The badge was a device for the control of the prisoner's movement within the prison. Its significance did not merely reside in the erasure of individuation but was also linked to the objectives of 'the model prison'. The same principle can be applied to the mask.

This mask differs from the fourteenth-century hood worn by prisoners on their way to execution and the black hood worn in early nineteenth-century American prisons,[23] since it was a specially designed 'prison cap'. It was described as 'a peculiar brown cloth cap, and the peak of this [which is also of cloth] hangs so low down as to cover the face like a mask'.[24] The peak was designed so that it could be 'bent up, and no longer served as a mask to the face'.[25]

This was, then, a purpose-designed garment linked to the objectives of the 'silent' and 'separate' system of the 'model prison'. The intention was that the prisoner could neither communicate with others nor be identified by others. They were meant to identify with a reformed life rather than their past criminality. Additionally, this garment was intentionally degrading in its obliteration of facial expression and in the discomfort of breathing through cloth. It was designed to be deliberate visual and bodily control of the prisoner as part of the surveillant culture of the 'model prison'. It also exemplified the inconsistency of the Benthamite project. The mask reinforced the grey area between clothing the body to be seen and restraining the body as a disciplinary practice. The way in which masks were viewed by observers reflected the confusion as to the reasons for their being worn.

Mayhew and Binney recognised the inherent uselessness and humiliation of the mask-like contraption. Their view was that 'the imposition of these same masks – though originally designed, it must be confessed, with every kindness and consideration to the prisoners, in order that their faces might not be seen in their shame – cannot but be regarded as a piece of wretched frippery, and as idle in use as they are theatrical in character'.[26] They later refer to a description of the mask made when its abolition was first proposed in 1853.

> That the mask or peak does not prevent prisoners from recognising each other in the prison; moreover, that as prisoners see each other before they are brought to the prison, come in considerable bodies, and are assembled

together when they leave the prison, it would be desirable to discontinue it, since the use of it appears calculated to depress the spirits of the men, without obtaining any corresponding advantage.[27]

This statement provides an important contemporary insight into the way bodily impositions that were introduced in the 'model prison' were experiments of total control in line with the architecture and ideological concept behind the prison. Although designed with the supposed Utilitarian intention of rehabilitation through humiliation, the prison clothing and masks that were introduced in the mid-nineteenth century were later recognised as merely punitive.

In many cases the use of the mask led to insanity and the complete destabilisation of the prisoner.[28] This type of excess of the 'silent' system was ended in the late nineteenth century in America and modified in England in the same period.

Although not officially a form of prison dress, the notorious 'treadmill' was constructed as a visible bodily punishment similar to that of the mask and based on the principles of the 'separate system'. Prisoners mounted cell-like stalls and trod the wheel for hours on end.

It had originated in the early nineteenth century as a device to train prisoners in the production of grinding grain. Between the mid-nineteenth century and its demise as late as 1898, it became a despised mechanism of bodily endurance with no apparent purpose than to exhaust and torture prisoners. The reason for its eventual abolition was partially to do with proof of its inefficacy as 'hard labour'. Prisoners claimed they were sick or physically incapable of working the treadmill. They would see the doctor and were provided with exemption. The system was seen as unsuccessful because prisoners consistently failed to comply with the authorities' rules.

In this respect, prisoners themselves resisted bodily inflictions of punishment. Few critics of the nineteenth-century penal system make allowances for the fact that prisoners acted to resist what were both perceived to be and were experienced as intolerable and unjust forms of punishment.

Alongside the introduction of the mask, an attempt to impose uniformity of dress as a mechanism of control was made in Pentonville prison. The striped cloth used in prisoners' clothing had been imposed in the early nineteenth century in America and was introduced in the mid-nineteenth century in Britain and Europe. 'The peculiar gingerbread-coloured convict cloth, with a red stripe in it'[29] that was used to make up British prison clothing was often discrete as a mark of criminality. It is, for example, not visible in the engraving of the Pentonville prisoner (Fig. 2.1). But it was woven into the cloth and appeared not only on clothing but also on all prison items. In the steward's store, Mayhew and Binney discovered 'immense rolls of the convict cloth with a red stripe in it', and when convicts from other prisons arrived at Pentonville 'all the articles they wore – jacket, trousers, cap, and even their gray stockings – were marked by the red stripe which is characteristic of all convict apparel'.[30]

The stripe in British prison clothing was not as conspicuous as the black-and-white stripe markings initiated in Auburn in America. Nonetheless, it signified similar notions of the embodiment of punishment and visibility. The stripe both enabled prisoners 'to be seen from a distance differentiated from the guards...and easily spotted if they flee from the guards'.[31] Stripes on prison clothing continued in a number of forms throughout the nineteenth century in English and German prisons and 'in many penal colonies in Austria, Siberia, and even the Ottoman Empire'. However, they were not used in French penal colonies which preferred 'to dress convicts in a red tabard rather than a striped tunic'.[32]

In Auburn prison in America, striped woollen clothing for male convicts continued until the early twentieth century when it was abolished by the Mutual Welfare League.

Despite the variations in the stripes on the first prison uniforms in the West, the authorities' intention in introducing these markings was similar from country to country. The fabric used for prisoners' uniforms distanced the convict from the outside social world. Additionally, striped cloth had become a cheaper fabric to produce from the 1770s with the invention of Hargreaves' spinning machine, Crompton's mule-jenny and Jacquard's loom.[33] At the same time as striped cloth was fashionable in the early nineteenth century, and was used in luxurious fabrics such as silks and satins for furnishings and clothing, cheap striped cloth could be easily manufactured in the prison environment. In this way technological developments in fabric production and fashionability in wider society ran alongside the introduction of specific markings of punishment and criminal identity. Stripes were thus part of the development of technological improvements as much as they were linked to the emergence of the modern prison.[34]

In British prisons, male prisoners' clothing made up of the red stripe, masks, numbers and labels were above all distinctive from the clothing of the prison warders, who were 'habited in their glazed caps and short work-day jackets...with a shiny cartouche-box for prison keys projecting from the hip'.[35]

In 1842 prison warders' distinctive clothing was not dissimilar to police uniforms. This was no coincidence since the emergence of the uniformed police force first occurred in early nineteenth-century Britain in the same period as the advent of the modern prison. Officers' uniforms in a number of institutions from hospitals to schools, the military and the police force embodied the increasing power invested in their authority. One of the distinguishing marks of prison warders' clothing from that worn by the subjected was the shininess of the 'cartouche' or decorated key box. This embellishment in the warder's uniform conformed to the distinctiveness found in many forms of official uniforms in Europe and had its roots in the social stratification of dress codes that had originated in the eighteenth century.[36] The control of the prisoner resided not only in their increasing sartorial uniformity but also in the marked differentiation of their clothing from the conspicuousness of those in authority.

Despite the increasing systematisation of the 'model prison' and attempts to spread these conditions throughout the country, the use of prison clothing that marked the inmate as prison property varied throughout the century. The broad arrow mark, for example, was rarely used on prison clothing until the later nineteenth century (see later in this chapter), but it occurred sporadically in the mid-nineteenth century. In 1851, for example, it was reported in a local newspaper that on 19 December, a prisoner named William French escaped from Dartmoor prison and was caught by the local superintendent of police. 'On searching him Baker found two letters in his pocket addressed to William French, and on his shirt were the letters "D.P." with the broad arrow.'[37]

The broad arrow as a conspicuous marker of punishment was implemented at specific prisons, such as Dartmoor, where chain gangs worked outside the prison. This was a similar use of the iconic broad arrow that was implemented in Australia during transportation up to 1853.

The clothing of male prisoners in England in the mid-nineteenth century (see Fig. 2.1) also mirrored working class clothing outside the prison walls. The short jacket and trousers of the 'model' prisoner were in mud-brown cloth. Their cut, while not tailored, was similar to the clothing of labouring men. But the clothes were smarter than those of, for example, a 'nightman' portrayed in Fig. 2.2. The convict's shoes are clearly of better quality than those worn by the nightman. This aspect of the model prisoner's apparel signifies the control of the working class by middle-class Utilitarian reformers in training men to labour. Rather than returning to a life of slovenly impoverishment, the criminal would gain a type of labouring self-respect.

In this way prison clothing emulated middle-class ideals of an ordered class-ridden sartorial hierarchy in mid-Victorian England. In reality there was widespread financial impoverishment and a lack of manual jobs available for urban working class men during this period. However, middle-class social reformers considered, for the most part, that the rough quality of street clothing was 'a personal short coming' on the part of the poor and that 'a graduation from sartorial negligence to a respectable smartness paralleled a turning away from crime towards legal employment'.[38] Prisoners in the model prison were thus provided with clothing commensurate with the purpose of turning criminals into labouring men.

It is no coincidence then that the 'model prison' at Pentonville was a hive of production, particularly as far as 'the trades of weaving, tailoring and shoemaking'[39] were concerned. However, there was a stratification of prisoners employed in these trades according to physical 'type'. This aspect of the labour system in the prison was an extension of the mania for categorisation. It also led to late nineteenth/early twentieth-century social Darwinian theories of criminality and the scientific categorisation of 'criminal types' through the examination of their physiques. 'In the distribution of these employments, the officers look principally to the physical and mental capabilities of the convicts. Strong, broad-shouldered men are put to weaving and to mat-making, whilst the more feeble class of prisoners are set to work as

LONDON NIGHTMEN.

[*From a Daguerreotype by* BEARD.]

Figure 2.2   London Nightmen, 1850s. Mayhew, London Labour and the London Poor: The London Street Folk, Vol. 1. (1861), Griffin, Bohn & Co. Stationers Hall, London.

tailors.'[40] Prison clothing and uniforms for men reflected mid-Victorian values of rigid class and gender distinctions.

gendered prison clothing

Changes occurred in the prison conditions for men and women in mid-nineteenth-century Britain. As was the case with men's clothing, female prison attire prefigured middle-class reformers' attitudes to working class women and their place in the broader stratification of society. In this respect, the earlier moralistic attitude of Elizabeth Fry prevailed.

Yet, there were inconsistencies in the segregation of men and women. Laws passed in the 1820s in England, America and France provided for the separate accommodation of men and women within the same building. This separation reflected the wider ideological gender construct prevalent in the nineteenth century based on the social organisation of 'separate spheres.'[41] Women with financial means were, for the most part, destined to care for the home and men to the world outside it. This gender division of labour within industrial society was predicated on tasks suitable for female and male physical attributes. But there were numerous exceptions to this ordering in wider society as there were in the implementation of separate prisons for men and women.[42]

However, this separation was hesitantly introduced through the nineteenth century in American and European prisons. This material and ideological gender differentiation was reflected in the marked differences between women's clothing in prisons and the more punitive practices that characterised men's uniforms. This difference was also based in part on the relative paucity of female criminals in comparison to men and the nature of female criminality. For the most part, women's criminal activities in the mid-nineteenth century were less heinous than those of men. Prostitution and petty theft comprised the main crimes of women. For this reason, women's prison clothing tended to be less obviously punitive.

In Fig. 2.1, this difference is visually magnified through the man and woman's appearance together, although they are separate engravings and incarcerated in different prisons. The woman in Millbank Prison is dressed in the clothing prescribed by Elizabeth Fry as 'plain decent clothing'[43] and no longer 'half naked' as in earlier portrayals.

This difference in the clothing of prisoners also occurred in America at this time. Men in Auburn prison, for example, wore the horizontal black-and-white striped woollen garment associated with American prisoners. Women wore loose cotton dresses with large aprons. These garments were similar to clothing worn by poorer women outside the prison walls.[44] In French prisons in the same period, women wore clogs, aprons and mob caps similar to those worn by peasant women.[45]

In Fig. 2.1 the dress of the woman convict approximates to that of a poorly paid servant. This is not the aspirational dress that many servants acquired through a variety of means, whether small retail establishments or hand-me-downs from the lady of the house. The woman's clothing indicates a degree of uniformity in line with reformers' concerns to provide the poor with clothing in keeping with their remaining on the straight and narrow.[46] It was an improvement on the ragged clothing in the 'picturesque' representation of women prisoners in the early nineteenth century. It did not, however, provide women with the respectability in clothing that they might have experienced outside the prison. The matron at Millfields explained that 'the women are mostly in for common larcenies...and many of them have been servants; some have been gentlemen's servants, and a good number have been farm servants; but the fewest number are, strange to say, of the unfortunate class in the streets'.[47]

Mid-nineteenth-century women prisoners' clothing was largely in keeping with middle-class reformers' notions of domestic respectability within women's ascribed station outside the prison. However, this approach did not entertain the consideration as to whether it was the exploitative experience within these situations of employment that had motivated women's original 'criminality'. Thus, women's prison clothing provided different restraints than that of the more conspicuously punitive clothing of male prisoners.

Throughout Mayhew's account there are examples of the appeal of docile women prisoners in their claret-brown garments, aprons and mob caps obediently carrying out domestic tasks such as needlework and embroidery and sitting outside their cells in straight lines along the corridors of the prisons (see Fig. 2.3). Yet, women resisted this imposition. For example, they expressed their resistance through making bundles of their bedding and wearing them as early versions of 'bustles' in their desire for a degree of fashionability in the 1860s. The matron explained that the reason for the bedding piled up outside the cells in the corridor was to prevent them from doing this in their cells.[48] Women expressly resisted the uniform 'respectability' of prison clothing. They saw it as a punishment since it prohibited their ability to express an identity that was seen by the authorities as above their station. As in the broader field of fashion and dress,[49] prisoners asserted their identity in clothing despite the attempts of the authorities to impose prison and bodily uniformity.

The apparent distinction between men's and women's punitive apparel, however, varied in actuality. Punitive clothing for women did occur and took the form of straight jackets in Millbank Prison:

> a coarse canvas dress, strapped over her claret-brown convict clothes. This dress was fastened by a belt and straps of the same stuff, and, instead of an ordinary buckle, it was held tight by means of a key acting on a screw attached to the back. The girl had been tearing her clothes, and the coarse canvas dress was put on to prevent her repeating the act.[50]

The warder considered the girl had reformed, but as Mayhew passed the cell the prisoner was heard laughing. Mayhew's interpretation of this reaction to harsh

FEMALE CONVICTS AT WORK, DURING THE SILENT HOUR, IN BRIXTON PRISON.

(From a Photograph by Herbert Watkins, 179, Regent Street.)

Figure 2.3   Female convicts at work during the silent hour in Brixton Prison 1854. H. Mayhew and J. Binney, *Criminal Prisons of London* (1971/1867), Frank Cass & Co., London.

asylum-like punishment was that she was hysterical or mad. But her laughter could have been an indication that women prisoners did not meekly accept this form of punishment.

Both the matron at Millbank Prison and Mayhew demonstrate a contemporary response to female transgression that was typical of authorities in the period. Women were considered reformed through conforming to their allotted role as domestic servants or labelled uncontrollable if they resisted punishment. In some cases, however, their resistance demonstrated deliberate agency in their disruption of the physical confinement of dress. For example, they were known to cut up the canvas dress with bits of broken glass that they would break by taking out the bones of their stays and smashing the glass with them.

It is of particular note that the punitive prison clothing of men was designed as visibly integral to the self-regulatory nature of the building in Pentonville. In contrast, at Millbank, there was an inherent disjuncture between the visually non-punitive servant's dress and the material restraint of the straight jacket that constrained women behind closed doors. This gender distinction is consistent with Bentham's Utilitarian system whereby the authorities registered knowledge about the nature of punishment appropriate to the individual prisoner within the broader ideological construct of groups of male and female working class criminals. Utilitarian penal reformers believed that differences, whether 'primary' (according to the degree of crime committed) or 'secondary' (according to the natural divisions of 'sex' or 'age') should be taken into account in terms of length of sentence, punishment or institution to which prisoners were allocated. Bentham's reforms, as laid out in his *Principles of Morals and Legislation*, represented a complex system of categorisation within the prison system that was dependent on ideological precepts.

The gendered prison clothing of the servant dress was consistent with Bentham's characterisation of women's social and class position as biologically determined. 'The health of the female is more delicate than that of the male...in point of strength of intellectual powers, and firmness of mind she is commonly inferior.'[51] The canvas punishment contraption was similar to the masks men wore in Pentonville prison. But it was used, in this case, as a control of behaviour inside prison rather than as a measure of the crime previously committed. It was, therefore, an unseen physical constraint that was part of an internal prison procedure. It was not a punitive visible design integral to the conception and construction of the all-seeing surveillant prison, as was the male criminal's mask in Pentonville prison.

The 'model prison' in Millbank was an experiment and the premises upon which it developed have informed much prison thinking and construction until the present. But there was a disjuncture between the belief in the reform of the criminal and the designs of punitive prison uniform. Bentham's Utilitarian social order was informed by mid-Victorian patriarchal values that considered women intellectually and physically inferior. This ideology accounted for the gender distinctions in prison clothing that were as much about hierarchical control as about modernisation.

Throughout the nineteenth century, middle-class penal reformers extended 'the practice of governance...making a world safe for capital through the regulation of the working class', in this case in the designs of prisons and prison clothing. They were also 'the carriers of the modernising offensive...which [was]...a vehicle for the regulation of the bourgeois class itself, as a whole...in favour of sobriety and restraint'.[52] In setting out patriarchal attitudes across class lines, Bentham's philosophy demonstrated the disjuncture between the conception of the controlling structure of the modern prison and the experience of those who inhabited it. Residual penal practices co-existed with newly introduced designs of buildings and clothing and in turn jarred with prisoners' knowledge of the world of modernity outside the prison walls. The contradictions inherent in bourgeois reform policies become transparent in the issue of clothing. Bourgeois reformers ridiculed the extravagancies of 'conspicuous consumption'[53] of the female middle classes outside the prison. If there had been consistency in their approach, they would have applauded women prisoners' thriftiness in making bustles out of bedding. Yet, they were critical of working class women clothing themselves beyond their station.

Essentialist systems of gendered prison clothing continued in prisons in Europe and America throughout the nineteenth century. Despite inconsistencies in its realisation, the 'model prison' introduced the concept whereby the design of the institution and its cultural practices ordered the social relations within it. In this way we can see that prison clothing was integral to current thinking about the rehabilitation or punishment of criminal behaviour.

institutional control and disparities in prison clothing

The 'model prison' in mid-nineteenth-century Britain reflected some of the political imperatives of general society. Mid-Victorian England was dominated on the one hand by hegemonic notions of Empire and the economic and cultural expansion of its power throughout its colonies and on the other hand by the domestic emulation and punitive regulation of labour as the cure for social inequality. Both organised working class dissent and movements of social reform increasingly contested this apparent hegemony.

Social historians have argued that the 1840s marked a low ebb in terms of 'the imperial idea'.[54] But it was also a period of domestic consolidation from which more aggressive imperial strategies were to be unleashed in the latter half of the nineteenth century.[55]

The politics behind the architectural and ideological reform of the prison were echoed in developments in museums and other cultural institutions. Reformers considered that art and culture could also be used as forms of working class self-regulation. The museum, the library and the gallery had 'the task of producing the worker who will not only not frequent the public house, but who will no longer wish to do so'. The working class would reform themselves and be 'oriented to the production of the progressive self'.[56] Bentham's panopticon design of the prison, the introduction of masks and the 'silent system' were similarly conceived as mechanisms of reform and self-regulation.

The idea behind the 'model prison' implied hegemonic control in its overall design. In practice it proved only partially workable when, as yet, there was no centralised control of prison services. Even after the 1860s when local prisons were bought into line with State prisons, anomalies persisted between prisons.

In July 1863, the Select Committee of the House of Lords reported that there were a number of systems in operation in different prisons. Prison conditions varied from the 'separate' system to complete 'solitary' confinement, from the 'silent' system to the 'associated' system (where prisoners could communicate with one another).

In terms of clothing, convicted prisoners in Leicester prison wore 'the prison clothing' that consisted of 'a frock as the sailors wear; it is made of a stout grey frieze for the winter, both the frock and the trowsers; they also have a check shirt and a flannel shirt and flannel drawers, worsted stockings and shoes'.[57] Prisoners in Bristol Gaol, however, did not wear uniforms but masks. They wore 'a bag down to their shoulders, which they can see through exceedingly well; but they cannot recognise each others' features, or the make of the shoulders behind'. With regard to 'respiration', 'it is perfectly free; it is nothing more than a veil after all' and all prisoners, both untried and convicted, wear this bag in order that 'ill disposed prisoners are prevented from having communication with the well-disposed prisoners'.[58] However, at St. Albans Gaol, unconvicted prisoners wore their own clothing.

The 'model prison', then, acted as precisely a 'model' of punishment practices as far as clothing was concerned but there were different interpretations in local situations. The Governor of West Sussex County Gaol, for example, talked about 'parti-coloured clothing' for 'penal' categories of prisoner, while 'plain clothing' was to be worn for the 'industrial' class of prisoner. All prisoners started as 'penal' prisoners and 'advanced' to the 'industrial' category.[59]

In all prisons, however, some sort of system of marks and categories were worn on the clothing of prisoners. These took the form of red arm bands as rewards and punishments for behaviour or 'parti-coloured' clothing for different categories of prisoners.

The stripping of prisoners on reception, the shaving of hair, bathing naked in front of prison officers and bodily inspections were universally introduced during this period. All these practices were designed, in one form or another, both to cleanse prisoners and to strip them of their identity. They were institutional practices in line with the precepts behind the design of the 'model prison'. Yet, they diverged from the overall regimented control that Bentham had envisioned. Also prisoners them-selves were aware of the haphazard absurdity of the failings in the system.

the provision of prison clothing in mid- to late Victorian Britain

In his memoirs D_S_ [Donald Shaw], who was imprisoned for 18 months in the 1880s, mentions that he was 'scrutinised "inside and out"'[60] on entry to the House of Detention, divested of all his clothing and bathed and dressed in prison clothing. He was then moved to Coldbath Fields Prison where he 'selected a nondescript pair [of shoes], tied by a cord, as unsuited a couple as ever were united, the right foot of which would have fitted an elephant, and the left have been tight for a cork leg'.[61]

The provision of clothing was arbitrary during the latter half of the nineteenth century although the period saw the increasing centralisation of the distribution and maintenance of clothing and bed linen in prisons. Much of the clothing was produced in prisons but there was also an increasing philanthropic hand-me-down culture of the wealthy providing clothing for the poor.[62] As Donald Shaw mentions, sacks of clothes were presented to prisoners. 'The contents of these, being thrown on the floor, were discovered to be boots, not new ones, or even pairs, but very old and dirty, mended and patched with lumps of leather on the soles, on the heels, and in fact everywhere. We were now invited to "fit" ourselves.'[63]

There was also a variety of procedures for the maintenance of clothing. For example, the prison laundry in a civil prison serving the Queens Bench in London contracted out the washing of bed linen between 1843 and 1862. A Mrs. Elizabeth Main was employed to wash the bed linen of the 'poor prisoners'. By the end of this period all the prison linen was washed in the prison.[64] However, it is unclear how wealthy prisoners washed their linen in the first half of the period. It can only be assumed that they still sent their clothing out to be privately laundered well into the 1860s, although their bed linen was washed within the prison.

Different systems for the provision of clothing in prisons prevailed until the Prison Act of 1877 when direct control of local prisons was transferred to Central Government. Until this time there was an uneven development in the mainten-ance of prisoners' clothing. Prisoners' humiliation was caused by the haphazard and inadequate provision of clothing and the imposition of a constrictive uniform. However, despite the more regularised central maintenance of clothing from the 1870s, washed apparel was still often returned to different owners.[65] But also during the period a system of privileges was still in operation in some prison institutions.

The production, distribution and maintenance of prison clothing in mid-Victorian Britain did not amount to a self-contained system. Rather it reflected aspects of broader social and penal reform developments that advocated centralisation, when in reality eighteenth-century practices such as privileges for the wealthy persisted inside and outside the prison walls.

the broad arrow in Britain and the US black-and-white stripes

The experience of prison clothing recounted by prisoners in late nineteenth-century Britain varied significantly. Many disliked the labelling by numbers, enjoyed the relatively good quality of prison clothing and hated the broad arrow marking.

For example, Captain D_S_'s account of clothing in the 1880s mentioned that wooden labels were attached to the clothing the prisoners received in bundles in Coldbath Fields Prison. The contents included 'a pair of blue worsted socks, a blue striped shirt, a blue pocket handkerchief the thickness of a tile, a towel as coarse as a nutmeg grater and a suit of clothes'. He considered the suit of good quality moleskin and well cut.

However,

> the otherwise agreeable effect is somewhat marred by the broad-arrow Government mark, which appears to be applied regardless of all symmetry and indeed of all expense. No general rule apparently exists as to the marking of this cloth, which one must conclude is left entirely to the discretion and good taste of the individual armed with the paint-pot. This want of uniformity thus lends an agreeable variety to the different appearances of individuals; for my part I always felt that I resembled the 'Seven of Spades'.[66]

This was said somewhat tongue-in-cheek but demonstrates the random nature of the application of the markings.

The broad arrow marking was also used on soldiers' great coats at this time 'to deter soldiers from selling them'.[67] But these had been discrete marks inside the clothing rather than daubed all over its surface as was the marking on prisoners' garments.

British prisoners' accounts of the broad arrow marking and photographic records demonstrate that it was only widely used as visible bodily punishment inside British prisons during the latter half of the nineteenth century and into the early twentieth century. This was 40 years after the introduction of the 'model prison'. During the period of British colonial pre-eminence in the early to mid-nineteenth century, the iconic broad arrow marking as visible stigmatisation of criminality was not as visible as it was to be later in the century.

Its introduction in Britain in the late nineteenth century coincided with a more aggressive colonialist policy in response to threats from its colonies and continued into the twentieth century when Britain's Empire was in decline. The broad arrow was not abolished until 1920 and continued in existence until the 1930s (see Chapter 3).

In the USA, the black-and-white striped iconic uniform had been introduced in the early nineteenth century. During this period America's power as a nation-state was not yet fully established and yet it was at this historical juncture that a visible embodiment of punishment was introduced within early American prisons. The demise of the American uniform occurred between 1900 and 1914 at a time when US economic and political pre-eminence was in the ascendant.

This paradigm suggests that nation-states' assertion of power through the embodiment of criminality was at a premium domestically when their political and socio-economic pre-eminence was either not yet highly advanced or under threat. At the very least the iconic prison uniform as public manifestation of the Government's control of criminality did not occur in Britain with the initial introduction of the 'model prison' but later in the century.

A prison photograph (see Fig. 2.4) of inmates at Gloucester prison, in the late nineteenth century, shows men wearing ordinary hard-wearing workwear with discrete broad arrows in a few places on the clothing. These are less indiscriminate markings than those described by D_S_ in Coldbath Fields Prison and by the Suffragette Sylvia Pankhurst (1882–1960) when she was in Holloway prison in 1906. 'The broad arrows daubed with white paint on the dresses were fully four inches long',[68] she wrote.

But not only was prison dress marked with the broad arrow, the soles of boots were also indelibly imprinted with it, so that prisoners' identities as government property would be left in the ground on which they trod:

> But weren't they boots? Fully fourteen pounds in weight. I put them on and the weight of them seemed to fasten me to the ground. It was not that alone, but the sight of the impression they left on the gutter as you looked at the footprints of those who walked before you, struck terror to your heart. There was the felon's brand of the 'broad arrow' impressed on the soil by every footstep . . . the nails in the soles of your boots and shoes were hammered in an arrow shape so that whatever ground you trod you left traces that Government property had travelled over it.[69]

The broad arrow, then, did exist and across genders. It was this mark on British prison garments that, similarly to the black-and-white stripes in America, were to become iconic signifiers of criminality for the public spectator.

This bodily labelling of criminals was in keeping with the thinking of Cesare Lombroso, the late nineteenth-century criminologist, and the early writings on penal reform of Havelock Ellis.[70] Although Havelock Ellis later repudiated Lombroso's thinking, in the 1900s he adhered to the science of criminal types. Lombroso proposed individual punishments for prisoners based on physiological measurement and the increased use of photography as criminal identification.

The British broad arrow and striped American uniforms were not individual but collective markers of criminality. They were visible embodiments of criminality and

Figure 2.4 Men in Gloucester prison c. 1900.

type cast prisoners as knowable by the authorities and outsiders. In this respect, the uniforms were integral to the surveillant and ideological role played by prison authorities and the public gaze in the control of the criminal.

resistance to prison uniform as criminality – Ireland

There were a number of dress practices in the latter half of the nineteenth century that conformed to some type of uniformity throughout American and European prisons. Individual prisoners resisted these forms of embodiment of punishment through small everyday changes such as the *ad hoc* construction of 'bustles'. Additionally, prisoners affiliated to political movements resisted uniformity that labelled them as criminal rather than political. Most notably this occurred amongst Irish Fenian prisoners in Britain in the 1870s.

In France 'political status' had been granted in the early nineteenth century as a right.[71] However, this right had to be fought for amongst Irish political prisoners within the British penal system. Irish political prisoners demanded political status or 'combatant' status that required British prison authorities to recognise their different identity from criminal prisoners. This meant that they should be permitted to wear their own clothes.

From the 1870s to 1900, Ireland saw successive attempts by William Gladstone's Liberal Government (1809–1898) to introduce Home Rule Bills which Conservative

Governments set out to block. As a result, there was both class war and national-ist upheavals. Laws were enforced against Fenians, Land League proponents and London socialists and radicals affiliated to the struggle in Ireland. Political status in prisons became as confused an issue as the political situation outside the prison walls. On the one hand, those imprisoned in Irish and English jails suffered even harsher measures than ordinary criminals. On the other hand, concessions were made in 1889, whereby 'the government of the time offered prison-issue civilian-style clothing as a possible way to resolve the issue'.[72]

However, many prisoners refused to wear jail clothes of any description even if they were 'civilian-style'. They objected to doing so on the grounds that it was their right to wear their own clothes rather than a privilege to wear prison issue clothing of any type, bestowed on them by prison warders.[73] This resulted in a confusing situation whereby a number of different practices existed. Individual Irish political prisoners and those who were arrested in support of the Irish cause had to nego-tiate their clothing status within the prison walls according to the balance of power outside the prison.[74]

The demand by Irish prisoners for political status established an important con-stituent of the Fenian movement. Particularly this was the case when Fenian prison-ers were sentenced to penal servitude and experienced even harsher conditions than criminal prisoners. This was the situation for Michael Davitt (1846–1906) and Jeremiah O'Donovan Rossa[75] (1831–1915) in the 1870s when they were forced to wear prison uniforms with the broad arrow branded on their boots and clothing.

William O'Brien (1852–1928), who was sentenced in the 1880s for organising tenants to stand up to evictions meted out by landlords, demanded substantial changes in clothing conditions. As a result of O'Brien's demands, prisoners such as Wilfrid Blunt (1840–1922), who was arrested in 1887 for organising against the evic-tions, followed his lead in fighting to obtain political status for prisoners. Although Blunt at first thought O'Brien's demands were exaggerated, 'it now seemed to me one where a stand needed to be made'. He refused to part with his own clothing and was threatened with force by the Governor. In response, he wore little clothing. He adds, 'in order to obtain humaner treatment for all political prisoners I should fortify my complaint of the violence resorted to…a different treatment was con-ceded and by the end of the year the former [political prisoners] all wore their own clothes and were relieved from menial duties'.[76]

Despite this success, the British Government was reluctant to acknowledge it. A. J. Balfour (1848–1930), who was Irish Secretary in Lord Salisbury's Conservative Cabinet from March 1887, said in the House of Commons that 'he made no diffe-rence in his treatment of political and common prisoners'.[77]

In the late nineteenth century concessions were made. These came about partly as a result of acute public awareness of the issue of Home Rule. The Liberal Party incorporated them into their agenda that was promoted by Gladstone and they were widely supported by members of the Opposition Party. Landlord evictions in Ireland

and the brutal response of the police to protests against the conviction of Irish leaders such as O'Brien also contributed to the granting of these concessions. Two protests, for example, one at Mitchelstown in County Cork in September 1887 and 'Bloody Sunday' in Trafalgar Square in November 1887, resulted in the deaths and injuries of hundreds of Irish people. In order to legitimise the harsh British response in the eyes of the British public, the Government responded to demands within prisons once the leaders were convicted.

Thus, it was during this period that demands for the wearing of their own clothes as 'political status' were first raised by Irish Republican prisoners and were met with a degree of success.

resistance to prison dress as criminality – Russia

Fyodor Dostoyevsky (1821–1881) did not consider himself primarily involved in organised politics. He was nevertheless arrested and sentenced in 1850 to 4 years penal servitude in Russia for his part in the Petrashevist conspiracy. This political movement allegedly conspired to overthrow the monarchy.

The novel, *The House of the Dead*, refers to prison conditions in Russia as unconducive to the reformation of the criminal. It describes the conditions of forced labour and solitary confinement as draining 'the vital sap from a man...and then presents the withered mummy, the semi-lunatic as a model of reform and repentance.'[78]

In 1845 Tsar Nicholas I had proposed a system of solitary cells in Russia along the lines of the model prison in Pentonville. This system was adopted in Russia in certain penal institutions for certain categories of prisoners. In Dostoyevsky's novel there are references to prison dress practices based on the uniform adopted from England and other European institutions, as well as more feudal systems of exchange and bartering of clothing. Archaic practices included 'ragged clothes, branded faces, shaven heads and the sound of chains'.[79] There was also the uniform worn by convicts that was similar to the 'parti-coloured' prison dress introduced in the early model prison at Gloucester. 'Each category of convicts was distinguished by the clothes it wore; the jackets of some were half dark-brown and half grey, as were their trousers – one leg grey, the other dark brown.'[80] At the same time 'some men earned money by doing nothing but buying and selling secondhand goods. Every last scrap of cloth was prized and was used for some purpose or other'.[81]

The House of the Dead is a fictional account of the journey made by one particular prisoner through a life of hell to the re-evaluation on his release from prison of what it is to be free in a philosophical sense. He refers to extant prison conditions in Russia at the time consistent with other European prison practices. He details the ways in which prisoners, whether as a protest for 'political status' or through the setting up of systems of exchange, made meaning for themselves in a world circumscribed by rules of dress as a category of criminality.

Dostoyevsky makes parallels in this novel and in *Crime and Punishment* between personal imprisonment as alienation and institutional incarceration. He considered that the humiliating nature of the prisoner's material conditions contributed to the experience of alienation and despair and not to reform. 'It is not the horrors of a convict life...nor his shaven head and ragged clothing that had broken him...the fetters he did not even feel...it was the wound to his pride that made him fall ill.'[82]

Peter Kropotkin (1842–1921), who served time in Russian and French prisons a little later than Dostoyevsky, saw prison dress as integral to the way prisons functioned as extensions of a malevolent capitalist system and considered that it created rather than deterred criminal cultures. This led him to argue in the late nineteenth century for the abolition of prisons. Kropotkin had been employed to conduct an enquiry into the Siberian penal system during the reform period in Russia between 1859 and the early 1860s. However, the report was ignored in subsequent clamp downs that took place from the 1870s. Kropotkin was arrested as a political activist in 1874 and spent time in Russian prisons before he escaped to Europe where he joined a number of anarchist organisations. He was arrested in France in 1882 and imprisoned for 5 years in Clairvaux Prison where he experienced the 'special conditions' political prisoners enjoyed in nineteenth-century France. Although separated from ordinary criminals, whether as an observer or as a result of his 'political status', Kropotkin was in the position to comment on a variety of European prison conditions during the late nineteenth century.

In his report, conducted in the mid-nineteenth century, Kropotkin observed that despite certain reforms in Russian prisons, such as the abolition of the branding iron, the worst conditions were experienced by prisoners sentenced to hard labour in Siberia. They had to make the journey from St. Petersburg in inadequate clothing and under exhausting conditions in inclement weather. They were regularly beaten and put in irons and one woman said that after 'three days' march...my feet were wounded, and my stockings full of blood'. A man was found 'quite naked' and others experienced 'the terrible damp and cold, without anything of the nature of a blanket'.[83] This situation, reminiscent of eighteenth-century 'malign neglect', continued in hard labour camps well into the twentieth century, despite agitation for reform.

However, Kropotkin experienced, as a prisoner himself, the equally deleterious conditions in the newly built model prison in St. Petersburg. He mentions that despite its cleanliness, prisoners were kept in irons and in solitary confinement for years on end. Uniforms consisted of 'grey clothes, with a yellow diamond on the back, and open shoes'.[84] As in other European prison systems, prisoners exchanged primitive conditions for the iniquities of the 'silent' and 'separate' system, where either uniforms or inadequate dress were additional punishment to the loss of freedom. Kropotkin observed that conditions in French prisons in the 1880s were more congenial than in Russian prisons. However, he said that they were run unscrupulously whether by the State or by 'private undertakers'. In Lyons prison, where Kropotkin spent the first

3 months of his incarceration, private provisioners – 'undertakers' – supplied prison uniforms to the convicted prisoners. They consisted of a 'brown jacket, all covered with multicoloured rags roughly sewn to cover the holes, and the patched up trousers six inches too short to reach the immense wooden shoes – they [prisoners] came out quite abashed with the ridiculous dress they had assumed…a dress which is in itself a story of degradation.'[85]

Kropotkin visited England in the late 1880s on his release from Clairvaux Prison. He observed that prison clothing, including the numbering of prisoners' identities, was similar to French and Russian prison conditions and was equally deleterious to prisoners' rehabilitation. Prison clothing in the model prison imbued the convict 'with the utmost contempt for human feelings. He divides the world into two parts: that to which he and his comrades belong and the outer world represented by the governor, the warders, the employers. A brotherhood rapidly grows between all the inmates of a prison against all those who do not wear the prisoner's dress'.[86]

Prison dress was central to Kropotkin's avocation of penal reform. He explicitly saw the iniquity of the embodiment of punishment as grounds for his socialist belief in the transformation of society based on equality of wealth, employment and education. These were the only conditions that would enable the realisation of 'self'. The humiliation of 'self', whether espoused by political systems based on the inequality of capitalism or regimes of punishment, merely encouraged anti-social feelings. Kropotkin deliberately made this link between prison clothing, prison reform and radical social and political change.

Although he recognised that there was worth in the medical treatment and care of the mentally ill in prisons, he criticised late nineteenth-century criminological theories such as those of Lombroso. Kropotkin did not agree that criminality was biologically determined. Rather criminality was caused by social 'difference of the circumstances under which they were born and have grown up'.[87]

conclusion

Nineteenth-century penal developments in Europe and America focused on the increasingly controlled and regimented punishment of the individual. In line with this type of penal thinking were a variety of attempts to implement uniforms as conspicuous punishment. By the end of the nineteenth century this ethos was changing towards more rehabilitative notions of confinement as therapeutic.

However, prison uniforms, the labelling of prisoners as criminal types and the humiliation of prisoners through the enforced loss of identity in prison dress were to continue well into the twentieth century.

Nineteenth-century punitive regimes still veered between prison clothing conditions of both malign neglect, as in the eighteenth century, and severe uniforms imposed within the model prison. Welfarist and socialist penal reforms as well as the more radical alternatives proposed by Kropotkin would effect prison clothing in Europe and America at the beginning of the twentieth century.

seams of change: the abolition of iconic uniforms, 1900s to 1930s

But that the dreadful thing about modernity was that it put tragedy into the raiment of comedy, so that the great realities seemed commonplace or grotesque or lacking in style. It is quite true of modernity...Our very dress makes us grotesque. We are the zanies of sorrow. We are clowns whose hearts are broken. We are specially designed to appeal to the sense of humour.

Oscar Wilde, *De Profundis* (London, 1911/1905)

A wardress shouted: 'Make haste and get dressed!' as she hung...some clothing over the door – strange-looking garments, all plentifully marked with the 'broad arrow', black on light colours, white on dark; stockings of harsh, thick wool, black with red rings round the legs; long cotton drawers, red striped to match the chemise; huge, thick petticoats – as bunchy and full at the top as those of a Dutch peasant, but without their neatness, cobbled into a broad waistband of capacious girth...and tied with tapes fastened in front; a curious sort of corset reaching from neck to knees...a Dutch bonnet with strings under the chin, and two pieces of cotton stuff, blue and white plaid...One of them with tapes stitched to it was to be worn as an apron, the other was the weekly handkerchief. Did I say weekly? Weekly in theory; even in the reformed period of 1921...I have known prisoners to be left six weeks without a change of clothing.

Sylvia Pankhurst, *The Suffragette Movement: An Intimate Account of Persons and Ideals* (London, 1931)

introduction

The words of the prisoners quoted above focus on prison dress as demeaning and risible at the turn of the nineteenth and twentieth centuries.

Oscar Wilde (1854–1900) was imprisoned for 2 years between 1895 and 1897 for homosexual offences and the Suffragette, Sylvia Pankhurst was imprisoned for short stretches of time during the years 1906 to 1914. Although both were upper middle class, they were on the fringes of respectable bourgeois society. Oscar

Wilde was a radical aesthete. Sylvia Pankhurst was a socialist and later communist Suffragette. Their writing about the indignity of prison dress and life at the turn of the century in Britain is informed by their class position outside the prison. However, they articulate issues relating to prison dress that are consistent with accounts of prisoners across class and gender.

This chapter explores the increasing visibility of the criminal as receiver of welfarist policies in Europe and America in the early twentieth century. But prison reform was not achieved without a struggle. Nor did it progress evenly.

early twentieth-century modernity and prison dress

Oscar Wilde's reference to modernity links prison dress specifically with the expansion of the fashion system within the wider social and political context of fin de siecle Europe and America. The demeaning nature of prison dress was particularly evident to the wearer and the spectator in a world where fashionability visually dominated the city streets. People were commercially exhorted to transform their experience of the everyday through the consumption of things and clothing.

In Britain colonial expansion was accompanied by the increasing import of fabrics from India and China. Additionally, industrial and technological change in the production of dress led to an increase in the turnover of available clothing. Glittering palaces of consumption[1] were subsequently built as department stores to display and sell, amongst other things, exotic fabrics and apparel in London and Paris. This was at the same time as America's establishment and exportation of streamlined industrial practices of mass production and consumption. These developments provided both more inclusive and also exclusive forms of aesthetic, social and economic public participation in the novel and the new. The fashion system was inextricably woven into the condition of visible modernity at the turn of the century.

There were also those without the economic power to buy into the new or too exhausted by the demands of assembly line production and gruelling domestic service to enjoy it. Thus, in London, East End girls working in the rag trade in close proximity to the wealthy show case of the West End were seduced but embittered by what they saw:

> There were about fourteen of us, seven either side of the table, working on each dress, and when the Court dresses were finished we were all told, 'no more work, off you go'. We used to go up to the West End every so often to see if there was any work...They were all dressed up in their diamonds, jewellery and beautiful clothes, and we used to stand there, bitter, thinking to ourselves, 'fancy, they're all dressed up and there's us, we can't even get a job to live on.[2]

Charles Baudelaire (1818–1883), the poet and cultural commentator of late nineteenth-century Parisian life, foresaw in the 1860s social world the predicament Wilde and Pankhurst wrote about in 1900 and between 1914 and the 1920s, respectively.

He was prompted to see the debilitating effect of modernity on the people in the city. In his prose poem *Paris Spleen* he writes of a man taking charge of two children 'all in rags' looking at the 'new dazzling café' in which Baudelaire was sitting: 'The eyes of the father said: "How beautiful it is!...All the gold of the poor world must have found its way onto those walls." The eyes of the little boy: "How beautiful it is...But it is a house where only people who are not like us can go." ' Baudelaire comments, 'Not only was I touched by this family of eyes, but I was even a little ashamed of our glasses and decanters, too big for our thirst.'[3]

Even more damaging is the exchange of gaze between the 'self' and the crowds when instead of rags, the poor are dressed as clowns. Baudelaire describes an old man 'as though he had exiled himself in shame from all these splendours...I saw a pitiful old clown...the ruin of a man...Here absolute misery, and a misery made all the more horrible by being tricked out in comic rags...He was mute and motionless. He had given up, he had abdicated'.[4]

The clown's 'abdication' from participation in modernity is not that of the radical's refusal but that of the poor's almost suicidal disengagement and alienation. Oscar Wilde makes similar connections with Baudelaire, between poverty and dress compared to the luxurious apparel available to those with money outside the prison. As a result of this visible disparity, the prisoner is humiliated by the laughter aroused by prison garb. The way in which prison and political authorities mediated the appearance of the 'criminal' type reinforced their culpability in the public gaze in the early twentieth century.

The tragedy of the clown and the prisoner dressed in parti-coloured uniform or the broad arrow mark and ill-fitting clothing, as Sylvia Pankhurst mentions, is highlighted by their witnessing and being viewed by the glittering world of modernity.

The need for welfare reforms, including conditions in prisons, in the first half of the twentieth century was partially informed by a growing awareness of the economic disparity between classes. As a result of the increase in conspicuous wealth in Europe and America in this period, middle-class philanthropists, Liberals, Socialists and working class movements were prompted to promote welfarist causes.

The first decades of the twentieth century saw penal reforms throughout Europe and America, including reforms in prison dress. Concepts of prisoner rehabilitation began to gain ground. In this respect, clothing could play an important role, reinforcing self-esteem by permitting the expression of an individual prisoner's identity.

Reforms were premised on notions of the 'normalisation' of the prisoner inside prison, in order that they might find employment and live 'normal' lives outside prison. Prison reformers recognised that ex-prisoners' social inclusion was dependent on a variety of enabling provisions within the prison walls. Thus, during the early twentieth century, prison regimes experimented with improving prisoners' educational and social conditions including prison clothing.

Reforms gradually abolished uniforms that visibly stigmatised the prisoner as criminal. In 1904 the striped uniform in Auburn prison in America was abolished with preference given to workwear 'greys'. Many Federal prisons followed suit in 1914. In Britain the broad arrow was legally abolished in 1920, although it continued to be worn into the 1930s. In some cases this led to the introduction of the prisoners' wearing of their own clothes. For example, the complete abolition of prison uniforms in Russian prisons took place in 1918 just after the 1917 Bolshevik Revolution and led to prisoners wearing their own clothes (see Chapter 6).

Prison staff uniforms followed a similar pattern to the uniforms of authority outside the prison walls. Uniforms worn by prison staff, the police force or military and uniforms that embodied corporate identity or professions and public institutions, communicated their status within the social fabric of the everyday.[5] These uniforms have a history of a fluctuating relationship with fashion based on conspicuous identity integral to the workings of specific organisations within broader visible social and political networks such as the police force and nursing. Prisoners' clothing, however, was largely hidden from sight, as were the prisoners who wore it.

One of the differences between prisoners' clothing and other forms of institutional dress at this time was in the economic condition of its provision. Prisoners did not participate in the everyday exchange of money and clothes. Clothing was provided as public[6] rather than as private consumption. Thus, change in prison clothing depended on the availability of Government funds in line with prevailing attitudes towards criminality. The provision of functional workwear for a cheap work force of prisoners also vacillated according to the economic conditions of the time. Contemporary occupational and working class dress, as we have seen in the previous chapters, influenced prison clothing changes in line with penal reforms.

The development of prison clothing in line with fluctuations in welfarist policies did not traverse a straight line towards more and more leniency.[7] Yet, significant changes occurred in this period.

the impact of international working class movements on prison dress reform

The Enlightenment, the French Revolution and the American War of Independence had influenced early nineteenth-century reforms of Howard, Fry and Bentham. Early twentieth-century penal reform movements in Europe and America were influenced by the work of Karl Marx (1818–1883) and working class, socialist and nationalist organisations in the late nineteenth and early twentieth centuries.

In Britain the Chartist movement in the 1840s had led to the establishment of workers' rights through the recognition of Trade Unions, the emergence of the Independent Labour Party and demands for suffrage. In Ireland, the growth of the Fenian movement in the late nineteenth century meant that demands for the same rights as 'prisoners of war', negotiated by Germany and England in the First World

War came to the fore. The British Government granted the Irish the right to wear their own clothes in 1917. However, they were only granted these rights 'on the condition that the prisoners elect a commandant who would be responsible to the governor for discipline'.[8] The British authorities recognised prisoners' 'political status' according to a hierarchy of internal disciplinary measures. This right proved to be a moveable feast, a concession that was removed or reinstated according to the political mood of the time.

For example, 'political status' was not granted to militant working class organisations such as the Clyde workers in Scotland in the same period. They had organised strikes, rent strikes and a campaign against enforced conscription for the war. Among socialist leaders and Clyde workers who were arrested in Glasgow in 1916 was John Maclean (1879–1923). He was sentenced to 3 years' hard labour, first in the still existing 'separate and silent system' of Calton Jail in Edinburgh and then in Peterhead prison. He said that in the prison system at Calton Jail, 'he lost his identity and became convict 2652'.[9] He compared the harshness of the Scottish prison system with the more favourable situation in France, where political prisoners were allowed their own clothes. 'But in bourgeois Scotland they were allowed none of these privileges. They were criminals, and nothing else.'[10] The response by the British establishment to the demand for 'political status' in prison clothing fluctuated from one prison to another, from domestic to colonial rule.

In India, the British imprisoned Mahatma Gandhi (1869–1948) on a number of occasions for civil disobedience in the run up to independence in 1947. Gandhi wrote of the complexity of 'political status' and prison clothing in the colonial context. The demand for distinction from criminal prisoners rested not merely on the wearing of prisoners' own clothing. Between 1908 and 1913, Gandhi suggested that Indian Nationalists should wear *khadi* (home-grown and spun cotton)[11] in order to boycott imported, expensive British cotton goods. Clothing was a broader political issue than merely one of 'political status' in prison. He was critical of the demand for 'political status' that privileged and distanced himself and other political prisoners from ordinary prisoners. He considered identification with ordinary prisoners to be as important as the demand for 'political status'.

He said,

> it is difficult to observe jail rules and yet maintain one's self-respect. Some of these rules are naturally humiliating. For instance we have no choice but to let ourselves be confined in a cell. We must, thus, respect the rules which apply to all prisoners. At the same time we should firmly oppose any measure which is intended merely to humiliate us.[12]

Gandhi identified how the issue of prison clothing and political status embodied specific political conditions within different nationalist and anti-imperialist contexts. Indian prison clothing, simply made up of *khadi* cloth, was introduced after independence in 1947. It was symbolic of Nationalist identity and anti-colonial struggle.

the gendering of prison clothing:
the Suffragette experience in Britain

The prison experience of the Suffragettes in Britain publicly exposed the notorious broad arrow markings of prison dress. This was partly as a result of the imprisonment of articulate political activists who were used to writing to the press and addressing meetings to raise awareness of radical causes, prison conditions and in this case prison clothing. When released, activists visited comrades and friends inside prison and continued to impart to the press the demeaning nature of imprisonment.

For socialist Suffragettes this was a way of exposing how the poor were treated, given that the majority of the criminal population were from the poorer classes. For middle-class agitators who were not socialists (as were many Suffragettes in the Women's Suffrage and Political Union, WSPU), the conditions in prisons were a source of moral indignation as to the way they themselves and prisoners in general were treated.

Constance Lytton (1869–1923) dedicated her writing to prisoners. Her appeal to prisoners to 'lay hold of your inward self and keep tight hold'[13] was condescending. However, she specifically mentioned that the exchange of experiences between ordinary prisoners and Suffragettes contributed to a radicalised middle-class understanding of impoverishment and criminality. The Suffragettes used prison dress and the conditions in prison as a form of propaganda for their cause.

In May 1909 the WSPU held a bazaar to raise funds at the Prince's Skating Rink in Knightsbridge and in April 1910 they held another in Cross Halls in Glasgow, Scotland. These bazaars combined simulations of the prison conditions they had experienced in prisons around the country with stalls for cakes, flowers and bric-a-brac. The organisation of the space was such that stalls were placed in the middle and around the walls were prison cells and a polling booth. Within the prison cells women re-enacted the life of Suffragette prisoners. Postcards (see Fig. 3.1) depicted women such as Emmeline Pankhurst (1858–1928) and Annie Kenney (1879–1953) dressed in broad arrow clothing, aprons and bonnets and large wooden prison number labels pinned to the front of their dresses.

In the re-enactments at the exhibitions in 1909 and 1910 the prison garments were replicas. The measurements of the broad arrow markings were possibly exaggerated for propaganda purposes. Nevertheless, they demonstrated the demeaning nature of the broad arrow that Sylvia Pankhurst describes as 'daubed with white paint and fully four inches long'.[14] Women sewed, mopped the floor or stood vacantly looking at the barred window. Also in the exhibition hall was a reconstructed prison cell in which a male political prisoner was incarcerated. The catalogue of the exhibitions described the reason for this inclusion. 'The cell of this political offender is twice the size of the ordinary cell... He is able to wear his own clothes.'[15]

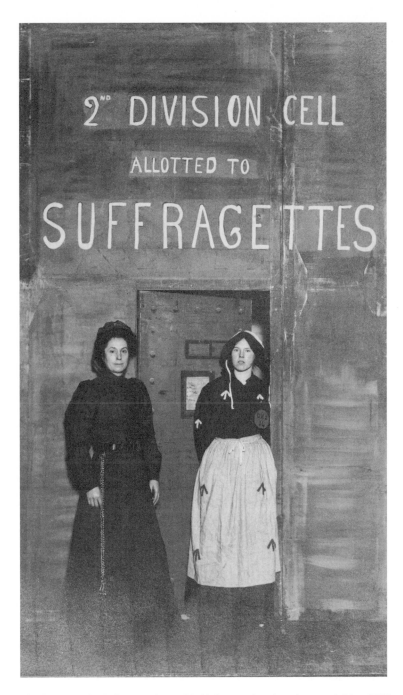

Figure 3.1   Postcard of a Suffragette dressed in Holloway prison broad arrow clothing, 1909.

The Suffragettes saw 'political status' and the wearing of civilian clothing as a right that crossed the gender divide. In 1909 and 1910 they considered that their lack of 'political status', in comparison to that of 'the political offender' (Irish prisoners), represented women's inequality. However, the Suffragettes' catalogue does not consider the struggle of the Irish prisoners historically. The Irish struggle for 'political status' had been waged throughout the nineteenth century.[16]

But it was not until after the Easter Rising in Dublin in 1916 that they were granted 'the same rights as "prisoners of war" '.[17] These rights had partly been won by long struggle and partly a consequence of the First World War agreements.

The Suffragette movement had started in the late nineteenth century. It was not until their campaign became aggressively agitational and broadened to include mass campaigning, between 1906 and 1914, that it gained sufficient public support to challenge the Government. It was during this period that the demand for 'political status' was added to the demand for women's right to the vote. As a propaganda tool the simulated WSPU exhibitions and the attenuated texts in the catalogues raised questions in the public domain about the inconsistency of 'political status' practised within British prisons. The main branch of the WSPU stopped their Suffragette activities in 1914 at the outbreak of the First World War. In Britain, propertied women over 30 were permitted the vote in 1918 at the close of war. Universal suffrage for women was not granted until 1928. The Suffragettes eventually gained what they had set out to achieve in terms of suffrage and also raised concerns for the general condition of women in prison.

Broader questions of how women prisoners were dressed and the effect imprisonment was meant to have on women's transgression of the social codes and ascribed gender roles within Edwardian society were taken up by penal reform organisations. During the last years of the nineteenth century and early years of the twentieth century in America and Europe there was recognition that, for the most part, the harsh punishment regimes of the mid-nineteenth century were inappropriate for women. Female crimes mainly amounted to petty theft, prostitution and alcoholism for which they were sentenced to short periods in prison. As a result, Local Reformatories in Britain were established on the American model[18] and were separate from State prisons. Women alcoholics made up a large percentage of admissions to Local Reformatories in the early years of the twentieth century. There was also an attempt to segregate women who were deemed incapable of being reformed by imprisonment because of their 'weaker mental health'. They required 'more flexible regimes in women's prisons'.[19] Women prisoners were increasingly allocated to rehabilitative regimes for the perpetrators of persistent misdemeanours rather than severe crimes. The few hardened women criminals were relegated to tougher regimes of punishment.

It was in these tougher conditions that Suffragettes found themselves as they challenged current gender stereotypes of impressionable and weak-minded wrong-doers across class boundaries. Instead, activists such as Sylvia Pankhurst,

Kropotkin and others who campaigned for 'political status' voiced the construction of the prisoner 'self' as political. The writing of these political agitators integrates the construction of the 'self' with prison dress changes within the broader political analysis of disciplinary society as a whole.[20] In turn the prison authorities branded them as criminals in convict clothing. As a result of this treatment, political activist prisoners could proclaim to the outside world the ways in which the early twentieth-century prison provided mechanisms for ensuring the continuity of disciplinary punishment. They also exposed the contradictions inherent in these systems. For, at the same time as branding them criminals, the prison authorities sought to feminise the Suffragettes' political voices. They were forced to carry out traditionally feminine tasks such as knitting socks, scrubbing floors or sewing. Although prison reforms took into account current notions of treatment of prisoners as opposed to punishment, a type of essentialism regarding the gendered nature of incarceration practices was still evident. Yet, the garments themselves belie this gendered embodiment of criminality. The broad arrow was a form of non-gendered prison dress and indiscriminately labelled all prisoners as criminals regardless of gender. Thus, women prisoners, whether Suffragettes or incarcerated for other convictions, were denied the ability to express notions of femininity through clothing. This is not to essentialise women as merely concerned with their appearance, since male prisoners were equally demeaned by iconic prison clothing. But it clearly indicates the contradictory nature of prison institutions' clothing practices in relation to the gender expectations of the rehabilitation of women and the resultant confusion in the minds of women prisoners.

The Suffragettes in Britain were categorised and bodily demarcated as 'Second' or 'Third Division' prisoners. Their clothing was coloured accordingly, although the broad arrow remained. 'Waiting by the office', wrote Sylvia Pankhurst, 'I saw again my fellow Suffragettes with a few others of the Second Class. Dressed in dark green to distinguish them from the rest of us in the Third Class chocolate brown, they were regarded as a trifle more respectable than the common herd'.[21] The Suffragettes had all been charged with the same sentences and for the same misdemeanours outside the prison walls. Yet, inside prison the garments embodied further categorisation based on whether a prisoner's behaviour was 'good' or 'bad'. Additionally, Sylvia Pankhurst's description of prison clothing indicates that the make of the clothing, the lack of fit and the coarseness of the cloth and stockings were uncomfortable and ungainly. 'The prisoners were scrambling for dresses of dark chocolate coloured serge in the heaps on the floor... I pulled from the pile a skirt many feet too wide... and a bodice with several large rents, badly cobbled together.'[22]

Although Sylvia Pankhurst and many of the Suffragettes were from upper middle class and professional backgrounds, there were also working class women such as the cotton mill worker Annie Kenney. Working class women, imprisoned as Suffragettes, felt equally demeaned by prison clothing. The importance of clothing to working class girls' self-esteem was clearly evident from the late nineteenth century. The knowledge of the importance of dress to young girls had come about as a consequence of the 'economic system of a household [that] might provide a means to a child's understanding of herself'.[23] Implied is not merely an understanding of 'self' through the acquisition of clothes but that additionally suitable clothing meant that marginalisation, whether in terms of class or gender, could be minimised in the gaze of others. At the turn of the twentieth century class consciousness in relation to clothing was evident at a time when fashions were widely seen in newspapers and magazines, on postcards and in the street on billboards.

Yet, there was a denial by prison authorities that the harsh clothing practices of early twentieth-century prisons militated against women's construction of sartorial identity and rehabilitation. But prisoners themselves were aware that the demeaning nature of prison clothing prevented the motivation to self-improvement. The demoralisation of the prison experience was expressed in women's body language as Sylvia Pankhurst mentions when she describes the exercise yard in Holloway prison. 'Then I turned to the prisoners, plodding round with dull gaze bent downward, treading without heed through the water on sunk stones, though there was dry ground within reach.'[24] Sylvia Pankhurst's education and class background enabled her to voice a common experience of many prisoners in their consciousness of ruptured identity through the wearing of prison clothing.

In October 1906, the Home Office ordered the Suffragettes, Sylvia Pankhurst amongst them, to transfer to First Division status. This meant that they could wear their own clothes. The fight for 'political status' had achieved minor concessions but it was not until later in the 1920s that the broad arrow was abolished for all prisoners. When Sylvia Pankhurst was released after 14 days of imprisonment, she extended her political activity to 'secure prison reforms, not for ourselves, but for the ordinary prisoners'.[25] She saw that it was the dirtiness of clothing as much as the lack of design of garments that was disturbing to any prisoner. This was particularly the case for working class women and girls who saw 'decent clothing' as a 'means of entry into the social world'.[26]

political resistance and prison clothing in America

The incarceration of political prisoners was equally harsh in America in the early years of the twentieth century when 'thousands of wobblies [an abbreviated name for the International Workers of the World or IWW] were arrested and given long prison sentences'.[27] Amongst the more prominent women imprisoned for agitating for suffrage and women's rights through improved conditions at work were Elizabeth Gurley Flynn (1890–1964) of the IWW and the anarchist Emma Goldman (1869–1940).

Goldman had been imprisoned a number of times in the 1890s and was imprisoned again in 1917 'under draconian wartime legislation' for organising 'a

No-Conscription League'.[28] In the 1890s she had been imprisoned in 'the tombs' in the prison on Blackwell's Island Penitentiary near New York City. She described prisoners as 'blue and white striped figures [who] slouched by, automatically forming into a line'. She talks of 'the monotony of the regulation dress in baggy and ungainly attire' and 'the daily degradation of being forced to march in lock-step to the river, carrying the bucket of excrement accumulated during twenty-four hours'.

She saw the day-to-day humiliation of prison conditions as part of a broader political critique of capitalist society in which 'crime is the result of poverty'.[29] She was again imprisoned in 1917. Some conditions had improved, such as the abolition of the black-and-white striped uniform. Nevertheless prisons still administered punishment through the distribution of humiliating and ill-fitting regulation clothing.

In the early twentieth century in America organised radicals and labour men and women were arrested when they went on strike for the introduction of the 'eight hour day' and increased wages in a number of industries. These included textiles and garment workers, coal miners, Ford workers and those in the steel industry. As James Cannon (1890–1974), a member of the IWW and later the Communist Party of America, wrote in 1926, 'the mills of capitalist justice grind out victims for the penitentiary. If you put your finger on any corner of the map of America...you can say with certainty: "In this state is a penitentiary which confines labour prisoners"'.[30]

Although penal reforms in America had led to the abolition of the demeaning black-and-white striped uniform, harsh conditions and inconsistencies existed. In the 1920s American industrial power was reinforced by the rigid control of the labour force in the mechanised assembly line conditions in factories. When organised labour and radicals objected to these conditions they were incarcerated. As a result, political activists exposed the conditions in prisons whereby prisoners provided a cheap labour force that benefited the American economy. These work conditions in prisons meant that clothing needed to be functional and hard wearing as a replacement for the striped prison uniform. But it is also clear that there were inconsistencies in the abolition of the striped uniform. Prisoners themselves were aware of these irregularities. As one prisoner said, 'the prisoner is compelled to don a suit of the striped clothing, which as a prison-uniform was abolished some years ago, and must wear it for at least two months after his release'.[31]

Amongst the harsh measures instigated in American prisons at this time was penal servitude. Prisoners worked in the quarries and built their own prisons, such as the Folsom Prison built between 1916 and the 1920s. As a result prisoners in chain gangs, at times, still wore black-and-white stripes in order to deter their escape. In most prisons in America the notorious striped prison clothing was abolished in 1914. However, it was to enter the world outside the prison walls as a visible embodiment of the criminal type in early American films.

In 1917 Charlie Chaplin produced *The Adventurer* in which he saves a family from drowning. He is an escaped convict and appears in striped clothing until, after nearly drowning himself and near naked, he is put in the family's bed. When he wakes up he sees striped clothing hanging over the chair and imagines he is back in prison until he realises they are striped silk pyjamas. He is only recognised by the family as a prisoner after they see his photograph in the striped convict's clothing in the newspaper. Chaplin's identity as an escaped convict is concealed from the family he saves through his lack of striped prison clothing. It is only the media representation of him in the stripes that alerts them to his identification as a criminal. It is this confusion of identity that is the main focus of the film. But the absurdity of the situation lies in the audience's recognition that Chaplin makes fools of the rich family, their inability to question appearances and accept the man who saved their lives.

In 1920 Buster Keaton, in *Convict 13* (see Fig. 3.2), dreams of a prison situation where he, like Chaplin, makes fun of the authorities through a variety of antics dressed in black-and-white striped clothing. Amongst these is a 'gallows humour' gag whereby the rope used to hang him is elastic and prevents his death. The prison authorities are fooled rather than the prisoner. The striped clothing, as in Chaplin's film, presents the viewer with immediate recognition of the heroic underdog humiliated by the clothing, who demonstrates the ability to outwit the authorities.

In the inter-war years, the chronological slippage between the abolition of striped prison garb and its entry into cinematic visual vocabulary provided mass audiences with an immediate fictional stereotype of prisoner identity, despite the demise of the uniform.

But political resistance to stereotyping, whether in striped prison garb or regulation clothing, was not merely a cinematic fiction.

In the early 1920s Marcus Garvey (1887–1940), the organiser of the black nationalist movement of the Universal Negro Improvement Association, was imprisoned in America for supposed fraud.[32] At his trial his clothing communicated resistance to the authorities' essentialist identification of 'negritude' with the 'experience of the slave as servile'.[33] His brown suit, gold monocle and heavy gold watch chain extravagantly subverted bourgeois sartorial dress in 1920s America and demonstrated his defiance. His clothing style was intricately interwoven into Garvey's identity as an African Jamaican. This was one of the first aspects of his political identity the prison regime deliberately attempted to eradicate through the imposition of the prison uniform 'grey' during the 3 years of his imprisonment. His sentence was later proclaimed a miscarriage of justice although he was still deported back to Jamaica.

In the early twentieth century, the international working class movement highlighted the political nature of prison dress. These radical movements affected penal policies and the gradual prison dress changes proposed by reform movements.

Figure 3.2 Buster Keaton in black-and-white striped prison uniform in *Convict 13*, 1920.

early twentieth-century ideas behind penal and dress reform

European countries established prison reform policies domestically in the last decade of the nineteenth century and during the years up to 1914. These were simultaneous with late nineteenth-century imperialist policies that resulted in punitive systems of punishment in the colonies. After 1885 France, for example, relegated recidivist criminals to detention in penal colonies. It was partly owing to the development of technological surveillance mechanisms, such as fingerprinting and other more sophisticated forms of identification, and partly owing to domestic fears of mounting imprisonment rates that French legislation of the 1880s resorted to transportation.[34]

Britain established brutal mass imprisonment camps in South Africa in 1902 and continued to inter and bodily regulate Indian subjects in South East Asian colonies. British colonial imprisonment practices in the mid-nineteenth century had relied on the physical measurement of criminality through the bodily identification of individuals with a tattoo as suspicious, since 'marginalised social groups tended to carry out tattooing'.[35] This practice continued into the early twentieth century alongside the imposition of a complex hierarchy of prison clothing and uniforms. At the same time, the British convict system in Australia was being dismantled.

Throughout the period penal reforms domestically, as in the colonies, did not take a linear direction. As we have seen in Britain and America, the relaxation of prison dress vacillated between the thinking that accompanied broader penal reform and the restrictive conditions of specific incarceration policies. The turn away from the bodily punishment of prisoners as a general social grouping meant that distinctions were increasingly made between types of criminals. These demarcations appeared visibly on clothing or, as in the British colonies in South East Asia, as tattoos.

Early criminological thinking, medical science and the emergence of organised radical politics in Europe and America informed penal reform in this period. In the late nineteenth century, as we have seen, the Italian professor and early criminologist, Cesare Lombroso had highlighted the relationship between the mental and physical characteristics of the criminal mind that resulted in the claim that criminality was inherited and could be identified biologically. According to this line of thinking criminal types could be identified through the measurement and registration of physical abnormalities and be individually treated. Lombroso had drawn partially on early Eugenics studies, whereby it was believed that undesirable human hereditary traits could be improved by State intervention. He also adhered to Social Darwinist thinking that considered social change was driven through competition between individuals, groups and nations. Influenced by this thinking penal reform presaged a turn away from the universal punishment of the criminal and instead introduced a more intensive surveillant culture based on the classification and physical identification of criminality.

Lombroso's theories were particularly applied in France by the Law Enforcement Officer Alphonse Bertillon (1853–1914) who devised rigorous 'scientific' devices for registering criminal identity.[36] These devices for measuring the cranium or physical irregularities of criminals often amounted to a type of physical torture. Yet, the clothing in French penal establishments was never marked with visible signs of punishment, such as stripes or the broad arrow as was the case in British and American prisons. The severity and thoroughness with which French institutions implemented the 'anthropometric' method of criminal identification replaced the perceived need for signifiers of punishment in visibly carceral dress.

Instead of using eye-witness accounts, increasingly police officers resorted to the physical measurement and subsequent labelling of individuals as physical criminal types in order to solve crimes. At the same time as these procedures were introduced, the standardisation of the photographic mug shot of the criminal provided visual evidence for the physical identification of the criminal type. For many penal reformers in Europe, prior to the First World War, the social and material conditions that fostered criminality were a lesser consideration than the biological and scientifically identified characteristics of the criminal.

Scientific explanations for the necessity to reform a number of areas of social and political life from penal to dress reform became popular in the fin de siecle period. In the 1880s the Dress Reform Association, for example, pronounced that dress should be 'healthy' and 'comfortable' rather than embodying the restrictions of the bustle or corseted crinoline. Dr. Gustav Jaeger provided 'rational' justification for utopian socialist, feminist and aesthetic ideas concerning the simplification of dress espoused by movements in Europe, America and Britain during the latter half of the nineteenth century.[37] However, although wool next to the skin was advocated as healthy, in practice it proved itchy and uncomfortable.

There were contradictions inherent within the pronouncements of the Dress Reform Association as there were in the thinking of penal reformers at this time. Yet, dress reform ideas affected mainstream fashion as early criminological, Eugenicist and Social Darwinian ideas influenced conditions in prisons. One of the conditions affected was prison dress. The iconic American and British uniform of embodied punishment that stigmatised all prisoners as criminal was not appropriate to regimes where individual types of criminality were meticulously identifiable. But this did not mean that the demise of the broad arrows and black-and-white stripes was rapid nor that the humiliation of prison clothing was eradicated.

Penal reformers in Britain were influenced by these European developments. The radical sexologist and later member of the Fabian Society, Havelock Ellis (1859–1939), for example, said in the preface to the 1900 edition of his book *The Criminal*, 'but it must be the business of science to deal with the criminal. We used to chain our lunatics. Our lunatic asylums during the past century have become mental hospitals. Our prisons must now really become what it was long ago said they ought to be, moral hospitals'.[38] He said that in order to 'treat' the criminal 'we need to possess full knowledge of the individual criminal'. In his early work he extolled the notion of the prison as a rehabilitative institution through the registration of knowledge about prisoners.

Ellis' ideas about penal reform demonstrate the ambiguous position in which many penal reformers and radicals found themselves at this time. As a socialist and member of the Fabian Society he agreed with the Eugenics movement and Lombroso in their attempt to visualise an improved, utopian world based on medical science and selection. However, later in the 1900s, he criticised Lombroso for his lack of societal analysis as to the cause of criminality.[39] He was influenced by reading Michael Davitt's *Leaves from a Prison Diary* and Kropotkin's *In Russian and French Prisons* that were based on prison experiences. He saw that the deprivation and discipline of prisons was detrimental to the rehabilitation of prisoners. In a later edition of *The Criminal*, Havelock Ellis, along with other penal reformers in the inter-war years, proposed that prisons should therapeutically treat prisoners rather than punish them and that prison reform should not be disconnected from wider social and political reforms. 'We may neglect the problems of social organisation, but we do so at our peril.'[40]

Early socialist welfare policies merged with early criminological ideas to drive changes in prisons in Europe and America. One of these was the eradication of iconic prison clothing that gradually occurred in the early twentieth century. Penal reform movements reflected early twentieth-century 'nonconformity, [which] presented itself, in one aspect at least, as a *modernising* [emphasis in the original] force, on the side of progress and change'.[41]

prison reforms and prison dress changes in America and Britain

Non-conformist views, whether cultural or political, converged at the turn of the century in Britain, espoused by Liberal governments between 1906 and 1922. At the same time international prison commissions took place during this period, the last of which was held in Washington in 1910. The most important agreement of the Congress was the approval of the indeterminate sentence. It stipulated that 'the prisoner would stay in prison until reformed – with a maximum limit'.[42]

This measure had been introduced during the reform years of the late nineteenth century in America and was supported by Havelock Ellis and the Fabians, amongst others, in Britain. The indeterminate sentence emphasised the rehabilitative nature of imprisonment as opposed to punishment. Yet, it also meant uncertainty about release for the prisoner.

Other reforms associated with the international agreements included the centralisation of prison institutions and the provision of education and training for prisoners to be employed in 'useful work'. Prisoners were further categorised. Younger prisoners in their teens were separated from the mainstream prison population. These 're-socialising' measures were meant to prepare 'the inmate for returning to free society'.[43] Socialists in America, such as Eugene V. Debs (1855–1926) and progressive prison reformers such as Thomas Mott Osborne (1859–1926), who had founded the Mutual Welfare League, were, in part, in agreement with these measures. This organisation had been responsible for the eradication of regimented practices in American prisons such as the 'lock-step' and the striped black-and-white uniforms. But, in America, as in Britain and many other countries, these reforms often meant little change for the experience of the prisoner. As one American prisoner said, 'control was still control, whether called treatment or some other euphemism, and life in prison remained grim and forlorn'.[44] Although, in 1904, Auburn prison ceased to dress prisoners in black-and-white stripes,[45] the majority of American prisons did not stop this practice until 1914. And in Britain a report published in 1922 on *English Prisons Today* demonstrated that demeaning punishment practices, such as the use of irons and chaining prisoners to the floor, were still in use.

Despite reforms, and the gradual eradication of iconic uniforms such as the black-and-white stripes in America, prison dress changed little in Europe in the years up to the First World War.

prison dress in France and Britain

The form and placement of the broad arrow in Britain between the 1880s and 1920 when it was abolished varied from prison to prison. In a Home Office photograph (see Fig. 3.3), women prisoners in Gloucester prison in 1900 are dressed in loose clothing, tied at the waist by apron strings. The broad arrow is daubed in black paint at the knee of the dress or apron of the woman prisoner on the right. The cap the prisoners wear is misshapen and has no connection with clothing outside the prison walls. The fitted staff clothing is tailored and in this respect connects with the outside world of fashion. It is as though modernity has passed the female prisoner by and this is all the more evident in contrast to the dress of the prison staff. The prisoners are posed kneeling in the garden of the prison. The photograph gives the impression that the prisoners are being trained in productive work. But clearly they merely touch the grass in their pale coloured calico clothing unsuitable for the task. It is no coincidence that the height differential between standing female prison officers and kneeling prisoners visually demarcates the power relations between prison staff and inmates. The photograph is staged for the benefit of the viewer – the prison authorities and Home Office personnel – in their depiction of the visual embodiment of order and control over prisoners.

Similarly in Fig. 3.4, male prisoners at Wakefield prison are shown in the useless activity of sewing mail bags in a workshop in 1914. The shape of the caps and the marks on the clothing approximate to the lowest rungs of the Army or Navy. The broad arrow mark is underlined by three stripes on the arm. This indicates the

Figure 3.3 Women prisoners in broad arrow clothing in Gloucester prison, c. 1900.

Figure 3.4 Male prisoners in broad arrow clothing, Wakefield Prison, 1914.

'Third Division' status of the prisoner. Additionally there are broad arrows on the cap and a wooden prison label hangs from the lapel. The men are differentiated from the prison officers who are dressed in peaked caps denoting their higher militaristic status equivalent to that of major. This differentiation is reflected in the spatial organisation of the photograph in which an officer stands on a table at the end of the room higher than the seated prisoners.

In France, 'le costume penale' for women prisoners consisted of similar clothing to that of the women at Gloucester. They wore loose-fitting long skirts, white aprons, white bonnets and a white 'fichu' or neckerchief over the shoulders. However, there was no broad arrow marking. This type of prison clothing is evident in a series of photographs taken in a variety of French prisons by Henri Manuel. Although these photographs were taken in the 1930s the clothing had not changed significantly since the early years of the twentieth century. The clothing was not dissimilar to that worn by the French rural poor. However, as in Britain, the clothing was produced in prisons and the quality varied from prison to prison. Men's prison clothing in France did not show distinguishing marks such as the broad arrow but similarly resembled workwear outside the prison walls. However, a bodily identification of men with criminality was the universal shaving of the hair.[46] The clothing itself did not embody punishment practices in France in the visible way that it did in America and Britain. Yet in the penal colony on Devil's Island and other islands in French Guyana, bodily punishment reminiscent of the eighteenth century continued from 1852 until 1946. The condemned were either chained to prison walls or 'forced to work naked in the jungle'.[47]

The unchanging nature of prison clothing in Europe affected men and particularly women. Rather than encouraging women to renounce crime on release from prison, the lack of self-esteem embodied in the wearing of prison clothing marked them as perpetually shamed. This was in contrast to the sartorial aspirations of women outside the prison during the early years of the twentieth century.

> Dress both declares a woman's femininity to the outside world and is one measure of her own self-esteem...And although individuality could be accentuated by the new pleasures – if only by lifting each person momentarily out of the uniform drabness of poverty – the process was under way long before the advent of cheap consumer goods in the 1930s.[48]

The inter-war years saw the continued harsh sartorial punishment of men and women. Even babies, who had either been born in prison or were imprisoned with their mothers, wore prison clothing in some prisons. For example, in Barlinnie Prison in Scotland in 1922 babies wore clothing consisting of blue-and-white striped heavy cotton material (see Fig. 3.5). No one seemingly evaded the bodily marking of criminality through dress, despite attempts at international reform.

Figure 3.5   'Prison clothing worn by a baby, Barlinnie Prison, 1920s.'

the dawning of the abolition of the Broad Arrow

The first penal institutions in Britain to implement abolition of the broad arrow marks were those housing youth offenders. Penal reformers and prison authorities recognised there was a distinction to be made between youth and adult offenders. From the mid-nineteenth century to the early reform years of the twentieth century, the Reform School Movement in America and Northern Europe vacillated between youth offender militaristic regimes and regimes that 'looked to normal schools to produce trained cadres of reform school personnel'.[49]

Incarceration practices veered from corporal punishment and solitary confinement to reform schools that trained boys to be industrial apprentices and inculcated family values into girls. Nineteenth-century reforms continued into the early twentieth century in the provision of 'scaled down prisons for juveniles'.[50]

In Britain this scaling down took the form of a recommendation in 1911 that prison clothing for youth offenders should not display brandings such as the broad arrow. In the early twentieth century there were also attempts, particularly in America, to 'individualise treatment', minimise restraints on the inmates and allow young offenders to wear their own clothes. For example, instead of providing a militaristic model, the superintendent at Whittier State Reform School in California introduced sporting activities to inculcate notions of 'team work' to transform inmates' characters.[51] This initiative heralded moves in Britain to introduce recreational activities into youth offenders' institutions after the First World War. As a result, in the early 1920s clothing followed suit. Although the prison authorities saw these changes in purely functional terms, they were influenced by broader social changes in recreational pursuits in the 1920s. In 1922 the Prison Commission issued a circular proposing that boys' breeches 'with a strap below the knee' were 'not suitable for hard work' as well as requiring 'constant repairs'. As a result prison tailors' shops were instructed to provide 'breeches...shaped like a pair of football shorts coming to an end at the middle of the knee-cap. The stockings will be turned down like a pair of football stockings, and will have a coloured top, the colours (red or yellow) corresponding to the colours of the Divisions in the Institution.'[52]

These stockings were knitted in the tailors' workshop in the prisons and additional yarn for the coloured tops had to be ordered. The detailed consideration of changes in prison clothing is emphasised later in the circular when it is mentioned that everyday shorts for boys would be distinguished from 'Sunday shorts'. It was suggested that a piece of material should be sewn onto the working shorts for this purpose. Importance was given to prevailing notions of sartorial clothing practices outside the institution. The authorities considered 'Sunday best' clothing was a process of normalisation and re-entry into society. Measures were taken to deter boys who wished to wear 'Sunday best' shorts everyday as they would find it hard to acquire a suitable piece of material to sew on to the workday shorts.

Prison authorities thought that boys who were, for the most part, from impoverished backgrounds, would aspire to being better dressed in quality clothing everyday. So they sought preventative measures to curtail these desires on the part of young offenders. The authorities interpreted these as trickery or even an extension of criminality.

Street football teams and 'junior clubs' were, throughout the pre-war and into the inter-war years in Britain, an important part of young boys' experience outside the Borstal. 'Despite the density of housing in most urban areas it was not difficult to find unused land' on which to play football. Consequently 'the teams who before 1914 might have played on the street drifted on to waste ground or municipal parks'.[53] So youths felt relaxed in the sports clothing they were given in the institution. It was, after all, an honorary boy's passion to be a football fan.

The prison authorities misjudged young boys' sartorial preferences in so far as they were more likely to want to be dressed in football-like attire than 'Sunday best'. As much as instigating regimes of power through the increasing knowledge of the individual, prison clothing reform demonstrated an ideological class imposition of values. These constituted false knowledge based on premises deriving from the prison authorities' position of control rather than social investigation.

However, despite the patronising and ill-informed reasons for changes in prison clothing on behalf of prison authorities, reforms did occur. Changes in prison dress practices were influenced by a variety of factors, not least by sartorial class values. Clothing for young offenders was increasingly seen as requiring different prerogatives to that of the adult prison population.

the abolition of the broad arrow

Changes in young offenders' clothing contributed to the drive to abolish the broad arrow marking. A circular from the Comptroller of Prisons to Governors of Borstals in 1916 stated that young offender clothing had 'been modified' and 'since 1911 was only marked with the ' "broad arrow" on the inside of outer clothing'.[54] However, there was an anomaly. Young prisoners who were sentenced to a month or under 'are clothed in the ordinary male prisoners' garments and . . . the articles are marked on the outside with the broad arrow at the time of manufacture'.[55] It was considered difficult to change this practice since it would mean providing a separate stock of clothing in male prisons and that this would prove 'uneconomical'. It was thus suggested that prison clothing throughout the prison system should be changed.

However, since this circular was written during the First World War years of 1914–1918 when prison reform was not a priority, inconsistencies in penal practices occurred. The circular mentioned that despite reforms in young offenders' institutions during the years leading up to the war, there had not been time subsequently to implement them thoroughly. Economic viability was of prime importance for change in prison clothing to occur. This took precedence over broader influences such as considerations of penal reform or clothing developments outside the prison walls.

From 1916 to the 1920s prison authority debates took place as to Borstal Institutions spear-heading wider changes in the abolition of the broad arrow for adult prisoners. In 1916, the reasons given for the initial proposal to abolish all broad arrow markings were that the practice was reminiscent of a past era when convict clothing was 'conspicuous and repulsive'. The marking had served as a deterrent to escape and other less conspicuous marks on clothing could provide the same purpose. But its actual demise did not occur until the 1920s.

This one document raises a number of pertinent issues in the way prison clothing practices changed in the early years of the twentieth century. The official documentation demonstrates a lack of urgency in the abolition of the broad arrow mark. It is only through the accounts of prisoners at the time that the extent of its use and the effect it had on prisoners are revealed.

Although prison historians have dated the abolition of the broad arrow as 1920,[56] there is evidence to show that the practice continued into the late 1920s. Wilfrid McCartney's account of his time in Parkhurst prison in 1928 mentions that he was provided with 'dirty looking trousers sprinkled with broad arrows...and a drab coat with hundreds, as it seemed to me, of broad arrows, all over it'.[57] He was a Communist imprisoned in 1927 for 10 years for obtaining information 'calculated to be useful to the enemy' (the USSR). He describes clothing with broad arrows in a variety of British prisons well into the 1930s.

There is a discrepancy, therefore, between the official documentation and the experience of the prisoner. A Home Office circular, for example, went out as late as March 1924 stating that the broad arrow should not appear on the inside or outside of prisoners' clothing or bedding.[58] The stamp 'HM Prisons' was to replace the broad arrow and prison Governors were asked to itemise the way clothing was marked. It is clear from the documents submitted by the authorities in response to the circular that although the broad arrow had not disappeared, it was intended that it should only be found inside the garments.

Another aspect of prison clothing is mentioned in the 1920s Home Office circulars. Types of cloth used for making up garments in the prison workshops varied from prison to prison. Calico, for example, was used in Holloway prison for shifts, petticoats and knickers. Flannel in blue, brown, green and grey was used for skirts and jackets according to the category of prisoner. Canvas was used for slippers. All these fabrics were economical and had been in use for everyday clothing since the seventeenth century in Britain. In the 1920s these materials were, however, rarely used for mainstream fashion garments. Calico was commonly used for 'toilles' or prototypes for testing out the design of a garment before it was made up in fashionable fabric. This accounts for the repeated mention, in prison diaries, of the 'coarseness' of the feel of prison clothing as a sensual deprivation experienced by prisoners.

In comparison, in the 1920s, prison staff uniforms were, largely, tendered to tailoring and uniform production companies under the auspices of the War Office. Only a small proportion were made up inside prisons. Distinctiveness in dress between officers and convicts resided not only in appearance but also in the garments' fabric and construction. Prison staff uniforms were on a par with military, navy, air force, post office and police uniforms. They consisted of such fabrics as 'fleece linings' for 'great coats', caps of 'fine blue wool dyed' and 'cuffs trimmed with mohair braid'. Female staff 'frocks' were made of 'pure sound 3 fold woollen yarn'. Such items as caps, belts, boots and shoes were under tender to outside companies. Whereas prisoners' clothing was roughly cut, finished, sized and varied from prison to prison, staff uniforms were standardised in terms of cloth, patterns and production across the prison system. They were also inspected regularly by the Clothing Inspectorate rather than, in the prisoners' case, reported to the Home Office by individual Governors.[59]

The centralisation of the production of staff uniforms was similar to the increasingly standardised mass production of clothing outside the prison walls in the 1920s and the 1930s. For example, inspections of standards of clothing production were established at this time in department stores such as Marks & Spencer. Prisoners' clothing, however, was exempt from such industrial practices that had travelled over the Atlantic from America. Partly this was due to cost and partly due to the simplicity of construction of prisoner clothing. But it is also evident that prisoners' clothing was considered inferior to staff uniform construction and clothing produced for mass consumption outside the walls.

Although the majority of fabric and clothing for prisoners was produced in prisons, a few items were contracted out to companies. Amongst these were the supply of leather for boots and shoes and the necessary tools for the production of clothing, such as needles, thread, white zinc buttons and yarn. Some stays and roll-ons for women that required specialist production were also made by outside companies and stamped with the requisite prison property mark.

The 1920s and 1930s saw industrial shortages and economic depression. The provision of prison clothing was affected by these conditions outside the walls. It is evident from the itemising of prisoner clothing by the Manufacturing department of the Prison Commission at the Home Office, that the production, provision and maintenance of clothing comprised a complex industrial system. It was a system determined by demand within each individual prison and centralised budget restraints. Additionally, the population for which the system provided was constantly in flux. To some extent, this accounts for the reiteration in every prison clothing circular to Governors that 'present stocks of articles, and materials should be used until exhausted'[60] before new clothing was produced. Consequently change in prisoners clothing was sluggish.

Government and prison authorities were only too aware that prison supplies relied on the public purse. The provision of clothing was a system of public consumption[61] dependent on the State. Prison budgets fluctuated in relation to general economic trends as well as Government penal policies and public opinion as to the severity of the treatment of prisoners.

The State provision of clothing in prisons in Britain in the 1920s and 1930s foresaw Austerity and Utility schemes in the 1940s. There was a similarity between prison clothing provision and the complexity of the nation-wide provision of rationed clothing instigated by the Board of Trade in the Second World War.

There were thus economic and political reasons for the gradual phasing out of the broad arrow marking. Its eventual actual demise in the 1930s saw the disappearance of a prison garment in existence for more than a century since its first appearance as colonial convict clothing in Australia, Tasmania and New Zealand.

media representations of the broad arrow after its demise

Despite its abolition the broad arrow continued to appear in cartoons and media representations of prisoners as a mark of criminality. The longevity of the representation of the broad arrow is partially due to Government and prison authority secrecy surrounding the nature of imprisonment and prison conditions at this time. As a result there was a lack of public awareness of how inmates were dressed. Partly the broad arrow was and is an immediately visible iconographic sign of embodied punishment. In the nineteenth century little was communicated to the public about prison conditions and newspaper and court reports concentrated on the crimes and the perpetrators of crime rather than visual identification.

However, throughout the nineteenth century, *Punch*, as a relatively conservative magazine, had familiarised its British readership with the broad arrow. Thus, a readily available visual language connected to the identity of prisoners as criminal entered mass circulation. The criminal increasingly became the popular subject of both fictional and news depictions for public consumption in the early twentieth century.

Partially the lag between the demise of the physical garment and the continuity of its representation was owing to the increase in the mass production of visual media during the twentieth century. Printed media, film and television increasingly resorted to the use of a shorthand visual embodiment of criminality. And *Punch* continued to rely on its original iconographic formulation.

In *Punch* between 1941 and 1986 there were six cartoons depicting the broad arrow. In the *Punch Almanack* for 1941 during the Second World War, for example, two army personnel with guns passively observe an escapee in the broad arrow uniform. 'He's not one of ours', says one, meaning an army deserter. Thus, the broad arrow garment replaces the man himself. He is just a criminal. In June 1955 a broad arrow garment lies discarded on the ground against a high wall with the notice 'Summer Bay Nudist Camp' and in 1966 an image of a man in the broad arrow looks pleadingly up to the sky and freedom. In March 1967 (see Fig. 3.6), prison officers review a row of men in the broad arrow garment with arrows pointing in different directions towards the 'responsible' criminal. In December 1968, a man in the broad arrow skis over the wall of the prison as prison officers comment, 'its Ferguson from the carpentry shop'. In 1986, prisoners in party hats and the broad arrow circle an electric chair. They are playing musical chairs while prison

". . . and so, if none of you are prepared to tell me who's responsible . . ."

Figure 3.6 *Punch* cartoon of the broad arrow prison clothing, 8 March 1967.

staff play the piano and comment, 'we try never to let a birthday pass unnoticed'. These cartoons provide instant recognition of embodied criminality on the part of the illustrator and viewer of the sketch and additionally denote the 'justified' punishment of the criminal. As Oscar Wilde mentioned in the 1900s, bodily humiliation of the prisoner was partly bought about by the risible nature of iconic criminal attire. Thus, the broad arrow continued as representational currency long after its abolition on clothing.

Increasingly film in the early part of the twentieth century and television post-Second World War focused on the criminal as actor in the outside world (see Chapter 7). British audiences were also aware in the early twentieth century of the American equivalent cinematic type, dressed in black and white stripes (see earlier in this chapter for reference to these film types).

prison reform and prison dress reform in the inter-war years

Penal reforms took place in Britain and America in the inter-war years. Yet from prisoners' accounts in Britain, it is clear that prison institutions were inconsistent in their application of reform.

George Kirby, for example, was a persistent young offender in the 1930s. He was from a poor family and describes being sent to an approved school for breaking into a cricket pavilion and stealing a needle and cotton to repair his trousers. The approved school was a Farm School in Liverpool run according to ideas from America. Treatment of young people was more liberal than had previously been the case in adult prisons. However, he attempted to escape a number of times. After many escapes from a variety of institutions he was arrested in 1938 and sent to an adult prison, Walton Gaol in Liverpool. They gave him

> brown clothes to wear; they put a little badge on the lapel which stated what part of the prison I was located...I felt like some sort of exhibit...it was rather coarse and it was ill fitting, I mean the lapels were cock-eyed, shirts were the same – all ill fitting...the clothes seemed like they were made in the dark ages on a very primitive loom and the shoes were equally as primitive. It made you feel inferior...it was like wearing sack cloth and ashes sort of thing.[62]

Eventually he was sent to Feltham Borstal, and with many other prisoners, he was released in 1939 when war broke out.

The importance of this account is that it is given by an ordinary prisoner rather than a political prisoner. Although the intention was to establish separate institutions for young offenders, some were still treated and clothed in the same way as adults. Continuity ran parallel to change in prison clothing practices and proposals for adjustments were integral to penal reforms in Britain and America during the inter-war years. The broader implications of imprisonment in terms of human rights issues were considered by a broad spectrum of liberal-minded reformers as well as radicals. They called for the establishment of regimes based on rehabilitation rather than punishment within the context of social and political change.

During these years the Labour Party came to power in Britain for the first time led by Ramsay MacDonald. Although there were vacillations between Conservative and Labour Governments during the period, radicals such as Sidney (1859–1947) and Beatrice Webb (1858–1943) and the socialist writer Bernard Shaw (1856–1950) of the Fabian Society pressurised for an evolutionary change to socialism through a succession of reforms. As Labour Members of Parliament, radicals such as Sidney Webb in 1924 and Fenner Brockway (1888–1988) in 1929 exercised socialist legislative authority for the first time.

An Enquiry Committee Report published in 1922, entitled *English Prisons Today* and a later publication in 1927, *English Prisons under Local Government*, by Sidney and Beatrice Webb, with a preface by Bernard Shaw, proposed radical reforms aligned to other welfare policies. Although these reports were sidelined by the 1925 Criminal Justice Act and the immediacy of the 1939–1945 war period, they re-emerged in the 1950s as frameworks for prison reform post Second World War. Fenner Brockway had been imprisoned during the First World War as a conscientious objector and his own experience of prisons, combined with his socialist background, informed the writing of the 1922 Report. This experiential component of a Parliamentary report provides evidence for the suggestion, at the beginning of this chapter, that the imprisonment of radicals and Left-wing militants during the first half of the twentieth century internationally influenced penal reforms of the period. Prison dress was one of the substantive considerations of these reforms.

Fenner Brockway's report highlights prison dress as in need of reform. The report historically considers that the imposition of uniforms in the nineteenth-century prison was as much to 'humiliate the wearer as to facilitate discovery'.[63] The report, unlike its nineteenth-century counterparts, did not proclaim that it was a 'scientific' investigation into prison conditions. Instead it relied on ex-prisoner evidence for its validation. The enquiry considered that after the demise of the 'arrows denoting [a prisoner's] criminality', the general condition of prison clothing as humiliation should be reformed. Demeaning clothing denied the prisoner's individuality and identity that was at the heart of the proposals for rehabilitation rather than punishment:

> Again and again our ex-prisoner witnesses protest against the degrading effect of the prison uniform. 'After I put on the prison clothes', says one, 'I had difficulty to retain my self-respect. The ugliness of them, the dirty colour and the patches in the coat and trousers...the disc bearing the number of my cell – all had a degrading effect, making me feel less a man and more an outcast.'[64]

The report highlights the way in which the introduction of prison uniform had become an embodiment of the way the State neglected to consider the self-esteem of a prisoner as fundamental to their rehabilitation. One of the aspects of prison clothing mentioned in the report is the recycling of 'underclothing'. The procedure of recycling underwear was just as degrading a measure as the imposition of prison uniforms. It was an issue that concerned prisoners and denied them a sense of self. Regardless of impoverishment or the nature of their crime, personal hygiene was often a mark of a prisoner's self-respect instigated in childhood outside the prison walls. The disregard for prisoners' clothing and in this case underwear, as much as outer clothing, was a hindrance to self-improvement. 'If the memory of everything else in connection with my prison experience grows dim, my recollection of the clothing, underclothing particularly, I was compelled to endure in prison will vividly remain...pants that hang in strips and have to be tied round the leg, if there happens to be a string or tape to tie them with...and ill-washed.'[65] Prisoners would prefer to wear underclothing for a month than the supposedly 'clean' garments which were 'dirtier than those I had on'.[66] Not only was this a sanitary hazard but it also affected prisoners' ability to construct a sense of self-worth and it was a form of sensual punishment invisible to the outside world. It was not merely prisoners' testimony to this practice but warders also considered that 'the prison garb is an unnecessary degradation'.[67] Warders also felt that the improvement in the provision of adequate clothing and decency would raise the morale of prisoners and as a result their own lives would be made easier. The report considered that clothing was aligned to other aspects of prison reform and not disconnected and trivial. The inter-war radicals perceived prison conditions as part of socio-political change and that the individual prisoner's physical condition rather than merely their psychological condition was in need of 'treatment'.

In appendices to the report, experiments conducted by the reformatory movement, organised primarily by the Mutual Welfare League in America, are cited as exemplary in providing 'rehabilitative aims and aspirations'. These were progressive attempts 'to get away from the tradition of punishment...to the view of criminals as members of human society'.[68] Amongst those mentioned was Dr. Katherine Bement Davis (1860–1935), Superintendent of the Bedford Women's Reformatory in New York, who was cited as one of the prime prison reformers at this period and had instigated the abolition of the black-and-white stripes.[69] The reform movement in America at this time stated that 'nothing is more likely to retard the prisoner's development' than 'tattered clothing which fits the prisoner like a gunny sack' and 'should not be tolerated.'[70] As a result, in many reformatories, once the 'ridiculous stripes had been abandoned...the dress was quite smart' and 'in some prisons each prisoner has his own marked underclothing'.[71]

The report continued to mention the need for the improvement of the conditions of prisoners in the colonies, particularly in India, and proposed the introduction of improved standards within the prison walls. These included the provision of clothing on a par with that of the clothing preferences of prisoners outside the prison. It is unclear from the report what exactly this meant. However, from research into Indian prisons earlier in the century, there is evidence to show that conditions varied between different prisons. In 1915 British colonial and middle-class Indian attitudes to criminals were based on 'rather vague ideas about collective morphology that remained ill-defined'.[72] Inspectors of Police reported that criminals attempted to disguise themselves in the clothing of 'devout men' and 'handbooks commonly detailed the types of clothing particular groups wore'. As a result, colonialist prison authorities had imposed a 'reconstruction of Indian' on prisoners whereby 'reformed women and men wore saris and turbans'.[73] Nationalists, such as Mahatma Gandhi, resisted these colonialist prison clothing stereotypes in India in the 1930s.

Fenner Brockway and Stephen Hobhouse's report recognised that prison clothing issues were aligned to politics and the nature of colonialism. They proposed domestic reforms that were progressive and attempted an international perspective. Many of these reforms were not implemented until the 1950s in Britain.

A report by Sidney and Beatrice Webb that extended reform ideas expressed in the 1922 report followed in 1927. However, the Webbs' report focused on conditions in local prisons that had previously been ignored. Their argument revolved around the premise that, owing to the centralisation of the prison service, there was no accountability in local facilities. As a result, conditions including prison clothing provision in local prisons were worse than in the central prison system. Additionally, they identified a core infringement of human rights. 'The prison has become "a silent world", shrouded, so far as the public is concerned, in almost complete darkness. This invisibility of the criminal, far from being improved in the inter-war years, had deteriorated and prisons operated an administration where there was "No admittance except on business."[74] The report suggested that it was as a result of the secrecy around prisons that the public was misinformed about the reality of prison conditions, whether in terms of human rights or the humiliation of prison dress. George Bernard Shaw in his preface to their book reiterated the Webbs' argument for more transparency in prisons. He explicitly counters Lombroso's earlier characterisation of the 'criminal type' as genetic and physically measurable. 'What it means is that the criminal type is an artificial type, manufactured in prison by the prison system.'[75]

The Webbs and Shaw did not consider everyday human rights as trivial. They saw prison reform and changes in the provision of prison clothing as humane and necessary and part of a socialist vision in a capitalist system that was itself criminal:

> The depredations of the criminal are negligibly small compared to the militaristic holocausts and ravaged areas, the civic slums, the hospitals, the cemeteries crowded with the prematurely dead, the labor markets in which men and women are exposed for sale for all purposes, honorable and dishonourable, which are the products of criminal ideas imposed on the entire population.[76]

These welfarist proposals in Britain, Europe and America were put on hold until after the Second World War.

conclusion

The early twentieth century saw the emergence of penal reforms that included major changes in prison dress. The period ended in the 1930s with regimes of 'malign neglect' and punishment as extermination in prisons in the USSR labour camps in Siberia and, in the most extreme case, in Nazi death camps during the 1940s.

As Victor Serge said of the late 1930s, 'We are on the eve of a new cycle of storms and that is what darkens our consciences. The compass needle goes wild at the approach of magnetic storms'.[77]

CHAPTER 4

inside out: from extremes to reform, resistance and back, 1930s to 1990s

Prisoners crouched in stale straw...where they...deloused themselves and crunched the lice between their teeth.

Victor Serge, *The Case of Comrade Tulayev* (London, 1968/1948)

[Although] pyjama like striped clothes that have become familiar to us might have been issued to most of the prisoners in the early years of the camp...later on it was a case of any clothing that was available...and those inmates who wore the striped clothing were 'kapos' who became overseers in the camps...and the prison number was printed on the back of the clothing.

Evelyn Le Chene, *Mauthausen: The History of a Death Camp* (London, 1971)

The clothing [in 1955] had come from army surpluses...Blue slacks and jackets from the WAAC's, seersucker dresses from the Waves, and long sleeved well tailored dresses of a deep blue, with large pockets, came from the Coast Guard. By swapping around I finally got two of these and felt real dressed up. The slacks were made for men, usually shapeless, a hideous dark green or khaki colour...They treat us like a child, dress us like a man – and then expect us to act as a lady...Garments could and should be made new for all.

Elizabeth Gurley Flynn, *The Alderson Story* (New York, 1963)

introduction

In Europe and America prison clothing had become less severe in the first half of the twentieth century. In the 1930s two of the harshest systems of imprisonment emerged under totalitarian Governments of different persuasions. The policies of the USSR under Joseph Stalin (1878–1953) led to the establishment of labour camps for dissidents against Stalin's communist regime as well as common criminals. Adolf Hitler's (1889–1945) National Socialist Party was elected in 1933 and Nazi concentration camps were established from the mid-1930s until the end of the Second World War in 1945. The German concentration camps were based on National Socialist eugenics ideas proposing the elimination of 'life that is unworthy of being lived'.[1] Conditions in the labour camps in the Soviet Union and German concentration camps[2] exceeded disciplinary measures in prison regimes that had existed previously. They were deliberately constructed forms of incarceration that were outside democratic legality.

It is almost a travesty to investigate prison clothing in incarceration systems that led to the death of millions. Yet, clothing was an integral part of these camps and to avoid them would be both historically inaccurate and give the lie to those who survived and subsequently wrote about their fear, humiliation and their experience of prison dress.

Prison dress was different under these regimes as was the nature of their totalitarian politics. The form of dress provided in these camps was determined by specific historical and political conditions. First, these differences depended on the type of prison system that had existed in the country prior to the accession to power of the totalitarian regime. Second was the regime's attitude to incarceration pertinent to their purpose as repressive mechanisms of the denial of life rather than the rehabilitation of the prisoner for social re-entry. Thus, the Soviet Union's lack of uniforms in 1930s labour camps evolved from two historical factors. There had been an absence of adequate protective clothing in Siberian prisons in the late nineteenth century. Prison uniforms had been abolished in 1918. Prisoners wore their own clothes directly after the Bolshevik Revolution of 1917. Thus, the neglect of prisoners in the Gulag not only served the repressive purposes of the USSR in the 1930s but also had historical antecedents. The German concentration camp practice of labelling and branding types of prisoners for different punishments or types of death could be said to be the embodiment of a logical extension of some of the European scientific approaches to the physiological identification of criminality prevalent in the late nineteenth century. These were taken out of their reforming context and distorted for the Third Reich's purposes of annihilation.

Both regimes significantly enlarged their camps of incarceration in the 1930s that were based on brutal punishment and ruthlessly exploited convict labour. Under the Nazis, camps became spaces in which to gather 'undesirables' for death and the 'Final Solution' that resulted in the extermination of thousands of Jews.

This chapter examines survivors' testaments as to their experiences of clothing practices under these regimes. After the Second World War international agreements attempted to safeguard against the re-emergence of regimes of punishment that were 'removed from the law and judicial oversight'.[3] Amongst these international decrees was the inclusion of the abolition of extreme forms of clothing practices. These international agreements led to subsequent penal and prison dress reforms in America and Europe in the 1950s and 1960s. There were, however, inconsistencies in the implementation of rehabilitative penal measures that had repercussions for the condition of prison clothing. Increasing rates of incarceration, particularly of black prisoners in America, the rise of the Civil Rights Movement and prison unrest in the 1970s led to a backlash against these reforms that was to spread internationally in the 1980s. The prison riots of the 1960s and 1970s highlighted the beginnings of a more visible punitive politics of incarceration that led to an increase in prison numbers and was embodied in the return, in the 1990s, of the iconic black-and-white striped prison uniform.

labour camp dress in Soviet Russia

There was a brief period immediately after the Revolution in 1917 when the Bolshevik Party in power in the USSR experimented with progressive policies. These included the right for women to have abortions, the legality of homosexuality and an enlightened approach to imprisonment. Prison uniforms were abandoned and prisoners were allowed to wear their own clothes. This policy had a number of consequences for prisoners in the turbulent years of the 1920s and 1930s.

The political situation in the USSR after the Revolution was a complex one. Between 1917 and 1920, opposition from other Parties, such as the Mensheviks, threatened the Bolshevik Party internally. Increasingly from the early 1920s domestic opposition was met with the beginnings of 'systematic repression'.[4] Between 1922 when he became ill and his death in 1924, V.I. Lenin (1870–1924) was preoccupied with the problem of dealing with dissent. Stalin, against Lenin's advice and as People's Commissar for the Affairs of the Nationalities, instigated the increased bureaucratisation of internal affairs and the subsequent repression of Bolshevik critics within the USSR. In order to deal with opposition to USSR policies in emerging communist nations, he 'institutionalised' repression of opposition to 'the foreign policy of the Soviet state'.[5] Later in the 1920s, repressive measures such as the establishment of convict labour camps provided cheap labour for the industrialisation programme of the USSR. Convicts were forced to carry out heavy manual labour for which purpose there was a lack of appropriate clothing. Functional clothing design for workers in factories had been instigated by revolutionary constructivist designers such as Liubov Popova (1889–1924), Vavara Stepanova (1894–1958) and Alexander Rodchenko (1891–1956)[6] in the early years of the Bolshevik Government. This clothing was not introduced in the work place or prisons owing to a lack of adequate funding. The economic priority in the USSR in the 1920s was industrialisation. Reform measures that had been introduced in the early years of the Revolution were increasingly incompatible with the development of economic stability after Lenin's introduction of the New Economic Policy in 1921.

These economic and political imperatives led in part to the authoritarian conditions of the labour camps in the USSR in the 1930s and after the Second World War. They were reminiscent of the 'malign neglect' of the eighteenth century in Britain with the addition of deliberate physical torture. Prisoners lacked sufficient clothing in the freezing enforced labour camps 'within the Arctic Circle'.[7] They were kept in conditions described at the head of this chapter by the writer and revolutionary Victor Serge (1890–1947).[8] But there were also conventional prisons in the USSR at this time. Although Serge's novel, *The Case of Comrade Tulayev*, is a fictional account of 1930s USSR, it is based on his own experience. He was deported to Siberia in 1933 due to his association with Leon Trotsky (1879–1940) who was critical of Stalin's policies. Serge describes conditions that were based on Bentham's 'model prison'. These were 'new, modern, built of concrete and located somewhere underground'[9] and were especially built for interrogations. Prisoners were kept in solitary confinement and their physical condition was unkempt. Serge mentions that one prisoner's clothes were filthy and 'shapeless'.[10]

The novelist Arthur Koestler (1905–1983) mentions similar conditions when he describes the authorities' 'stiff uniform with creaking cuffs'[11] compared with prisoners who were known merely by their numbers. He talks of a peasant prisoner whose 'toes were frozen blue'.[12] Whenever Gletkin (the prison guard) appeared, his 'stiff cuffs' were mentioned as a signifier of the authoritarian prison regime. Prisoners – whether 'political' or 'criminal' – were punished to the extent of torture in 'handcuffs which grazed the wrist' and had been 'screwed too tightly straining [the] arms while twisting them behind [the] back'.[13]

The early Bolshevik abolition of prisoners' uniforms meant that there was no incentive, in subsequent years, to increase State expenditure through the provision of adequate clothing in prisons. In this way the 'social phenomenon' of prison clothing reform is transformed into a political benefit in the augmentation of 'concrete systems of punishment',[14] in this case, the overtly authoritarian. Serge's experience in Russian prisons during this period was dissimilar to his previous experience in French prisons between 1912 and 1917. There, uniforms were issued rather than prisoners' being left without clothing as they were in the USSR. However, all prison conditions in his opinion were equally humiliating and 'depersonalised'. Prisoners had 'the same look of the hunted man'.[15] Serge characterises all prisons as 'insane machines' that 'grind on in every . . . country of the world' and are all equally 'useless and brutal'.[16]

However, conditions in the USSR were particularly extreme in the labour camps after 'the 1938 Moscow purge trials' when 'the number of political prisoners in the Soviet Union was seven million . . . one that remains so enormous that it is virtually incomprehensible.'[17] Vast numbers of prisoners died.

There is little visual evidence of the prison clothing and conditions of Stalin's labour camps and secret prisons. Depictions of the extremes of Gulag punishment have depended on the written word. For example, the writer and Russian dissident Aleksandr Solzhenitsyn (1918–2008) describes the transportation convoys of prisoners to the 'rural prisons' in the USSR in the 1930s. He contrasts the well-clothed 'convoy guards . . . in their sheepskin coats' with 'the doomed prisoners in their summer clothes' when 'they marched through deep snow'.[18] Accounts of the labour camps repeatedly mention the cold and the rags. 'Each day around the fires, a dozen or so huddled human beings gathered wrapped in every rag they owned.'[19] And 'clothed in wretched and thin rags, the convict continuously suffered from the cold and froze'.[20]

These conditions continued into the 1950s in the Eastern European 'Gulag'. The naturalised British subject and British Communist Party member Edith Bone (1889–1975) was held in solitary confinement for 7 years, between 1949 and 1956, for allegedly being an 'English spy' in Hungary. In her memoir she mentions that she was issued with inadequate clothing for the cold weather. 'As the weather grew colder I again demanded warm clothing, but was fobbed off with promises, until I went on hunger strike'.[21] This situation continued until she was taken to the sick-bay having 'been found unconscious in the bathroom'.[22] Edith Bone was at this time 66 and although as a political prisoner she did not have to wear prison dress, she was prevented from wearing adequate clothing. A doctor who treated her in the hospital was also a prisoner and had been arrested as a foreign spy. 'He wore trousers with narrow blue and white stripes; this was my first glimpse of prison dress'.[23]

The inconsistency in the way in which prisoners were treated within the USSR and in Eastern Europe becomes clear in accounts of prison clothing. However, whether amounting to torture or neglect, there was a consistency in the deliberate lack of provision of adequate clothing. The striped prison clothing that Edith Bone mentions is reminiscent of the pyjama-like garb of prisoners in Nazi concentration camps despite the USSR's opposition to the Nazi regime and its previous liberation of Nazi concentration camps in 1945. Stripes were thus used as iconic prison clothing regardless of the politics of different authoritarian regimes.

clothing in Nazi concentration camps

Before the Second World War, Weimar Germany had established severe regimes of punishment that were advanced by Adolf Hitler and his National Socialist Party when they came to power in 1933. During the Second World War, National Socialist imprisonment policies were 'perverted into a tool of systematic repression and extermination'[24] in the concentration camps in Germany and Nazi-occupied Europe. Concentration camp conditions were widely broadcast in photographs, documentaries and feature films after the allies liberated the camps in 1945.[25]

Evelyn Le Chene survived the concentration camp at Mauthausen. In her memoirs (see quote at the beginning of this chapter), she mentions that the blue-and-white striped pyjama-like garb worn by many of the inmates was just one of the ways in which the Nazis organised the camps. The blue-and-white striped pyjama garb (Fig. 4.1) has become an iconic garment indicative of concentration camp categorisation. Film footage of the liberation of the camps shows mostly men wearing it. A few female survivors wore it and it was seen on corpses. Ruth Elias was a child who was transported in a wagon to Auschwitz. She mentions

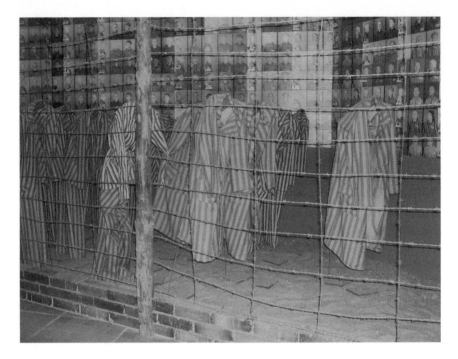

Figure 4.1 Striped prison uniforms in Auschwitz Museum.

being met at the station by 'people with striped uniforms. I didn't understand what this meant',[26] she said.

The Nazis did not invent this system of embodied incarceration evident in concentration camps up to 1941.[27] The blue-and-white striped clothing had existed in early nineteenth-century prisons in Germany.[28]

The Nazis used this uniform to stigmatise 'undesirable' social groups regardless of whether they had committed a criminal offence or not. Thus, Morton Piasek (see Fig. 4.2) was a Jewish survivor of Mauthausen and appears in the blue-and-white striped pyjama-like garb after the camp was liberated in 1945. Apart from the stripes' association with punishment, prison bars, grilles and exclusion, there is another meaning connected to striped clothing relevant to its use in the camps. The blue-and-white stripes have an association with pyjamas or nightwear. There is an implication that people wearing these clothes may also be protected, for example, at night, when they are most vulnerable.[29] In the case of the concentration camps, those dressed in the blue-and-white striped prison uniform were indeed protected as 'kapos' or organisers of inmates, at least in the early years of the Nazi camps. They were segregated from the worst indignities and horrors of the camps. The uniform, therefore, had a double meaning. The prisoners in the striped uniforms were labelled as punishable within the concentration camp system but were separate from the other categories.

Figure 4.2 Morton Piasek in striped prison uniform, after he was liberated from Mauthausen concentration camp, 1945.

The systematic nature of the bodily punishment that took place in the camps revealed more extensive malpractices than merely the dressing of prisoners in the pyjama-like uniforms.

On liberation inmates were found naked or dressed in meagre clothing amounting to rags. They were kitted out in an assortment of inadequate garments. Survivors recount how prisoners in the camps were ordered to undress in the courtyards under the guise of being disinfected. Survivors repeatedly mention the courtyards in front of the gas chambers or vans that transported prisoners to their deaths, piled high with clothes and their being ordered to collect the clothing. These discarded clothes were recycled to prisoners who were employed around the camps or as manual labourers.[30] Unlike the Soviet labour camps, the organisation of the concentration camps was also based on a scientific classification of inmates. The systematic nature of the Nazi regime extended nineteenth-century carceral knowledge and classification to its limits. Bodily identification of punishment and extermination was regulated through a colour-coded system of Stars of David and triangles.

Although this system was not explicitly to do with clothing, it was an embodiment of undesirability and 'bare life'[31] that was a preoccupation of the Nazi system of imprisonment in the camps. As was the case with the striped uniforms, there were historical precedents for the use of the Star of David that went back to the fourth and fifth centuries. Christians had used the Star of David as a sign of the exclusion of Jews. 'Where the Christians had said to the Jews you cannot live amongst us, the Nazis said you cannot live'.[32] In Germany after 1933, this practice of regulating Jews through the wearing of yellow Stars of David had already existed outside the camps. Nazi systems of bodily regulation were 'not only the exception and the rule…but also the state of outside and inside' that 'pass through one another'.[33] The Nazis normalised their lack of judicial procedures for the identification of punishment by introducing it into everyday social life.

The camps extended the system to include all classes and manner of social groups. Additional to the yellow stars were triangles 'with point upwards…and another with the point downwards', in red (political – mostly communists), green (criminals – thieves, fire-raisers etc.), blue ('migrants'), pink ('homosexuals') or black ('a-socials' or those considered lazy and malingered).[34] The history of the prisoner was visually registered and superimposed on the body in the form of a triangle. Additionally, black triangles signified gypsies and mauve triangles had to be worn by Jehovah's Witnesses and conscientious objectors.

The colour-coding system was established universally in the death camps after 1942 and extended to include all types of individuals or collective identities considered undesirable by the Nazi regime. The coding system also embodied a system of punishment intended to cause dissension within the hierarchy of the camps. At times, inmates displaced their antagonism against the Nazi political system and instead criticised the type in which they had been cast. Nazi camp staff nurtured these dissensions between inmates in order to deter revolts against concentration camp regimes. More than any other type or group of prisoner, it was the European Jewish communities who bore the yellow Star of David, whose lives were ended in their thousands. The Nazis bodily labelled individuals and collectives and on this basis assigned them to a systematic regime of death. 'From this perspective, the camp' was constructed as a 'biopolitical space'.[35] These Nazi categorisation techniques were, more than in any other system of punishment, embodied and deliberately made visible in the colour coding of 'existence' and the pyjama-like garb prior to annihilation. Distinctions were not based on types of criminality but on political, racial and cultural determinants.

However, there were also, at this time in Germany, prisons such as Traunstein that harboured men and women who were considered by the Nazi regime to be common criminals. Such was Louise Rinser, who had written a novel critical of the Nazi regime. She describes her fellow inmates in 1944 as 'this worn and tattered glory in the middle of the prison yard'.[36] Clothing worn by prisoners was made from old uniforms of the military and transported from the death camps, making up a sort of prison system of redistribution within its vast and brutal confines.

The gradual release of information about the sub-human cruelties of Nazi death camps appalled the world. For the next few decades after the end of the Second World War international penal policies, including prison dress regulations, were introduced as measures to prevent the return of such inhumanity.

prison clothing reform policies 1940s to 1950s

Governments were preoccupied with the war effort during the Second World War and few prison reforms took place. Wartime prison clothing conditions had varied considerably even within the same prisoner of war camp run by the Germans. For example, the Red Cross provided British and American prisoners of war in Stalag Luft 1 with clothing whereas Russian prisoners of war were 'clothed in grey rags that had once been uniforms'.[37] These visible inequalities contributed to British, Canadian, American and European prisoners' discussions of the ways in which society might be improved after the end of the war.[38] Political debates about societal restructuring after the Second World War also took place in wartime Britain. The Welfare State as provider of free education, health care and social welfare was debated by politicians and socialists eager to establish Labour Party policy once the war ended. Prison reformers who had been involved in the establishment of the Howard League for Penal Reform in 1920s Britain, and Alexander Paterson (1884–1947) who was Commissioner of Prisons from 1922 to 1947, continued to work on ways to encourage the rehabilitation of prisoners after the Second World War. Many of Paterson's ideas about prison reform appeared in the Criminal Justice Act of 1948, a few weeks after his retirement and death in 1947. (See Chapter 5 for prison dress conditions in British prisons 1950–1990.)

1950s American prison clothing

Alexander Paterson's formulation of the normalisation of the prisoner[39] characterised debates about prison clothing in the period of the 1950s to the 1960s. In his writing, Paterson made reference to the relative freedom of the American prisoner who was allowed to wear clothing similar to that worn by those outside the prison gates. He concludes his chapter on 'Food, Bedding and Clothing in Prisons' with the comment that European Governments

> have much to learn from American practice...The knitted pullover and lea-ther coat are common articles of American dress. Prisoners are allowed to buy these at the prison commissary or have them sent in by their friends...The men are also allowed to buy or be given their own ties, shirts, underclothes, socks with the result that the average prisoner looks much more like the aver-age civilian.[40]

Helen Bryan was convicted of Contempt of Congress in 1950 and was sent to Alderson Prison, the only Federal prison for women in the United States in 1950. She attests to Paterson's assertion that there was a degree of choice in American prison clothing in the 1950s. However, it was a limited choice and she was not able to wear her own clothing. When she arrived in prison, she was taken to a prison clothing store and tried on dresses, coats, socks, shoes and underwear, '"What size do you wear and what colours do you like best?", Louise asked me. "Size twelve and I like blues and greens"'. But the fit of the clothing only approximated to the size of the wearer and it was only through alterations that a reasonable degree of comfort was achieved. 'We would look as well in our clothes as we could.'[41]

Elizabeth Gurley Flynn (1890–1964), communist and erstwhile IWW cam-paigner, who was imprisoned in America in 1955, voiced a similar experience of prison clothing. The choice was limited and the onus was on the inmate to custom-ise clothing in order that it both fitted and embodied some degree of individuality. She wrote,

> most of our time in orientation was spent in repairing, fitting and sewing cloth-ing allotted to us. At that time we received either seven cotton dresses or five dresses and three slacks. Later the number was reduced. Some were old, faded, with unsightly patches. They were to be worn in all seasons – "tissue paper", the women called them in Winter. Women from the South and Puerto Rico suffered severely in cold weather. Socks, low shoes, slips, bras, and rayon panties, completed our wardrobes.[42]

During this period in America, women's fashions changed rapidly due to the intro-duction of ready-to-wear and casual dress in the 1930s. Sportswear started to be mass produced and the introduction of synthetic materials such as rayon in the 1930s and nylon in the 1950s[43] meant that popular fashions were easier to main-tain and less restrictive to the body. Young women's clothing particularly reflected these changes in the introduction of less formal but fashioned attire, such as pedal pusher trousers, casual fitted blouses and sweaters and shorter skirts to the calf or knee.[44]

Despite Flynn's mention of more contemporary fabrics such as rayon under-wear, the dresses were patched and shabby. There was a disparity between the slow changes in clothing that women inmates experienced in the 1950s and the diversity and speed of the turnover in female fashions that occurred in market-led, consumer-oriented America. Women's expectations and fashionable preferences were changing rapidly as Helen Bryan mentions when she expresses her hatred for a particular belt and shoes. 'It was a narrow cloth one that had once been black, but with many washings had turned a sickly grayish brown. Of my new possessions I most disliked this belt, and the brown canvas slippers.'[45] At a time when waists were nipped in, oversize dresses that were held in with a hideous belt were not merely unfashionable; for a young woman they were humiliating if she was seen in them by friends or relatives on visits.

In the West generally, it was not until the 1960s that menswear started to change more speedily in line with womenswear. It is important to avoid essentialist gender distinctions when comparing male and female inmates' experience of clothing; however, the deprivation of clothing for women at particular historical times, when fashion changes are at a premium, can reinforce a woman prisoner's sense of loss of identity of her previous self. As a result, imprisonment may be experienced as more poignant an embodiment of humiliation through the wearing of prison clothing than it might be for men.

Male prisoners in the 1940s and 1950s were mostly dressed in the equivalent of workwear as demonstrated in the retro American prison film *Shawshank Redemption* (1994).[46] The film follows Andy and Red's life inside from 1949 to Andy's escape in 1966 and Red's eventual parole. The clothes changed very little during this period although the 'greys' of the 1940s (grey shirts, caps and blue trousers) were replaced by denim jackets, jeans and white T-shirts in the early 1960s. There was little change in American mainstream men's fashions compared to womenswear during this period. However, the rupture to the inmate's sense of self between inside and outside prison is reflected in the comparison between the slow changes to men's clothing outside prison and the non-changing nature of men's functional clothing inside prison. Additionally, prison clothing was work related and there was no casual clothing or leisure time. At the end of *Shawshank Redemption*, Andy flings off his prison clothing immediately after his escape. He does not merely discard his clothing because he wants to avoid identification as an escapee in the outside world. The very exhilaration with which he throws it off is an expression of his individuality. As an innocent inmate, he had won his freedom and escaped over the border to Mexico. Prison clothing as an imposed institutional embodiment of the punished self becomes symbolically the disposable raiment of the free self.[47]

In America and Europe in the 1950s and 1960s prison reforms were prevalent. Rehabilitation rather than punishment was, largely, the focus of imprisonment. In prison clothing terms, garments were not meant to stigmatise inmates in the way in which black-and-white striped uniforms and broad arrows had visually demarcated criminality in the early twentieth century. Yet, penal institutions continued to confer control and power over prisoners through the provision and distribution of clothing. The way in which prisoners conformed to or resisted dress regulations were noted as marks of an inmate's rehabilitation or continued lack of responsiveness to the reform of individual behaviour. Despite the relaxation of prison uniforms in America that Paterson had observed, prisoners' accounts indicate that institutional clothing practices continued to embody humiliation. The ways that inmates adapted prison clothing or saw themselves in institutional garb are as much an indicator of prison clothing practices as the chronology of the ways prison apparel was reformed in line with penal policies.[48]

1950s international prison clothing reforms

The United Nations (UN) unanimously adopted the Universal Declaration of Human Rights in 1948. However, the Soviet bloc, South Africa and Saudi Arabia abstained. This declaration affected the conditions in which political prisoners were treated and ensured that there was the possibility for Human Rights organisations to investigate possible infringements of the agreement from this period onwards. Additionally, in 1949 the Geneva Convention was agreed that legislated for the humane treatment of prisoners of war. Most importantly, in 1951 the 'United Nations Standard Minimum Rules for the Treatment of Prisoners' was proposed. It stated that all prisoners' conditions and particularly clothing, should not be humiliating. This resolution had first been mooted in the 1920s and 1930s. Its reintroduction post-Second World War was instigated by the return of welfarist domestic policies in the late 1940s and early 1950s in many European and Scandinavian countries as well as America. This resolution foresaw changes in the provision of prison clothing internationally. The UN resolution was adopted in August 1955 at the First United Nations Congress on the Prevention of Crime and the Treatment of Offenders. It stated that adequate sanitary conditions for all prisoners should be provided 'as frequently as necessary' and that

> 17. (1) Every prisoner who is not allowed to wear his own clothing shall be provided with an outfit of clothing suitable for the climate and adequate to keep him in good health. *Such clothing shall in no manner be degrading or humiliating...* [emphasis mine]
>
> (2) All clothing shall be clean and kept in proper condition. Underclothing shall be changed and washed as often as necessary for the maintenance of good health...
>
> (3) In exceptional circumstances, whenever a prisoner is removed outside the institution for an authorized purpose, he shall be allowed to wear his own clothing or other inconspicuous clothing...
>
> 18. If prisoners are allowed to wear their own clothing, arrangements shall be made on their admission to the institution to ensure that it shall be clean and fit for use.[49]

In the 1950s, there were, then, international moves towards policies of normalisation. Prison conditions were to approximate as closely as possible to those pertaining in everyday society in order to customise prisoners to their return to life outside the prison walls. But, as we have already seen in 1950s America, the interpretation and adoption of more lenient clothing practices varied significantly from country to country and from local to central or Federal prison. The pace of change away from the dehumanising aspect of prison uniforms towards prisoners wearing and consuming their own clothes fluctuated dramatically. Simultaneously, more punitive measures were introduced alongside reforms that allegedly recognised increased freedoms for the individual prisoner.

trapped in a vice: American prison clothing: 1960–1980

Western countries did not adopt the 1955 UN declaration in its entirety. Variations in penal policy globally reflected broader political changes from the 1960s. Shifts in political allegiances, both within national boundaries and between different blocks of countries with competing economic interests, significantly increased in speed between the 1960s and 1980s. These positional changes were determined largely by the corresponding expansion and domination of global markets. Balanced against this jostling for economic power, there were domestic threats to national stability in many countries in the West. Radical political movements in the late 1960s and into the 1970s were, as a result, met with a show of force and harsh penalties. Globally, Right-wing penal policies developed in this period and were most significantly led by the USA which 'adopted and exported "law and order ideology" '.[50] Right-wing politicians saw criminals and prisoners as 'detached and useless or a danger',[51] whereas 1960s and 1970s American and European liberals believed that prisoners should be individually treated and reformed rather than punished. From this standpoint the causes of crime were seen to be able to be treated in the individual deviant rather than as failings in society.[52]

These shifts affected the experience of the prisoner in a confusing manner. In 1970, Jessica Mitford quoted a prisoner in a California prison who said that convicts saw themselves 'trapped in a vice between "the punitive nineteenth century guard and the 1984 headshrinker" '.[53] As far as clothing was concerned, these opposing imprisonment ideologies meant that while prisoners were beginning to be allowed to wear less restrictive uniforms, they were gagged and shackled in court if they were considered unruly.

It was in this context that the 'indeterminate sentence' was imposed on prisoners as a rehabilitative measure and against which black prisoners rioted in American prisons in the 1960s and early 1970s. The indeterminate sentence meant that prisoners were only released if they were considered by the authorities to have reformed. For Black Panther prisoners, who were inside for political offences, conforming to a model of rehabilitation held by the prison authorities meant foregoing their political beliefs. Their prison sentences were, therefore, lengthened by the nature of their 'crime' and their resistance to rehabilitation as a cure of criminality. A measure that was initially considered progressive had become punitive in the eyes of the Black Panthers and other groups of prisoners.

The repeal of the 'indeterminate sentence' was one of the main demands raised by Black Panther prisoners in San Quentin, Folsom and other American prisons in the 1960s and 1970s. It was against these conditions that other prisoners such as chicanos and black working class criminals became militant. They united with political activists in asserting their collective identity against the carceral power of a racist capitalist penal system.[54]

The revolutionary black American George Jackson (1941–1971) was imprisoned in the late 1960s at the age of 14 for stealing a purse. Later he was held in solitary confinement in Soledad Prison for 7 years. He said,

> from the first moment I'm brought into this scenario, I attempt to establish control over the exchanges that will take place between myself and my captors... There is only one type of inquisitional situation that I personally cannot control – the session that begins with violence. In those cases, guile fails and blacks learn to fight multiple opponents while handcuffed, or at least learn how to protect the groin area.[55]

He was killed in San Quentin prison in 1971. Bodily torture and restraint were practised against male and female black political prisoners in order to coerce confessions from them. Both out of view of the public eye and in court rooms throughout America, prisoners were gagged on a scale reminiscent of the nineteenth century.

Angela Davis (b. 1944) bears witness to this when she mentions the treatment of a woman prisoner, Joan Bird. She quotes Joan Bird as saying, 'they put handcuffs on me and turned me over face down on the ground and my hands cuffed behind me. Then they began to kick me and walk on my back and legs'.[56] This form of overt corporal dehumanisation was utterly against the UN declaration of 1955. Furthermore, it demonstrates the co-existence of punitive bodily control of women prisoners with more liberal forms of dress provision. Although these latter sartorial practices were limited and informed by the essentialist idea that women criminals could be normalised by their selection of apparel, as in Helen Bryan's case in the 1950s, they did not amount to brutalisation.

At the same time both female and male Black Panthers had to conform to prison clothing as opposed to wearing civilian clothes as political prisoners. As self-acclaimed political prisoners the way they chose to visually stand out collectively and express their politics bodily was through the espousal of the Afro haircut. The Black Is Beautiful Movement in America in the 1960s had rejected mainstream beauty ideals exemplified in the straightening of hair.[57] Despite the later appropriation of the Afro by the fashionable mainstream and its subsequent loss of political authenticity, the adoption of Afro-American identity by black prisoners continued for some decades (see Fig. 4.3). At this time in America prison clothing varied between Federal and State prisons. From black radical writers' accounts at the time, it mostly comprised scant clothing and a lack of uniformity.

Erica Huggins was imprisoned in Niantic State Prison in 1971 at the same time as the radical activist Angela Davis. She wrote a poem about the difference between the unkempt appearance of women prisoners and a Women's Liberation rock band that visited the prison:

> wild hair, fonky guitar (someone said
> bessie smith came to mind)
> hair-all lengths, legs, arms, smiles, music –
> SISTERS – and us...
> raggedy petticoats, cotton dressed, rocking,
> swaying,
> screaming[58]

In the Women's House of Detention in New York, where

> 95% of the prisoners were Black and Puerto Rican,...all personal effects down to...toothbrushes and clothes were confiscated. The sisters were left in their cells with nothing but the nightgowns they were wearing...and the hoards of cockroaches and mice.

Angela Davis continues to demystify the commonly held belief that, in comparison to the treatment of men in prison in America, 'the gravest problem [was] the tendency to "baby" the women captives...This is a myth which must be immediately smashed'.[59]

The Black Panthers outside prison in the 1960s wore flamboyant clothing that embodied and proclaimed their politics.[60] In contrast, their lack of 'political status', the condition of prison clothing scarcity and the physical brutality they experienced within the prison walls were, for the most part, hidden from public view. As a result of the inhumane conditions experienced by political prisoners in jails throughout America, organised black radicals staged non-violent sit-ins. Their demands included the right to 'political status'. For example, demands made in the Folsom Prison Manifesto in 1970 included 'that prisoners confined for political reasons be treated in accord with the Geneva Convention of 1954 and that their personal property be respected and allowed in their possession and that they not be manacled'.[61] Additionally, they proposed that ordinary inmates' salaries be improved in order that they could maintain their clothing in prison rather than rely on poor relatives outside. Prisoners in Folsom jail went on strike for 19 days and stayed in their cells. During this time prison officials refused to negotiate with them. Eventually the strike was violently broken up by prison guards.[62] After peaceful prisoners' strikes failed and the public announcement of the killing of George Jackson at San Quentin prison, in May 1971, Attica

Figure 4.3 Woman in an American prison, 1994.

Prison inmates rioted. The Attica demands were similar to those at Folsom. Despite initial negotiations between the prison authorities and the inmates, the rebellion was eventually put down violently. There were 39 deaths, and 88 others were wounded. These included prison officer hostages who had been kidnapped by the prisoners and some of the original inmate negotiators. Additionally, 'once the prison was retaken, the physical reprisals against the convicts began with vicious vengeance'.[63] Although many of the immediate demands of prisoners for improved conditions and clothing were not conceded, the more political and ideological demands raised by the prison protesters served to radicalise the prison population. This was in turn met by 'a harsher repression of convicts'.[64]

Race riots in American jails inspired international prisoners' organisations in the early 1970s. These included the Preservation of the Rights of Prisoners (PROP) in Britain that proposed there should be a Trade Union for prisoners, as did prison organisations in Sweden (KRUM), Norway (KROM) and Denmark (KRIM). Their agendas vacillated between advocating broad policies such as inmates' constitutional rights and the immediate demands for all prisoners to receive the everyday requirements necessary for survival. These demands related to prison dress in a number of ways. While in America and Northern Ireland (see Chapter 5) prison-ers demanded 'political status' and the right to wear their own clothing, in 1971, KRUM, an organisation of prison inmates in Sweden demanded that 'guards and inmates should wear civilian clothing'.[65] Swedish prisoners voiced these demands because they considered that the continued imposition of prison clothing was an inconsistent omission in the liberal prison experiments in Scandinavia after the Second World War. American prison race riots had inspired international prisoners' movements. They drew attention to prison systems based on class and race dis-crimination, bodily punishment and humiliation, despite liberal international agree-ments. Inadequate clothing and unsanitary conditions continued into the 1970s. Right-wing 'Law and Order' advocates used the riots as a reason to challenge wel-farist penal policies that espoused treatment of prisoners rather than containment. As a reaction against 'prisoner activism', 'the treatment model of penology was effectively terminated'.[66]

Despite the work of prison reform organisations in America, conditions in prisons did not radically change for the next 20 years. For example, the rules for women prisoners' procurement of clothing in Cook County Jail in Chicago in 1973 had not significantly changed by 1996. They stipulated that 'clothing, like everything else, is County property. Take care of it. Destruction of ANY County property may get you more time'.[67] Although some prisoners were given a choice of clothing in America from the 1950s, the inmate's appearance was controlled by the prison authorities. Clothing was procured at the prison commissary or took the form of imposed prison uniform, colour-coded according to inmate status. For example, white clothing denoted that an inmate was maximum security. Gary Gilmore, the convicted mur-derer, comments, 'they gave me a pair of white coveralls to wear and I hate coveralls. Too tite in the crotch'.[68] Coloured clothing characterised the uniform across gender, although its form varied. In November 1976 in Utah state, for example, Gary Gilmore appeared in Court in 'leg shackles…loose white pants and a long white shirt'.[69] However, in January 1977, he wore 'white coveralls' at a Tribunal in Salt Lake and his signature 'red, white and blue sneakers'.[70] This last appearance was after he had been on hunger strike to protest that his life sentence should be commuted to death rather than languish on Death Row for his entire life. The sneakers signified agency in his long drawn out fight for the right to die. Despite uniformity there were small personal details of clothing that inmates could select. For example, Gilmore insisted he was executed in his 'crazy red, white and blue tennis shoes he always wore in Maximum'.[71]

Despite individual sartorial expressions, the body of the inmate was controlled by clothing regulations and intrusive searches on a day-to-day basis regardless of gender. Women in the 1970s in Ohio Reformatory for Women attested to this:

> [They] look into your vagina and rectum and make you stand naked in front
> of them…You are told that this number is your new name and you are never
> to take off the bracelet or destroy it. You start losing your identity when you're

locked up . . . You can dress only one way, you can adjust your uniform only so far, you can wear shoes only so high.[72]

Although some penal institutions in America continued to 'individualize treatment of inmates' from the 1970s to the 1990s, strict codes of custody militated against the psychological help inmates were offered. The inmate's life was 'still regulated and dictated by the limits of the institution, and the majority of her choices are determined for her, not by her'.[73]

Prison dress codes also served to embody the strict demarcation of staff and inmates and the de-humanising nature of the prison regime contradicted more personalised forms of treatment. Prison authorities' perception of this mind/body separation was embodied in humiliating prison dress regulations that militated against therapeutic self-improvement in America during this period. This had a deleterious effect on the potential for inmates' rehabilitation. In 1970 a controlled psychological experiment was conducted at Stanford University. Two groups of college students wore either prison guard uniforms or inmate garb. In the experiment students in the role of prison guards meted out brutality and students allocated prisoner roles 'became servile, dehumanised robots'. ' "At the end of six days", wrote Zimbardo [one of the instigators of the Stanford experiment], "we had to close down our mock prison because what we saw was frightening . . . It was no longer apparent to most of the subjects (or to us) where reality ended and the roles began" '.[74] The implications of this experiment were not addressed in the subsequent relaxation of prison conditions including that of prison clothing. It was a period when law enforcement was a political imperative as opposed to negotiation and reform.[75] During the 1990s there was a further burst of public sentiment against the perceived over-protectiveness of prisoners on the part of prison institutions. This resulted in extreme forms of embodied criminalisation such as the reintroduction of chain gangs by some States in America. 'New uniforms with stripes reappeared for the first time since the nineteenth century.'[76] The re-emergence of the humiliating black-and-white striped uniforms occurred at the same time as an increase in the rate of incarceration, the beginnings of the building programme of high-tech super prisons and the advent of private prisons (see Chapter 6 for an account of these developments). These prison conditions in America are reminiscent of the nineteenth century. Despite attempts by reform agencies to promote the rehabilitation of prisoners through wearing their own clothes, more extreme forms of embodied punishment and strict penal dress codes prevailed in many American prisons. Prison clothing as the stigmatisation of criminality was reintroduced, intricately interwoven with an increasing rate of incarceration.

conclusion

In the early years after the Second World War, public knowledge of the conditions in which inmates had been held in the Russian Gulag and Nazi concentration camps influenced international agreements for the preservation of the rights of prisoners.

In the 1950s, attempts by the UN to legislate internationally against inhumanitarian inmate clothing conditions, combined with national prerogatives to reform prison cultures, led to limited improvements in the provision of less-stigmatised prison dress. Despite these reforms, black radical activists resisted racial discrimination and the continuation of bodily restraints in American prisons in the 1960s. There were shifts between the Right-wing backlash against the riots in American prisons in the early 1970s and welfarist penal reforms that called for the treatment of individual prisoners. These reforms included the normalisation of prison conditions and inmate apparel. However, the Right-wing 'Law and Order' ideology that espoused the tenets of a return to 'just desserts' in the punishment of the criminal, pervasively swamped more progressive approaches to the rehabilitation of the prisoner. Some States in America in the 1990s saw the re-emergence of the visually embodied stigmatisation of the prisoner in iconic black-and-white striped uniforms. A similar progression, although not as visually obvious as the re-introduction of black-and-white striped uniforms, occurred in other countries in the West after the Second World War and will be investigated in the next chapter.

consumption as redemption? Britain, 1950s to 1990s

From 1956 between the ages of 18 to 40 I was in and out of prison. I was mostly on the streets. I was dirty and had louse in my hair. I loved trousers I found in bins or public toilets. I didn't speak or look like a woman was meant to be so I paid the price of being myself. I was excluded and not wanted in society. When I was in prisons I was made to conform to other people's assessment of what a woman is.

Chris Kitsch, *Confessions of a Bag Lady*,
British Library Sound Archive, CD ROO230, 31–35

[1950s] By the time he got back with the coarse grey cloths [*sic.*] I was out of the bath. 'Here you are.' He said, 'I hope they fit but I doubt it and here's the best pair of shoes I could find.' I put this gear on and it fitted where it touched, and was as coarse as sack cloth. I felt like a right tramp and most probably looked like one too.

Frank Norman, *Bang to Rights: An Account of Prison Life* (London, 1958)

In prison I don't think the clothes themselves are dehumanising but I think they're depersonalising. You're given prison clothes and invariably they're clothes that don't fit. Clothing in prison is a controlling device. Everything is poor quality – why shouldn't it be – you're cons! But it adds to the whole sense of you being without power without an identity.

Interview with ex-prisoner (1984–2004), Hastings, December 2005

introduction

A variety of changes took place in prison dress between the late 1950s and the 1990s. This chapter looks at changes in Britain from the 1950s when major reforms took place in prison clothing policies that included the prisoner's right to wear his or her own clothes. At the same time, in the specific context of the Troubles in Northern Ireland, prisoners were denied 'political status' that led to the extreme situation of Blanket protests, hunger strikes and death. But even in the relatively benign conditions in which prisoners were kept in English prisons a gap between legislation and the humiliating experience of clothing provision remained. This chapter focuses on the way that systems of clothing provision interweave with prevalent political penal policies and are experienced by the prisoner. As demonstrated in the words of prisoners quoted above, prison dress plays a crucial part in the construction of identity, compliance or resistance to incarceration. Issues of dress are looked at in relation to gender and clothing, survival and the expression of individual or collective identity that became visible in different political contexts. Increasing rates of imprisonment took place in this period throughout Britain and affected the provision of prison clothing and the lives of inmates. As one ex-prisoner said, 'on a day-to-day level clothes are definitely part of survival – that's staying strong! If I was scruffy I'd be struggling because part of my identity was to look smart despite my circumstances'.[1]

fashion and prison dress changes in Britain

In the 1950s, Britain's economy was unstable after the privations of the Second World War. In 1940s and 1950s Britain prison clothing was thus not a priority. Rationing and tight controls on the provision of clothing prevailed until 1952. During the Second World War the British Textile and Garment Industry was run down in order that manufacturing could concentrate on the munitions industry to provide armaments and machinery for the war effort. The Board of Trade had devised a plan for the use of existing stocks of textiles in a situation where the import of raw fibres and the export of cloth and garments had declined. As a result Austerity measures harnessed the consumption of clothing to its decline in production. The people of Britain were encouraged to recycle what they had and this was similarly the case within the prison walls as late as the 1960s and 1970s.

In 1942, the Board of Trade instigated the Utility line that was the functional couture inspiration for the 'Make do and Mend'[2] campaign whereby the majority of the population were encouraged to make their own clothing from material that was available in their homes. These restrictive clothing schemes were models of State design and provision that were to characterise functional prison clothing design and production until the 1990s.

Although the production and consumption of clothing in Britain slowly regained momentum, the British Textiles and Garment Industry was not modernised and never regained pre-Second World War levels of production. All these developments in the clothing industry affected the production of clothing in prisons for the following decades. Similarly, changes in the broader Fashion Industry influenced post-Second World War prison clothing. Paris couture houses had, to a large extent, closed down during Nazi occupation. However, France continued to produce a limited couture line, particularly in millinery, mainly for the benefit of Nazi officers' wives in occupied Paris.[3]

In 1947 the French fashion designer, Christian Dior (1905–1957) relaunched the Paris collections with what became known as 'The New Look'. The extravagant use of yards of material in a single Dior garment was greeted with public outrage in clothing rationed Britain. This was demonstrated in the pages of popular magazines such as *Picture Post.*[4] Gradually during the 1950s Parisian influences were reaching British women but without the extravagance of couture. Many women made their own adaptations or had pared down versions of the 'New Look' made up in local dressmakers. In Austerity Britain fashion passed by the prison uniform.

Despite a few changes in the length of hemline for women prisoners and from grey-and-white striped shirt to blue-and-white striped shirt for male prisoners, few changes occurred in the 1950s and 1960s. It was not until the 1970s that prison clothing changed for women and later in the 1990s that men's prison uniforms were abolished. These significant changes were influenced by broader fashion innovations in Britain. First were the radical innovations for female fashion. Although British fashion designer Mary Quant (b. 1934) established her retail outlet Bazaar in London in 1955, her influence did not spread widely in Britain until the early 1960s. Fashionable ideas were disseminated through a proliferation of magazines for young women. However, the availability of fashions was limited to those who could travel to the metropolis. Thus, particularly for working class girls in the provinces, there was a lack of London-inspired clothing, and many resorted to making their own clothes in the way their mothers had done in the 1950s.[5] It was only in the late 1960s that high street boutiques burgeoned throughout the country providing cheap women's fashions.

There was a marked convergence between developments in women's fashions outside the prison walls and changes that took place for women prisoners in 1971. Women prisoners were for the first time allowed to wear their own clothes rather than prison uniforms. This was in contrast to the lack of changes in men's fashions outside and men's uniforms in prisons in the 1970s. Although sub-cultural Teds and Mods clothing in the 1950s and 1960s appealed to groups of working class youth outside London, few retail shops catered to their needs. Counter-cultural sartorial flamboyant menswear was largely limited to outlets in the capital. Whereas the expansion in young women's fashion outlets was greeted by the prison establishment as an encouragement to normalise young women as consumers, sub-cultural and counter-cultural men's fashions were seen as a threat to traditional masculinity. This gendered approach to clothing was reflected in male prisoners only being granted the right to wear their own clothes in 1991.

The historical time lapse between the change in women's and men's prison clothing reflected the comparative lack of fashionable provision for men in the 1970s in the broader fashion industry. These prison clothing changes raise the question of institutional gender assumptions in the treatment of men and women in prison. Prison authorities took an essentialist position with regard to the domestication and normalisation of women through their right to wear their own clothes.

There was a presumption that women would re-enter the outside world as consumers of clothes not only for themselves but also for their male partners and children. This policy overlooked groups of women prisoners who, out of choice for some and necessity for others, returned to their previous codes of dress outside the prison rather than re-modelling their sartorial aspirations on the high street. In contrast, behind the protracted decision to allow men to wear their own clothes, there was the assumption that men were less concerned about their appearance and were not potential consumers of clothes. These differentiated gender policy changes in British prisons provide an insight into the ways in which reforms in the production and provision of prison clothing reflected contemporary penal thinking and broader fashion and industrial prerogatives. Prisoners' perceptions of these changes are considered here in relation to the way prison authorities represented inmates to the public. A case study of these changes in Britain between 1970 and the 1990s historically situates the political and cultural complexity of the issue of prison clothing.

prison conditions in 1970s–1990s Britain

Britain's prison population increased during this period as did that of most countries in the West. One of the reasons for the expansion in crime and the subsequent rise in incarceration rates[6] was the increase in unemployment in the 1970s owing to the decline in traditional manufacturing industries. Working class communities had previously been relatively economically stable and were dependent on male employment and tight-knit families that from the 1970s became increasingly fragmented.

Although there is not a direct correlation between high rates of unemployment and an increase in crime, the statistics for the 1970s to 1990s period in Britain show a marked increase in unemployment and prison numbers in both male and female prisons. More men were unemployed in areas that had depended on traditional local industries. Women, who had previously largely taken care of the home, often took the place of men in order to provide for families. Increasingly they entered the expanding service industries such as the retail sector. Thus it was that within local working class communities 'the regulatory processes which had been in operation in the post-war period were gradually being transformed'[7] by the late 1970s. Different reasons have been given for the increase in female imprisonment figures at a time of growth in women's employment. One of the reasons is that men's unemployment contributed to increased tensions in the family, the subsequent increase in family break down and the growth of single parent families. Women suffered the double burden of economically and socially providing for children. This meant there was an increase in economic hardship and material inequality for both unemployed men and single parent women as well as for kids left unattended at home. Increasingly during the period single parents were also publicly stigmatised. Although poverty does not necessarily lead to criminality, the condition of social marginalisation[8] in which working class women found themselves accounts to an extent for their turn to minor offences such as shoplifting and prostitution that were the major forms of female criminality. At the same time, domestic tension in the family meant there was a tendency for men increasingly to commit domestic violence. This would partially explain the corresponding increase in rates of male criminality. Most criminologists agree that there was at this time a convergence of factors that meant the relationships between gender, employment and crime were complex.[9]

At the same time as the breakdown of local communities there was, in Britain, a decline in the provision of welfare agencies during the economic recession of the 1970s. Conservative Thatcherite policies of 'Law and Order' in the 1980s led to a corresponding increase in the provision of prison places and a vast prison building programme to combat a perceived increase in crime. As a result money was poured into prisons to alleviate conditions of imprisonment, amongst which were internal sanitation and the gradual provision of clothing choices for prisoners. There was thus a parallel decline in welfare agencies in communities and an increase in welfare provision within penal establishments. This development has been explained by the political and economic division of resources whereby the Government's 'Law and Order' budget under Thatcherism was unaffected by the comparative decline in Government spending on social welfare in local communities.[10]

the prison clothing industry in Britain 1970–1990s

At the same time as traditional industries and communities were on the decline, and in line with the improvement in prison conditions, there was an expansion in the production of prison clothing during the 1970s and 1980s. Textiles and garments prison workshops grew substantially during the post-war years. Prisons located in traditional clothing production areas such as Lancashire and Yorkshire employed local instructors who trained prisoners in the manufacture of clothing. Finished prison issue clothing was transported to prisons that, for example, specialised in the production of furniture for prison cells. In the 1970s and 1980s the vast complex of production and distribution of clothing and furnishing significantly grew to the level of a discrete prison industry.

Additionally, technological changes had affected the maintenance of clothing in prisons since the 1950s. For example, a complex network of laundries was introduced between 1955 and 1959.[11] The establishment of laundries in prisons came at a time when the middle classes were able to buy their own washing machines and communal laundrettes were built for those who could not afford their own. The provision of laundries in prisons meant an increase in washing facilities for prisoners in line with the democratisation of clothing maintenance outside the prison.

This aspect of the provision of prison clothing was extended in the 1970s and 1980s. The organisation of laundering clothing meant that specific prisons catered for other prisons in the region rather than contracting out washing to companies outside the prison walls. However, the centralised control of washing clothes often resulted in the failure of delivery that such a complex system incurred. This meant that prisoners' own clothing, 'with the individuating traces of its wearer',[12] was often not returned or in bad condition. Many prisoners complained about this when interviewed.

One man who was imprisoned in the 1970s said, 'they used to bleach the fuck out of pants and underwear and they were stiff with starch. It was just the thought of putting another man's underwear on was so humiliating and revolting'.[13] Another added, 'all the clothes had been boiled so it wasn't dirty but it stank foistiness'.[14] The re-distribution of washed clothing was experienced by the prisoner as a form of erosion of their identity by the institution. During the 1970s some prisons allowed a limited facility for inmates to wash their own clothes such as socks and T-shirts. However, the rate of modernisation of equipment or laundry systems varied from one prison to another with a corresponding range of experiences for the prisoner. The funding of prison systems' provision and maintenance of clothing was politically accountable and yet hidden from the public. Cost was at a premium in deciding factors for innovation whether technological, managerial or in relation to changes in clothing practices in prisons. For example, between 1963 and 1964, a number of Prison Governors in Britain[15] argued that buying clothing for Borstal girls would be too costly in comparison to the cost of prisons producing their own clothes. Not only did prisoners provide cheap labour for the prison population but the prison workshops also provided employment for instructors who had worked in declining industries outside the prison. An experiment took place in 1964 in the Holloway prison Borstal wing that was a precursor to the adoption of women prisoners wearing their own clothes in 1971. Girls were encouraged to bring in their own clothing that they had bought outside the prison; however, they were also expected to make their own clothes. Thus, the employment of instructors from outside was ensured. From the discussions that were held at this time about women wearing their own clothes, it is clear that the cost of the scheme was a priority. Women would have to be provided with their own clothing inside if they did not have the means to be provided with it from outside. Unsurprisingly, the introduction of women's right to wear their own clothes was initially not about enhancing the lives of inmates but about cost. Similar debates did not occur when men's prison clothing regulations changed in 1991. By this time the question of cost was controlled by the centralised administration of the distribution of prison clothing. Whether brought in from outside retail outlets or designed and produced within prisons, the provision of all aspects of clothing was by then firmly established as part of the 'Regime Services' under the auspices of the Home Office.

gendered prison clothing: 1950s and 1960s

In the 1960s the embodied discipline of male prisoners was regulated with military precision whether in Borstals or adult men's prisons. In the film *The Loneliness of the Long Distance Runner* (1962), a young boy – Colin – is arrested for stealing money from a bakery. He enters the youth offenders institution and is stripped of his clothing, possessions and his outside identity. He and the rest of the boys arrested are clothed in identical kit, comprised of roughly made jackets and trousers, and lined up in front of the Governor, who proceeds to lecture them on the necessity of obeying the rules and standing to attention. He infers that conformity will lead to behavioural change. In the novel upon which the film is based, Colin, rather than interiorising the stricture to behave as the prison sees fit, laughs and in that laugh there is resistance. Colin's repost is, 'well I could have died laughing, especially when straight after this I hear the barking sergeant-major's voice calling me and two others to attention and marching us off like we was Grenadier Guards'.[16]

Masculine penal normalisation was thus seen as militaristic institutional conformity. It was also about a return to the outside world as productive workers, integrated into the sombre world of sartorial masculinity where individual choice was limited. Prison issue clothing consisting of blue-and-white striped shirts, straight trousers and jackets was commensurate with a semblance of the embourgoisification of working class male attire. The thin blue-and-white stripes of the shirt retained a memory of smart city dress as well as signifying prison bars. The authorities saw male prison clothing as symbolically representative of the criminal's return as straight to the world outside prison. Yet, the experience of the clothing was one of impoverishment and shame. Male prisoners had a strong sense of the importance of clothing. As one said,

> even a scruffy officer would look smart in their ties and shirts, shiny shoes and his hat. There was a complete difference between officers and prisoners. A convict would wear a big old denim jacket, trousers that were too long, shoes that a hundred people had worn before him. You looked scruffy and you never polished your shoes...I realised about all the controlling mechanisms and one of them was clothing...The thing about clothing is it makes you feel a certain way. If you're dressed scruffily you feel lazy and unmotivated.[17]

This prisoner's personal technique of resistance was to take pains to retain his own sartorial smartness.

During the 1960s, women's uniforms consisted of loose, unfitted blue dresses made of cheap cotton (see Fig. 5.1). There were few seams and the dresses were made to fit all sizes. They were produced by prisoners with little dress-making training, in prison workshops around the country. These crumpled and worn dresses[18] and photographs of women in Holloway prison (see

Figure 5.1   UK women inmates' blue dress uniform, c. 1950s/1960s, NCCL Galleries of Justice, prison clothing archive (author's photograph).

Figure 5.2 Women in Holloway Prison, c. 1950s/1960s.

Figs. 5.2 and 5.3) attest to the lack of fit. The dresses contrasted with the official militaristic prison staff uniforms (see Fig. 5.4) that were contracted out to manufacturers in the same period. The staff uniform was more fitted and made of non-creasable lightweight cotton/rayon mix fabric. The fabric from which garments were made, as much as the absence of design, distinguished the incarcerated from those in authority. However, women individualised prison uniforms in the way they wore certain items. Women in Holloway prison in the 1960s demonstrated this in the way a collar was open at the neck or buttoned up (see Fig. 5.2), whether a cardigan was buttoned or left open, whether items bulged in pockets[19] (see Fig. 5.3). These small differences amounted to day-to-day choices that the inmate made in order to express individual identity in imposed dress. Despite the institution's attempt to stamp out prisoners' individuation of clothing, it persisted as survival techniques and limited forms of agency. In this case the way clothing was adjusted by inmates displayed involvement in and disaffection from their institutional stigmatisation as criminals. 'Prison clothing is anonymous...One's possessions are limited...the urge to collect possessions is carried to preposterous extents...these things are assiduously gathered, jealously hidden or triumphantly displayed.'[20] Yet, institutions tend to see men's and women's attitudes to clothing in prison differently. This is powerfully demonstrated in changes that occurred in British prisons between 1970 and 1990.

Figure 5.3 Woman in Holloway Prison cell, c. 1950s/1960s.

gendered prison clothing: Britain 1970s to 1990s

The changes between 1971 and 1991 trace the continuation of clothing as a gendered strategy of penal control. The 1971 reform whereby women were allowed to wear their own clothes in prison received public recognition during prisoners' protests in 1972. (The Preservation of the Rights of Prisoners (PROP)) co-ordinated a campaign for improved conditions and prisoners appeared on the roofs of prisons. The press

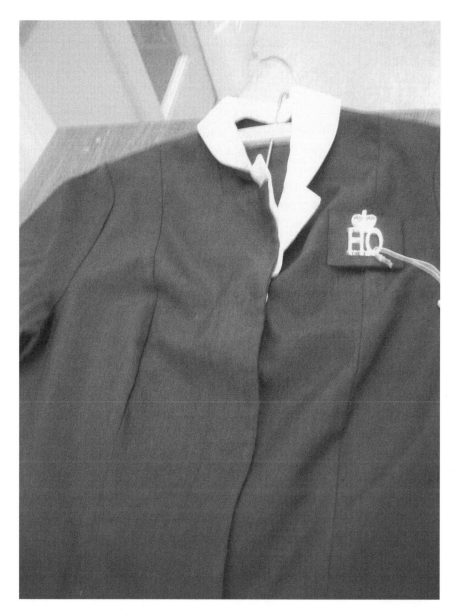

Figure 5.4 Women staff's uniform, c. 1970s. NCCL Galleries of Justice, prison clothing archive (author's photograph).

reported that 'girl inmates of Holloway prison staged a rooftop protest... The girls were not in uniform. They all wore ordinary clothes and one had a fur coat on'.[21] There is an implied sense of moral indignation at women prisoners being able to afford fur coats. The more serious issue of the demands of the prisoners is secondary to the gendered concern that female prisoners were permitted clothes above their station as criminals. In practice, the clothing women were permitted was highly regulated.

Nevertheless, the 1971 reform did permit limited choice to prisoners. Colourful blouses, for example, were allowed and clothing that had been obtained from high street retail shops could be brought in to prison so that inmates were able to retain a degree of fashionability (see Fig. 5.5). The distinction between staff and prisoners was broken down, to an extent, through the prisoner's garment providing a closer fit to the body than the previous loose-fitting uniform. However, there were new distinctions not only in the comparison between the militaristic and the civilian, but also between the cost of professionally tailored staff clothing and cheap high street fashions.[22] In a Home Office official photograph of a 1970s Holloway prison workshop (see Fig. 5.6), girls wear floral blouses similar to the one in Fig. 5.5. The photograph represents a stereotype of prison authorities' notion of the normalisa-tion of young women prisoners as consumers of fashionable clothing after they were allowed to wear their own. The reality for women in prison at this time often differed from this official visualisation.

In 1972, in the class I taught in Holloway prison, there was a variety of women none of whom appeared as the young women in the photograph. One group of young women had been prostitutes and 'serviced' the sailors in the Liverpool docks. They wore dungarees and sported naval-inspired tattoos on their arms. The authorities had attempted to physically eliminate their previous identification with prostitution. Yet the girls chose to wear clothing that identified them with their previous occupa-tion and geographical area outside the prison walls. A Hungarian woman, however, who had been charged with shoplifting and had no relatives to turn to for clothes to be brought into the prison, dressed in the same shabby clothes each week. The authorities had made little provision for the replacement, repair or maintenance of this woman's clothing. The poverty from which had arisen her original perceived need to shoplift showed in the clothing she wore. Additionally, despite women being allowed to wear their own clothing, the bodily humiliation of imprisonment experi-enced by women was evident in the increase in self-harming in this period. Women who, for the most part were imprisoned for minor offences, would come to the class each week with bandaged arms and the effects of self-harming through sticking pins and other objects into their arms. The 1970s saw the beginnings of an increase in self-harm amongst women and eventually also amongst men.[23]

For many women in prison, dress reveals their reduction 'as women by the pro-cess of criminalisation'.[24] This is at odds with the normalisation process whereby prison authorities see rehabilitation as being dependent on women's feminisation through the consumption of clothing. For other women, clothing was a marker of the continuity of their group identity outside prison. Neither of these groups feature in the official photos of Holloway prison in the 1970s. Rather, official photographs represent the feminised notion of the inmate that approximated to the prison author-ities' concern with their normalisation in the eyes of the public.

There is evidence of soiling on the 1970s woman prisoner's blouse (see Fig. 5.5) whereas the staff clothing is immaculate. Not only does this demonstrate

Figure 5.5 1970s woman prisoner's blouse. NCCL Galleries of Justice, prison clothing archive (author's photograph).

Figure 5.6 Holloway women's prison workshop, c. 1970s.

a distinction between fabrics that retain marks and those that do not, but it also shows that the clothing materialises the circumstances in which they were worn. Prisoners' clothing displays the same stresses experienced by the women who wore them rather than the fashionability represented in the prison photograph. There were similar distinctions between male prisoners' uniforms at this time and that of the staff. Whereas blue-and-white striped shirts produced in prison workshops in the 1970s were bulky, made of twill and revealed no wastage of fabric through their lack of shape (see Fig. 5.7), staff shirts had a number of pockets and were fitted (see Fig. 5.8). As an ex-prisoner comments, 'prison officers would wear their black and white uniforms and they were smart. There was a complete difference between officers and prisoners. Clothing is about dividing the relationship between prison officers and cons'.[25] The blue-and-white striped shirt signified contradictory processes of normalisation of the male prisoner. It was a form of sartorial respectability and yet the striped fabric was representative of age-old imprisonment. When the arm was raised the vertical stripes of the shirt met with the horizontal stripes to form a grid.[26]

When I was teaching in Wakefield Top Security Prison for men between 1972 and 1973, some men were dressed in the uniform blue-and-white striped shirts, grey sweaters and prison trousers and shoes. Others wore prison dungaree-type clothing if they worked in workshops. The staff wore uniforms similar to the police at this time. Apart from the distinctions between male prisoners' and staff dress, inmates' hair was forcibly cut. The normalisation of the male inmate was not through the consumption of clothing but through the imposition of a stereotype of English male respectability – the short-back-and-sides hair cut. As Richard Neville (b. 1941), one of the editors of the *Schoolkids OZ* magazine,[27] recounts when he was on remand in the early 1970s in Wandsworth Prison, 'the warder told us we would be taken to another wing to be "tidied up"'. Felix Dennis (b. 1947), another editor of *OZ* and in prison with Neville, 'whose luxuriant mop lay on the floor around him', mentions that there is a choice. '"Shearing now by this friendly inmate, or tomorrow by the official prison barber. Even shorter"'.[28] There was relish in the warder's tone when he ordered the editors of *OZ* to be shorn. Prison authorities saw the gendered normalisation of these icons of countercultural permissiveness as a visible and public embodiment of their punishment. In Wakefield Prison in the early 1970s, some long-term inmates were allowed to wear their hair minimally longer. There was, therefore, a degree of choice in the length of hair. The harshness of embodied punishment varied according to different prison cultures. However, extreme lengths of hair that were fashionable across classes in the early 1970s were seen as an infringement of conventional masculinity. The same men I met inside Wakefield Prison sported hair below their shoulders outside the prison walls. Most significantly there was a time lapse of 20 years between 1970 when women could wear their own clothes and 1990 before men were permitted to do so. The reform again set up new distinctions between

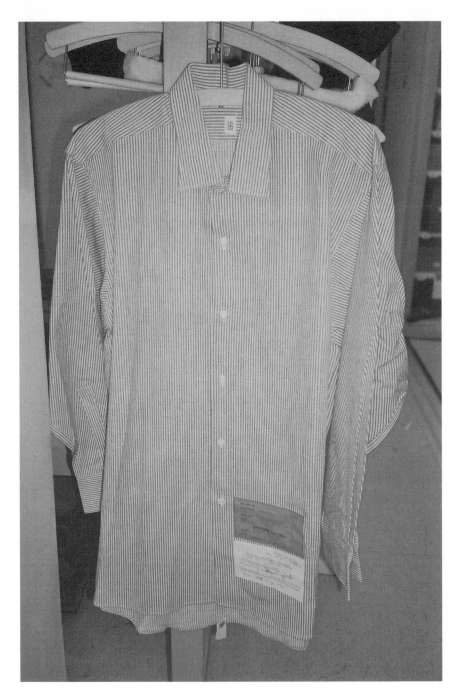

Figure 5.7 Blue-and-white striped male prisoner's shirt, c. 1980s. NCCL Galleries of Justice, prison clothing archive (author's photograph).

Figure 5.8   Male staff's prison shirt, c. 1980s. NCCL Galleries of Justice, prison clothing archive (author's photograph).

those inmates who could afford fashionable clothing and those who could not. For example, the East End gangster, Reggie Kray (1933–2000) owned a Harrods shirt.[29] The American astronaut Buzz Aldrin[30] (b. 1930) sent it to him in the early 1990s. The shirt was impeccably cut and made from quality fabric. It proclaimed the lifer's previous aspirational taste for aristocratic rather than middle-class clothing as sig-nifier of East End gangland status. Through the gifting of the shirt by an American celebrity, Reggie Kray's status was re-established as distinctive from other prisoners and the prison staff in their uniforms. 'When you could wear your own clothes they were sent in and then it was about prisoners who had cash. There were gangsters who had earned a lot of money outside and they were identifiable in relation to their clothing styles.'[31] However, it is uncertain whether Reggie Kray identified with the Harrods shirt since someone outside the prison had chosen it.

The shirt nevertheless signifies how after 20 years he was still seen by outsiders as a member of the East End gang. Studies of lifers' responses to the previous labels attached to them outside prison show that after years of imprisonment their self-perceptions may have changed and range from 'partial acceptance...through amused detachment...to total and bitter rejection'.[32]

The moments of change in 1971 and 1991 denote a shift from the uniformity of prison clothing as punishment to a system of control of the consumption of clothing. But many inmates still relied on prison issue clothing. Although this clothing no longer comprised a uniform it lacked fit and individuation. Despite this there were ways in which prisoners either learnt to circumvent privations or personalised the clothing provided. For example, a young man sentenced to a year in prison in 1998 had to 'hand everything over (even underwear)'[33] when he was inducted. He was issued with items of prison issue clothing that included a tight pink shirt and trousers that did not fit. It was only through his cell mate knowing how to get better clothing that he was provided with presentable jeans and T-shirt.

This is an indication of a technique whereby the activity of procuring clothing, permitting the 'self' comfort and a normative appearance within the prisoners' own dress code, is reliant on another prisoner's inside knowledge of the prison system.

Prisoners' voices whether written or oral reveal the extent to which the availability and maintenance of prison clothing, in the form of altering, washing or procuring it, continues to be an issue of privation for prisoners to the present day. Even after the 1971 and 1991 reforms, there was a continued lack of availability of prisoners' own clothing through poverty or the lack of friends and relatives outside the prison. Consequently, the provision of prison issue clothing continued as a mechanism of control marking distinctions of comparative wealth and status within the prison population.

Irish blanket protests 1970s–1980s

The extent to which prison clothing is a political issue is demonstrated by the lengths to which the British Government was prepared to go to diminish the rights of Republican prisoners during the 1970s in Northern Ireland. 'Political status', or the wearing of civilian clothing by Irish prisoners, was restricted in the 1970s. This resulted in the Republican prisoners' 'Blanket' and Hunger Strikes in the late 1970s and early 1980s. These events galvanised public opinion around the importance of the Irish 'Troubles' and the anti-imperialist struggle of Republicans. An Irish Republican prisoner mentions the political issue of prison clothing at this time. He was imprisoned three times during the 1970s. The first time was between 1974 and 1976 in Northern Ireland in Crumlin Road Jail and Long Kesh (the precursor to the Maze prison). In his induction he immediately 'claimed " status" '. During this time 'political status' prisoners were segregated from ordinary prisoners imprisoned in 'the cages' at Long Kesh. They were allowed to 'wear their own clothes for the whole time' while ordinary convicts had to wear prison uniform. He adds:

> When I first saw a prisoner in prison uniform it was a repellent thing. It was humiliating. It was something I was horrified by. It marked them down as convicts and non political prisoners. So I was looking at them thinking: 'Did you burgle or what did you do?' It was the mark of a criminal.[34]

This observation highlights the way ordinary prison uniform immediately identified inmates as criminals regardless of the nature of their crime. This comment is all the more poignant as it is made by an inmate whose 'crime' had been political and, at this time, was recognised as such by the prison authorities and British Government. As far as women prisoners in Ireland at this time were concerned, those from the '26 counties' (Southern Ireland) rather than from 'the oppressed minorities of the ghettoes of Northern Ireland' were unable to act as rebelliously as Republican women who had lived under the repression of the Northern Ireland police force. Despite this, one woman from the South had to remind prison officers that she had 'the right to wear her own clothes' when they took away the trousers she was wearing. Prison officers explained that her black trousers were too similar to the Republican uniform and that they were threatening to prison officers. They insisted that they would give her other clothes.[35] Eventually the Republican prisoner in charge of one of the wings of the prison provided her with a skirt that fitted and was considered appropriate both as 'her own clothes' and non-Republican uniform. Although female and male Republican prisoners were allowed to wear civilian clothing prison authorities controlled them.

The second occasion that the male prisoner was imprisoned was under the Prevention of Terrorism Act. He was held in English prisons for a total of 17 days. On this occasion 'I remember a burning sense of indignation when I was forced into prison uniform. You were wearing another man's underpants, another man's socks. Everything was ill-fitting. You felt completely humiliated. I can't describe it. It marked you out as a criminal'.[36] The third time he was imprisoned was in 1976. He was in Brixton prison in London and he was eventually granted 'political status'. In contrast, in Northern Ireland at this time, this right had been taken away from Republican prisoners as a 'punishment for causing a riot in 1974 and burning down the 'cages' in Long Kesh'.[37]

The notorious H-block of the newly built Maze prison was opened in 1976 on the site of the 'Nissen-hut dormitories' of Long Kesh internment camp. It was a formidable architectural structure designed to punish those incarcerated within its walls through constant surveillance. The denial of 'political status' was one of the prison regulations wielded by prison authorities as a punitive measure in line with the prison's 'fortifications [that] show the toughness of the prison regime and the seriousness of those responsible for running it'.[38] The architecture of the Maze, the regulation of prisoners' bodies through the denial of the freedom of association with others and the imposition of prison uniform were visible reminders of the lengths to which the Conservative Government in Britain was prepared to go to suppress the Republican cause. The interconnection between the politics of social and penal control with architectural and bodily design had characterised the nineteenth-century Model Prison. It was partly this aspect of the brutal construction and regime of the Maze prison that was opposed by prisoners inside its walls. There had been a long history of Republican prisoners demanding the recognition of 'political status' in their refusal to wear prison uniforms and in 1976 the protest took an extreme form. Prisoners wore no clothes at all rather than prison uniform, with merely a blanket around them for a degree of warmth. At the same time they refused to wash or take bodily care of themselves and these political acts comprised the Dirty Protest.

It was mostly Republican prisoners who went on the 'Blanket protest', although a few Loyalists also staged protests. These inmates considered that the taking away of their own clothes by prison authorities was a political act. Resistance to wearing the prison uniform was 'to say I'm holding on to my dignity and my political identity and I'm not accepting your authority. Those were the issues. No one had to articulate those issues. It was something engrained'.[39] In a Northern Ireland Prison Archive in Belfast there are 'examples of these blankets and the ways they were fashioned – sometimes as clothes, marching uniforms, marching regalia and even body armour for riot situations'.[40]

Restrictions and 'political status' regulations applied to women prisoners although not as strictly as for the men. Women Republican prisoners in Armagh prison were not forced to wear uniforms. However, their protest took the form of refusing to wash or change their clothes in solidarity with male prisoners. The part women played in the Dirty Protests was significant. They were aware of the subversive power they held in the collective refusal to care for and maintain their appearance as expected by the authorities. The contrast between unkempt prisoners and the female prison staff was a visible everyday reminder of the prisoners' resistance. One woman said,

> the more asexual we became with our loose-fitting jeans and streaks of dirt running down our faces, the more feminine [the screws] became, with their

elaborate coiffures, their waists nipped in tightly, great whiffs of perfume choking our nostrils every time we left the cells.[41]

The authorities' attempted strategy of criminalisation through the stripping away of Republican identities was met with resistance on the part of the inmates. Additionally, the Republican community outside the prison walls supported the prisoners' struggle. Eventually in 1981, after 10 prisoners had died on Hunger Strike, the British Government and prison authorities conceded on the issue of 'political status'. But 'the right to wear our own clothes instead of prison uniform…was the only demand that was met'.[42] However, although the Northern Ireland Prison Service under the auspices of the British Government agreed to this clothing demand, they adopted a policy whereby all prisoners could wear their own clothes, whether male or female, criminal or political.[43] In this way the prison authorities removed the political significance of the Republican prisoners' action. Thus, a special case was made in Northern Ireland prisons whereby male prisoners could wear their own clothing from 1981.

This transparent inconsistency in British prison clothing policies is demonstrated in the film *In the Name of the Father* (1993). It was based on the real false imprisonment of Gerry and Giuseppe Conlon from Belfast. In 1974 they were sentenced to 15 years for the Guildford bombing. The film demonstrated that through the staging of show trials and forced confessions, the police authorities were aware of their innocence after the real bomber had confessed. Yet, the Conlons were kept in maximum security units in English jails, dressed in branded clothing with yellow stripes down the side of the trousers and a large yellow patch on the jacket reserved for those at risk of escape. Although allowances must be made for cinematic exaggeration, the film was largely historically accurate. It shows that even after 1981, when Northern Irish jails had conceded 'political status', and despite the Guildford Four's wrongful imprisonment, Irish prisoners were visibly sartorially segregated, punished and discriminated against as criminals in English prisons. However, the granting of 'political status' and the wearing of civilian clothing were the first of a number of hard won victories for the Blanket protesters that paved the way towards negotiations and the Peace Agreement in the late 1990s.

the abolition of prison uniforms in Scotland: 1970s to 1990s

During the 1960s and early 1970s, prison regimes in Scotland were similar to those in England. Prison uniforms were the rule and the conditions varied between normalisation through therapeutic treatment to systems of punishment. In the 'Cages' in Inverness prison, for example, prisoners 'were kept naked' and 'prison staff were potentially violent'.[44] Prisoners rioted in response to these eighteenth-century conditions.

In 1973 a Special Unit for maximum security prisoners was initiated in Barlinnie Prison in Scotland and continued for 20 years. Jimmy Boyle (b. 1944), who was sentenced to life imprisonment in 1967, entered the unit when it was set up. One of the main premises upon which this special unit was devised was the recognition by prison reformers that prisons should 'be making offenders more responsible people so that on release they will be capable of playing a useful role in society'.[45] One of the responsibilities conferred on this small group of male prisoners in the unit was to obtain, wear and maintain their own clothing rather than wearing 'degrading and humiliating' prison uniforms. Prison staff proposed that they too should wear civilian clothing. Prisoners and staff argued that the scheme would be jeopardised if staff continued to wear authoritarian uniforms. Eventually this was permitted in order to carry through the principles of the unit. A committee of prisoners and staff resolved tensions between staff and prisoners, between members of staff and between prisoners. Prison clothing practices reflected the egalitarian regime in place within the prison system.

Before his release in 1982, Jimmy Boyle was returned to an ordinary prison for 2 years. Prison authorities did not provide an explanation for this move. He described the loss of identity he experienced in an ordinary prison. 'I feel anonymous wearing this coarse prison uniform.' Not only was the wearing of prison clothing degrading, every aspect of clothing was controlled so that he received a 'weekly change of socks, shirt and underpants'.[46] When he was finally allowed out of prison he wrote, 'once dressed in my own clothes I felt like superman. I seemed to smell and feel different'.[47] Boyle considered that the experience of spending a large portion of his sentence in a prison unit based on mutual respect for the identity of individuals contributed significantly to his rehabilitation. After the experimental unit was closed, prison issue clothing was re-imposed in prisons in Scotland in the early twenty-first century. The relaxation of distinctions in clothing that was evident in the Special Unit was undoubtedly a beneficial experiment. Yet, it was also costly. It was not adopted universally in Scottish prisons during a period of increasing prison numbers in the late 1990s and into the 2000s. Although remand prisoners are allowed to wear their own clothing, all prisoners, both men and women, wear prison issue clothing that includes 'blue denims, trainers, underwear, sweaters, work-wear and, in the case of women, 'cotton skirts and smocks'.[48] The clothing is bought in commercially by a variety of contractors. In 2001 a prisoner arrested for refusing to pay a £30 fine for demonstrating against the deployment of Trident by the British State was sentenced to a 7-day sentence in Barlinnie Prison. He wrote a letter to the Governor of the prison complaining about degrading conditions. One of these was 'underwear which seemed to be issued on a "one-size-fits-all" basis…I spent my time waddling around with my underpants below my crotch…Likewise my vest was half way up my chest'.[49] This inmate characterises the anonymity and physical discomfort of prison issue clothing as degrading as a prison uniform. This type of punishment has not been modernised in many contemporary British prisons.

current clothing systems of provision in English prisons

Prison clothing policies evolved between the 1970s and 1990s and were linked to the deliberate institutional encouragement and regulation of prisoner consumption as opposed to imposed uniformity. These changes were reflected in the expansion of opportunities to consume cheap clothing outside the prison walls. The expansion in the communications industry, the media and retail shopping precincts has meant that local communities are visibly encouraged to participate in the acquisition of goods such as clothing. Yet, there are few opportunities to gain employment. This gap has led to marginalisation where once the work place provided stability of income and roles of belonging in working class communities.[50]

In Britain, America and in other Western societies, prison establishments have increasingly encouraged prisoner consumption of clothing as normalisation into the world of late modern commodification. At the same time, in England, the cheap production of prison issue clothing has continued in prison workshops. Until the 1970s, training in the Textiles and Garments Industry might have led to a job on release from prison. However, owing to the decline in the industry in the West this is now unlikely. Thus, there is a gap between the social expectation to consume clothing and the possible employment of the ex-prisoner. The prison system professes to counter prisoner recidivism through their normalisation inside and thus their social inclusion outside prison. However, many prisoners are used as cheap labour within the prison walls with little prospect of an improvement in their situation on release.

In England, although inmates are encouraged to wear their own clothes, many do not have the means to achieve this. Thus, the centralised provision and distribution of clothing takes the form of a vast and complex industry. This system is called the Prison Regime Services and is run under the auspices of the Home Office. In terms of public expenditure, this provision accounts for huge sums of money both administratively and in terms of deliverables. Vast sums of public money go into State clothing provision, at a time when the prison population is expanding, alongside the expansion of both State and privatised prison building programmes.

state provision of prison clothing in England

The Prison Regime Services is a State-run provider of prison clothing. It currently runs alongside the encouragement of prisoners to supply their own clothing and the privatised distribution of clothing in private prisons. Thus, three models of clothing provision co-exist.

The State scheme has similarities to the Austerity Regulations that were set up in Second World War Britain in the 1940s. Clothing and fabric production are intricately linked to the pared down functionality of styles and designs. In the 1960s and 1970s, the State provision of clothing was run by the Farms and Gardens prison department. This organisation was later named the Prison Design Group and, in the 1980s and 1990s, it was responsible for the production and distribution of prison clothing and other requisites, such as cell furnishings. The establishment of this group as a Prison Enterprise, within the Regime Services and in collaboration with the broader Federation of Clothing and Designer Executives, occurred in 2003. Recently the production of prison clothing has expanded to incorporate professional designers and manufacturers. It was from these beginnings that the Textiles Department as part of the Enterprise, and Supplies Service, under the auspices of the HM Prison Regime Service, gradually developed into what is currently a huge manufacturing, contractual, distribution and clothing maintenance operation throughout the country.

Regulations within each prison concerning the clothing allowance for inmates signify the degree of control of prisoners and determine the State provision of dress. Every piece of a prisoner's property, such as toiletries (including nail scissors and shower caps) and clothing, are itemised by the prison authority. The prisoner is issued with a 'facilities list' in each prison that includes the clothing allowance permitted. This list is broken down into categories according to the status of the prisoner. These include those 'prisoners arriving through reception with no appropriate clothing', those on the 'basic and standard regime' and 'enhanced regime' inmates. They are given a limited amount of prison issue clothing 'for an interim period prior to receiving property from visits or by post', and those who are on the basic regime 'are permitted less clothing than those who have earned enhanced status'. The itemisation of property and clothing is in accordance with whether an inmate is allowed clothing from the outside, clothing that is 'bought' from the prison shop or applied for from mail order catalogues. The style and construction of garments and accessories are also regulated. For example, women's skirts are itemised as 'appropriate length', tops are 'not allowed to be see-through, no crop tops', Shoe heels – 'stilettos and platforms – are not acceptable, the heel must be no more than two inches' and stockings and suspenders are 'not permitted'.[51] The detailed itemisation of prisoner's clothing that is justified in security terms provides the prison authorities with a form of institutionalised knowledge of the prisoner. Additionally it is intricately broken down in production terms to types of design in relation to gender, security and 'decency'.

However, prison clothing requirements are contradictory. For example, in terms of gender, feminine nightwear is prescribed as normalisation for women inmates. However, there are limits to how 'feminine' these 'night-dresses' can be. They cannot be see-through, too long or too low at the neck. Prisoners could trip if they were too long and female inmates should not be embarrassed to wear clothing when male staff are in the vicinity. Issues of 'decency' are paramount and yet the facilities list provided to women prisoners on entry into prison in Holloway prison only mentions '2 nighties' and not pyjamas.

The contradiction lies in the fact that the majority of women in prison wear 'uni-sex track-suits, jeans or work-wear' so pyjamas would seem to be a valid option. This is born out by those working in prisons and on a number of occasions when I have visited women's prisons, whether in the 1970s or in 2006, as well as from prisoners' accounts themselves. Out of 14 women I talked to, all of them said they wore either track suits, jeans or prison issue clothing that comprised the same items. All of them, apart from one, mentioned that the only time they 'dressed up' was for visits.[52]

As far as male prisoners are concerned, even after the introduction in 1991 of their being able to wear their own clothes, the majority of men resort to wearing prison issue clothing. The State prison regime network, therefore, predominantly designs, manufactures and distributes men's clothing throughout the prison system. Regulations determine the entire system of the provision of prison issue clothing from the design and the choice of fabric to the manufacturing, the contracting out of specific garments, their delivery and maintenance. For example,

> fabrics have to be robust and not unusual fabrics. Some of them have been in use for twenty years or more…work-wear for men and women is made of poly-cotton mix fabric. Some of these are similar fabrics to outside but there isn't as much lycra used in prison-wear.[53]

This is partly so that garments fit all sizes and partly so as not to exhibit the body in terms of 'decency'. This requirement, in turn, has implications for designers employed by the Prison Enterprise Services. Regulations concerning the colour of prison issue clothing, their functionality, sizing, accessorising and manufacture as much as the type of fabric used, apply throughout the State provision. In terms of sizing, for example, there are 'twenty one sizes of jeans' in prison in order to cater to 'the extremes at both ends.' Men as well as women and young offenders are prone to eating disorders or are registered on drug rehabilitation programmes, in which case they might lose or gain weight.

> Sometimes its difficult to source underwear off retail shelves [such as Marks & Spencer] since the sizes are not big enough so the Prison Regime Services have to design them specially along the same lines as M & S knickers. But they are, in this case, not styled in the same way. 'G' string underwear, for example, is not permitted.[54]

In this sense, issues of contemporary fashionability are determined by functionality in terms of prison regulations, market availability and prisoner demand. Although prison regulations are the priority for design, prisoner demand is also an important consideration. For example, the standard blue-and-white striped shirt worn by male prisoners was altered in recent years due to 'prisoners cutting off shirt sleeves since long sleeves provided restrictive movement…Thus short-sleeved shirts replaced them'. Additionally, market changes in the cheaper production of lightweight rather than the previously heavyweight cotton used in the production of shirts has meant that 'the fabric has changed to a lighter cotton than previously'.[55]

Although prison issue clothing is regulated in the same way as any prison service, whether food, sanitation or building maintenance, the Textiles Department has introduced fully designed and fashioned, rather than merely functional clothing into the prison repertoire. For example, in 2001 a womenswear range of 'long fleece jackets and leggings was designed in fashionable styles and colours. However, there was a surprisingly low take-up'.[56]

From discussing this with women prisoners it is evident that the majority of women do not wear prison issue clothing since it makes them feel 'ashamed'. Even if clothing approximates to a fashionable design, they do not want to stand out from other prisoners or be seen by visitors, other prisoners or staff in regulation, stigmatised prison clothing. Another explanation for women's lack of acceptance of designer prison issue clothing is that many prisoners' needs in terms of clothing are not dissimilar from those outside the prison walls. Their clothing preferences are largely based on income and social and economic considerations rather than imposed designer values. When designer clothing is acceptable it is through their own choice or design. For example, in Italy in October 2006, a group of inmates in a women's prison designed clothing from their jail uniforms. These items constituted 'neutrally coloured T-shirts, reversible sweat shirts, pants and miniskirts'.[57] These items were presented on Milan catwalks as designer clothes in the outside world. They were not designer clothing produced as prison issue dress with the associated institutional labelling of criminality. These fashion collections demonstrate a transformative juxtaposition of originally stigmatised clothing with a fashionability of the inmates' choice.

The organisation of the State prison issue clothing system reflects certain aspects of the outside world of clothing production. Stores Clerks, Acquisitions Clerks or other functionaries in individual prisons act as types of 'buyer' although money is not exchanged. They take the orders for prisoners' clothing needs. These are co-ordinated and realised by the centralised Textiles Department in the Regime Service. Designers generate working patterns that are sent out to the prison workshops. Fabric orders are centrally decided and distributed to the workshops. Prison instructors control the quality of the made-up garments before they are circulated. Some clothing is also manufactured by or ordered from outside companies. For example, since there is less demand for women's prison issue clothing, most of the production of clothing, across gender, takes place in men's prisons. Since men are not permitted to make up women's underwear and nightwear, these garments are manufactured outside prison. Thus, a number of systems prevail even within the State sector. In this instance, the prison system and its internal rules and organisation are reliant on the broader clothing system outside the prison. Prison regulations concerning issues of 'decency' pertaining to women's clothing have to be conformed to by outside operators. As a result of more women wearing their own clothes than men, less female clothing is produced. This results in 'women's prisons buying in menswear such as jogging bottoms, track suit tops and other items which are unisexual'.[58] Gender issues are intricately bound up in the appropriate form of provision adopted as they are in the design of the garments produced.

In manufacturing terms, the State system mirrors the lack of modernisation in the Textile and Garment Industry outside the prison walls. Globalisation has meant that the British industry has largely moved to countries with supplies of cheaper labour. As a result the machinery in the State prison system is relatively archaic. 'There's little investment in machines. Vandalism occurs frequently and the machinery is, as a whole, not computerised'.[59] Wages are low since training in prison clothing workshops is provided as an incentive for those on 'good behaviour'. It is not, therefore, a form of lucrative employment for the support of families nor does it, on the whole, provide the inmate with future employment outside the prison since jobs in the Textile and Garment Industry have declined.

The distribution of prison clothing is equally complex.[60] It comprises a number of departments, geographical locations and the transportation of made-up garments from prison workshops to the central store and from central stores to individual prisons according to their respective orders. Additionally, vast quantities of internal contracts and paperwork are engendered so that financial outputs are publicly accountable.

There is also the issue of maintaining clothing, whereby garments are washed in a central laundry system and some prisons have 'wing laundries' or prisoners wash small items in their cells. In the main, when clothing is centrally washed under the auspices of the Prison Regime Services, prisoners are often not returned the same clothing. 'Clothing has a short-life since it is very vigorously washed. For example, boxer shorts only last a few months'.[61] Additionally, clothing has to be 'deinfested' as a 'security measure' and the detailed regulations as to each prisoner's individual property allowance has to be abided by and monitored.

The authorities, whether the officer within the prison responsible for overseeing these operations, or the Head of Textiles at the central prison Regime Services confer that 'the clothing issue is not deliberately demeaning...we have to supply clothing and launder it and it's a difficult operation'.[62] However, prisoners' experience is often one of the de-personalisation of clothing. They know that there is a risk of loss or the destruction of treasured clothing in the vast complex of laundering and maintenance of clothing in prisons. There have been cases when jeans, for example, were destroyed in the laundry or other prisoners have stolen clothing. These cases resulted in compensation appeals against the prison.[63]

There is a bureaucratic system whereby prisoners' complaints are sent to the Stores Clerk in the individual prison and centrally co-ordinated. But this is a complex process when the numbers of prisoners around the country are forever increasing. As a result authorities try to avoid appeals whenever possible.

Partly as a consequence of penal policies of mass incarceration, the stated intention of those in control of the State provision of clothing, in terms of its lack of being 'demeaning', is rarely fully adhered to. There has been a relaxation in the form of prison staff clothing over the past decade. Female staff clothing comprises black trousers and white blouses similar to the less military uniforms of male staff. But largely, staff clothing is contracted out to manufacturers and distributors. This procedure is similar to the provision of official military, police and other uniforms of authority. There is thus a continuity of a marked distinction between the clothing provided for staff and inmates.

clothing consumption in State prisons

We have seen how the State provision of prison clothing has run parallel with the introduction of the consumption of clothing that developed in prisons from the 1970s. In the contemporary State-run prison in Britain there are a variety of ways in which inmates can procure their own clothing. These are largely dependent on distinctions based on gender and pecuniary standing. In many men's prisons clothing shops do not exist. Instead prison issue clothing is available in stores that are run by prisoners. But the clothing that is available is restricted. The availability of mail order catalogues for clothing purchases fluctuates from prison to prison. Thus male prisoners largely depend on relatives or friends on the outside. When clothing from outside prison is received it makes a substantial difference to a prisoner's sense of control of their identity. As one male ex-prisoner mentioned,

> my cousin sent me my own Baedebeck track suit and I felt great. Even though I was in gaol I felt a hell of a lot better. I felt more human. It gave me some status as well on the landing...I was the gym keeper at the time and I looked smart. Years and years of that scruffy prison look means they're trying to take away your identity, your personality.[64]

During the 1990s and early years of 2000, the Women's Voluntary Service (WVS) ran a donated clothing store in Holloway prison.[65] But many women felt that this was equivalent to wearing 'hand-outs'. 'However good the quality of these clothes, it affected women's self-esteem and their ability for self-determination.'[66] In 2004 the second-hand clothing store was closed.

In Holloway prison, during 2004–2006, when there was no provision for women to buy their own clothing, there was a scheme called 'Dress for Success' that provided women with an outfit of clothing for interviews for jobs on release. This was recognised to be insufficient for the majority of inmates and there were plans to start a 'boutique'.[67] The shop 'Glad Ragz' was introduced in September 2006. This shop provides off the shelf high street clothing mostly from companies such as Primark as well as second-hand clothing. Access to the shop is permitted to women who have attained enhanced status and have earned sufficient credit on what is called the 'canteen card'. Some women appreciated the introduction of a clothing shop. When I visited the shop, a woman inmate was expecting a visit from her family in the afternoon and said, 'I'm spoilt for choice, I'm excited now... It makes you so depressed if your clothes don't fit'.[68]

However, a number of women are unable to buy clothes and their perception is that 'no-one can help.' Alternatively, their property cards were not updated and their applications to buy items were ignored. It was considered by some women that the system was 'unfair'.[69] The institution sees the consumption of clothing as a way of providing women with more choice. But the choice is limited to women who have enhanced status for 'good behaviour' and is controlled by the authorities. In order to resist this privation women personalise their clothing by 'changing the style and cutting legs and arms of prison issue clothing' and a black British woman 'added sequins as well as cutting them'. A trans-sexual who was on medication to change sex to be a man, wore men's dungarees and groomed his facial hair as a man.[70] Male inmates also customise the shape of the collar, cuff or hemline of prison issue shirts in order to personalise them.[71] These everyday clothing and bodily activities indicate ways in which prisoners transform the shaming prison issue clothing or replace their lack of access to the shop or catalogues. In this way they attain a degree of control over their personal appearance and the regulated consumption of clothing.

There are other everyday distinctions between prisoners in relation to clothing that perpetuate difference according to pecuniary wealth. For example, again in Holloway prison, women who have babies inside prison are differentiated according to whether they are on welfare benefits or unable to be provided for by the State (e.g. non-British nationals, asylum seekers and others). Those on benefits are able to procure baby clothing from Mothercare catalogues and those without welfare benefits have to resort to second-hand baby clothing. Thus, clothing distinctions continue to exist within prisons based on ethnic identity or monetary status.

All these practices amount to forms of controlled consumption. Yet, resistance to regulated clothing exists. For example, in 2006, on the counter of 'Glad Ragz' in Holloway prison there was a pile of red T-shirts, printed with small black markings of the broad arrow originally daubed over prison clothing for men and women in British prisons and stopped in 1920. The T-shirts were designed by prisoners and printed with the help of a company called 'Designs from Inside'.[72] They are marketed online for public consumption. The iconic sign of punishment so hated by prisoners in the history of the British prison system has become an ironic visible mark of fashionability in the outside world. In the same way American prisoners produce socks with grey vertical stripes on a white background and labelled 'Alcatraz' in yellow.[73] Tourists to San Francisco covet them as prison souvenirs. This could just be taken as a cynical marketing ploy on the part of the prison authorities. But, by turning historical practices on their head, prisoners display a wisdom about their own corporal and clothing history. These forms of subversion also challenge the way the media continues to depict criminality. The broad arrow in England continues to be used as a short-hand sign of punishment despite its demise.[74] Through the designs of iconic prison clothing, the Holloway women and American prisoners display ownership of their prison clothing heritage and subvert the history of their punishment. They also make use of newly acquired design skills with which to reveal this knowledge to the public, the prison institution and inmates.

During the years after the attack on the World Trade Centre in New York in September 2001, the erosion of human rights in Britain increased, particularly in the case of imprisonment without trial of 'terror suspects'. These measures affected domestic prison policies in relation to the public humiliation of prison inmates. Less obvious than American prisoners in pink in the streets of Phoenix Arizona (see Chapter 6), but nonetheless condemnatory, is the return of visibly identifiable prison clothing for offenders on community service in the streets of Britain. Fluorescent jackets,[75] as a visible revival of embodied punishment, replace the normalisation of the inmate in their own clothes. Outside becomes inside in indeterminate shame.

prison clothing in private prisons

Privately managed prisons were introduced in Britain in the 1990s and Britain has the most privatised prison system in Europe.[76] Although controllers, who are linked to the Government Home Office, inspect private prisons, private companies manage them. Additionally companies that run these prisons manage private prisons in South Africa and Australia. Globalisation thus affects the world's prisons as a system dependent on financial markets. Inmate training programmes and employment opportunities as rehabilitation are contracted out to outside companies with the purpose of motivating prisoners 'to work in an industrial environment'.[77] The express objective of private prisons is their expansion, typified by profitable deals with building contractors. This 'serves to stifle meaningful debate about the current prison population crisis'.[78] As a result, conditions in some private prisons are reported as 'abandoning prisoners in a hell hole of violence and corruption'.[79]

The clothing provision in private prisons for men and women follows the same pattern as inmate employment, laundering and the cleaning of the prison. Clothing is contracted to outside companies when inmates cannot afford their own clothing or have no relatives to provide for them.[80] There is no centralised provision as in State prisons and the supply of track suits for women and items of underwear and socks for men are provided on an *ad hoc* basis according to regulated demand. Since private prisons are dependent on making a profit and the prison authorities, in the name of the company, assess the needs of the prisoner, every attempt is made to keep costs down. As a result, there is a tendency to 'non-intervention, neglect and indifference'.[81]

conclusion

The system of provision of prison clothing in Britain demonstrates that the reform whereby prisoners could wear their own clothing approximated to some degree to the UN declarations of the 1950s (mentioned in Chapter 4). However, in the past four decades, waves of more lenient non-custodial prison clothing experiments such as in Barlinnie Prison in Scotland were interspersed with punitive clothing measures, exemplified in the Irish struggle. As prison numbers increase a number of prevailing clothing practices ensure increased expenditure on prison cultures and a continued sense of embodied shame experienced by male and female inmates, to the extent of self-harm and suicide.[82] This is despite the decrease in actual crime statistics and in conflict with proposals for more community treatment and a resultant decline in prison numbers.

Those who work in prisons, their centralised organisations and prisoners themselves perceive that there are inadequacies in the design, production, consumption and provision of clothing inside prisons. Humiliation prevails as the embodied experience of the inmate despite the different types of clothing available in place of the imposition of prison uniform. Imprisonment in Britain depends on huge public expenditure for the provision of clothing when survival rather than rehabilitation is the everyday experience of the inmate. This is equally true internationally as will be seen in the next chapter.

contemporary prison clothing: inside turns out

You're there in your combat BDU (Battle Dress Uniform) with the US flag facing the wrong way because you're 'charging towards the enemy' and I'm here in orange.

Moazzam Begg, *Enemy Combatant:*
A British Muslim's Journey to Guantánamo and Back (London, 2006)

Their dresses and headscarves were threadbare and torn...the next day Mariam allowed me to give out my clothing to the women who did not have extended family.

Dayna Curry and Heather Mercer, *Prisoners of Hope:*
The Story of Our Captivity and Freedom in Afghanistan (London, 2002)

introduction

This chapter examines international contemporary prison clothing between 1990 and 2008. The words of the two prisoners quoted above indicate a polarisation of prison clothing practices. Moazzam Begg was held by the USA in Guantánamo Bay for four years and the woman was held by the Taliban in an Afghan prison in the months running up to the US invasion in 2001. Between 11 September 2001 and Barack Obama's inauguration as President of America in January 2009, prison clothing re-emerged as a globally visible embodiment of criminality regardless of proof of culpability. This is most evident in the orange jumpsuits and hoods imposed on suspected terrorists by America and its Allies in this period. These extreme forms of clothing as embodied punishment were eerily reminiscent of early nineteenth-century uniforms and hoods used in Europe and America. At the other extreme, in the South in countries such as Afghanistan, prisons do not provide clothing, unless, as in the case above, women are provided with a *chawdur* or veil for religious reasons. Prisoners live hidden from the eyes of the world in the clothes in which they entered the prison unless relatives can visit and exchange the inmates' clothing. It is only through the observations of two Western Aid workers imprisoned in Afghanistan that we know that women inmates were living in rags. This condition of neglect exists in many parts of the world. It is similar to conditions in prisons in the West in the eighteenth century under regimes of 'malign neglect' before prison reforms were introduced in the 1820s. The above prison clothing conditions not only represent a re-enactment of the past but also provide an indication of the way in which history is embedded in activities and practices that indicate 'a dialectic of past–present relations.'[1]

There is a third model of prison clothing provision that lies between these two polar opposite conditions. A variety of prison clothing practices exist that approximate to the normalisation of the prisoner in their own clothes or prison issue clothing that has a resemblance to everyday wear outside the prison walls.

Yet, as the numbers of prisoners globally increase, imprisonment becomes more a 'holding'[2] operation than one that is rehabilitative. It is under these conditions that malpractices occur however ostensibly lenient the proclaimed penal policy might be in the permission they give prisoners to choose their clothing. For example, one of the prison inmate leaders of the Strangeways Prison riot in Britain in 1990, Paul Taylor, attributes the cause of 'the worst incident in the history of the prison service'[3] to overcrowding. Additionally, he explicitly mentions, amongst other unsanitary conditions that led up to the riot, that 'it was unacceptable for prisoners to go two weeks without a change of clothing.'[4] After the riot the practice of 'slopping out' (whereby prisoners had to use a pail as a toilet in their cells and empty it when the cell was unlocked in the morning) was, at least in the immediate aftermath, terminated. And male prisoners were permitted their own clothes and slightly improved washing facilities in 1991.

In all three of the above scenarios prison clothing is integral to the broader penal and political system in operation. First, the return of the visibly condemnatory orange jumpsuit (see cover image) was introduced for Guantánamo inmates by America in 2001. At the same time America suspended the Geneva Convention which had protected the rights of uncharged detainees from after the Second World War.[5] The extreme use of embodied surveillant practices was legitimated by the argument of the hyperpower that there was no need for a justification for the use of nineteenth-century brutality when America was threatened by terrorism.[6]

In the second case, in Afghanistan in 2001, prisons were run by the Taliban and the political ideology of extreme fundamentalism was the controlling mechanism. Westerners in Kabul prison received packages of clothing and other goods and food from Western embassies and the prisoners signed cards that were sent back to the West in acknowledgement of their having received the parcels. They were explicitly told not to share the goods with other inmates since ordinary Afghans should not be spoiled by Western luxuries.[7] Medieval prison conditions of overcrowding and lack of adequate clothing that were found in Afghanistan in 2001 exist in other parts of the world, such as South America, Africa and Asia. This is due to global inequality and impoverishment outside the prison walls in addition to neglect inside.

And in the third case, in countries that have normalised prison clothing provision, the increase in prison numbers globally since the 1990s has led to a lack of clothing provision and clothing maintenance facilities that militate against reforms instigated after the Second World War. The growth in prison numbers has not necessarily been linked to national increases in crime committed. Rather, criminologists have taken it as a standard measure of the parallel increase in punitiveness globally.[8]

Although there are underlying differences between penal regimes and their prison clothing provision in particular countries, there is a commonality in so far as the denial of freedom as punishment is central to the way criminality is embodied in dress practices. It is these differences, similarities and inconsistencies that will be looked at in this chapter in order to stumble towards an understanding rather than an assertion of global coherence.[9]

contemporary European prison clothing

In the early years of the twenty-first century, in Europe as in Britain there exist a number of types of provision of prison clothing. In some countries prisoners are allowed to wear their own clothing but this is dependent on a prisoner's financial or previous work situation outside the walls. As a result there is distinction within the ranks of inmates according to the clothing they wear dependent on relative wealth. Many prison institutions state that prison issue clothing or the wearing of inmates' own clothing is non-discriminatory. Yet overcrowding, the lack of facilities such as the washing of clothes and the subsequent inability of the institution to ensure that clothing is returned to their owners, often results in the lack of control of prison clothing on the part of the prisoner.

In Germany, for example, prison issue clothing is provided for those prisoners without the means to acquire their own clothes and it is explicitly 'not a kind of uniform. For leisure time, prisoners receive a special type of outer garment, which is not permitted to be discriminatory in nature. It must be similar to clothing that could normally be worn outside of prison. All prisoners receive basic clothing, and if needed work and sports clothing'.[10] The clothing is manufactured in the prison tailoring workshops and certain items are procured from retail shops. The provision of prison issue clothing, as in Britain, is a vast, complex industrial network whereby the specific designs and production vary according to the region and comprise a variety of weights of fabric and colours. These range from brown and grey and some striped material for work trousers to turquoise and yellow that are more ambitious colours for prison clothing. They show a degree of contemporaneity in choice of textile as well as their cross-gender design.[11] Recently, in a German Prison Act, it was proposed that prisoners could wear their own clothing if agreed by the prison warden and this varies between Federal prisons. The majority of prisoners choose to wear their own clothing because prison issue clothing is not 'personal prison clothing' but this is on the proviso that they wash and maintain it. The ability to wash their own clothes again depends on 'their respective financial situation'. If they wear prison issue clothing many prisoners do not receive 'the exact same articles which they handed in to be washed'.[12] In many respects, the German situation is similar to the British provision, whereby a number of practices exist. Although there is an attempt to be non-degrading and non-discriminatory in outlook, certain practices, such as washing clothing, the individual financial distinctions between those who can afford to wear their own clothes and the condition of overcrowding, militate against the execution of this policy. This results in institutional embodied control of the prisoner and his or her identity.

In France a similar situation exists. Male and female prisoners have worn their own clothes in State-run prisons since 1983. Those prisoners who work in the workshops as cheap labour for large companies, receive workwear made in the prison.[13] However, Fleury-Merogis, the supermax prison outside Paris that was built according to the American model in 1992 and houses 3,600 prisoners, operates a similar system to that found in private prisons in Britain. There are few resources in such large-scale prisons for the maintenance of sanitary conditions or the requisite provision of clothing for individual prisoners according to their needs or their rehabilitation.[14]

In contrast, Sweden is a prosperous and advanced industrial country similar to Germany and France and despite cuts in welfare provision in the 1990s, it remains wedded to certain social democratic principles. As a result it is 'comparatively lenient, with relatively low levels of imprisonment per head.'[15] However, it is one of the few European countries to consistently provide a prison uniform for all inmates whether male of female and whether maximum or minimum security prisoners. It is precisely because it has not forfeited its commitment to State provision as much as other European countries, apart from Finland, that it still sees rehabilitation in terms of providing prison clothing. Swedish prison issue clothing demonstrates a partial throwback to 1970s' and 1980s' broad social democratic principles. Thirty years ago socio-economic distinctions, whether within the prison walls or outside and whether in terms of dress or standards of living generally, were attempted to be overcome by the provision of material goods as signs of an increase in social equality. It was Sweden that initiated the cheap mass production of quality clothing and furniture in outlets such as Hennes and IKEA. It is debatable as to whether these successful global companies any longer represent social democratic principles. However, it is evident that notions of normalising prisoners through a uniformity of provision in high street clothing is central to the Swedish system (see Fig. 6.1). The colours are limited to beige, red and grey for all clothing and the garments comprise casual wear commensurate with clothing available in high street retail outlets. However, there is an inconsistency in the politics behind Swedish prison clothing since it is manufactured by a variety of cheap manufacturers in the Far East.

Figure 6.1   Swedish prison clothing 2007.

As in other countries in Europe, Sweden is integrated into a global market-led economy. Its internal political systems, including its prison system, is not isolated from, in this case, the global capitalist and exploitative fashion system. Rather than exploiting prison labour as in many countries in the West, it looks to the East for cheap labour as do corporate fashion companies. Additionally, the State maintains control of the identity of the inmate through the provision of a uniform, however casual the design. It is as though the prison system still retains vestiges of the idea of rehabilitation as material normalisation in a society which no longer espouses the social democratic policies that existed in Sweden in the 1970s.

Despite the increasingly prevalent turn towards the privatisation of prisons and the ensuing disregard for rehabilitation, there are attempts at reforms in which clothing features as a form of normalisation. For example, in Switzerland there are only two prisons for women and one of them, Hindelbank, provides predominantly for the rehabilitation of drug users. Neither the women inmates nor the prison staff, or 'gardiens', wear uniforms. The prison officers 'have mostly been nurses or social workers before coming to the prison'[16] and are paid comparatively high wages. Switzerland is a small country and does not have an overcrowded prison system relative to other countries in Europe. Within individual countries, then, there are pockets of innovation whereby attempts are made to break down distinctions between the punished and punishers through a change in clothing practices. This policy, however, requires substantial public funding. Most countries are reluctant to invest in reforms of this nature unless the numbers of prisoners are reduced.

In the Netherlands another form of experimental prison clothing has been instituted in a 'hi-tech' jail. The prison provides prisoners with 'electronic wristbands' and allows inmates to 'buy in' perks on a 'credit system'. This scheme permits them extra clothing provision or other everyday requisites. The system is cheaper[17] to run than a conventional jail since it bypasses the necessity for the provision of prison issue clothing. Instead, the embodiment of surveillant incarceration establishes another set of normalisation procedures. The constant electronic monitoring of the inmate by prison staff is reminiscent of a modern version of Bentham's panopticon in the nineteenth century. Additionally, inmates are encouraged to accumulate money in order to consume clothing. This mix of practices prepares offenders for release into a normative world inhabited by camera surveillance and a society that encourages the consumption of clothing as visible status. Developments in textile and product design technology facilitate these latest experiments in incarceration practices. Design is put to use to serve prison initiatives that reinstate political power as visible institutional knowledge of the individual. Similarly, in Britain, electronic tagging extends the mechanism of bodily control of the individual offender in everyday life rather than within the prison walls. This practice has proved to be a false economy. Rather than reducing numbers in prison, electronic tagging results in the eventual incarceration of prisoners for minor offences such as 'anti-social behaviour' when they do not abide by the bodily restrictions imposed. These technologies replace traditional prison uniforms with systems reminiscent of nineteenth-century surveillant regulations of the body.[18]

In some Eastern European countries more traditional forms of prison clothing exist. In the Czech Republic, for example, where overcrowding is an issue, most prisoners wear prison issue clothing. However, in 'minimum and medium security prisons they have recently been allowed to wear their own clothing', at certain times, and 'pre-release prisoners wear their own clothes'.[19] Prison issue clothing consists of limited colours – dark blue, brown, red and black – and is seasonal. Male and female clothing is similar in design and the clothing is centrally produced in one prison (Pardubice). Distinctions between prisoners as to who can or cannot wear their own clothing are controlled by the institution in terms of the type of crime committed. Thus maximum security prisoners are prohibited from choosing their clothing while inmates convicted of drug abuse and other less serious crimes can wear their own clothing. This is different from countries in Western Europe where distinction is controlled by the individual's financial status.

In Poland, however, a reform 'was implemented in the 1990s that took administrators and inmates out of official uniforms. Removal of the uniforms allowed both staff and inmates the chance to establish their own identity and further permitted a more personal level of rapport'.[20] This reform was introduced in the mid-1990s in an attempt to change the conditions of prisoners inherited from the Soviet period. Although conditions have improved, the increase in the prison population continues and the socio-economic situation in Poland has meant that the lack of 'appropriate funding' militates against such reforms in practice. Another result of diminished financial resources in Eastern Europe in relation to the increase in numbers of prisoners has been a parallel augmentation in health issues. One of the complaints of prisoners, in the Czech Republic for example, is that those who are forced to wear prison issue clothing in the summer, when there is not always the requisite amount of light weight clothing available, is that the heavier weight clothing irritates the skin and they refuse to wear it. 'Doctors try to give exception for wearing other clothes – and this is a problem.'[21]

Since the collapse of the Soviet Union in 1991, a number of clothing practices and prison conditions exist according to a variety of prison policies in Eastern European countries and Russia.[22]

contemporary prison clothing in Russia

For nearly a century prior to the 1990s Russia's penal institutions were disciplinarian and thousands of prisoners died through neglect, the harshness of the conditions and the imposition of hard labour. The Soviet economy had relied on the removal of dissidents from everyday life and the cheap labour of prisoners. Progressively after 1991 modernisation took place in Russia whereby, in some institutions, alternative methods of imprisonment were introduced that were based on rehabilitation. This meant that in some instances there was a move away from a policy of imprisonment as exclusion from participation in everyday life.[23] Alongside modernisation there was experimentation with alternative models of the provision of clothing. Before 1991 clothing for the most part had been sparse and the death of inmates occurred as a direct result of the lack of adequate clothing and footwear. One of the significant changes in penal policy and the form of the provision and distribution of clothing is the way in which some prisons have established links between local communities and the prison population. The improvement in Russia's record on human rights is seen by many reformers in Russia as a requisite connected to the modernisation of the penal system. One of the means of measuring change is in the prison's openness to outside involvement. Smolensk and Omsk strict regime prisons,[24] for example, have introduced a system of 'barter'. This means that local communities have a say in the conditions of work, wages and quality of products produced in the prison. In exchange, prison authorities and prisoners negotiate with the local communities for the provisions inmates require in exchange for the work done. As one local client involved in this process commented, ' "they (penal colonies) always need foodstuffs, we need parts for machinery. It's a mutually beneficial relationship." '[25] Rather than prisoners relying on friends, families or their own financial resources to acquire clothing, inmates are able to establish relationships with the local community in determining what work is needed and what they, in turn, require from the community. Local people and businesses profit from this arrangement[26] and in turn if an inmate needs new clothes or shoes he or she earns the right to request these from the local community. In a study of this system of bartering it is reported that there was a mixed response from prisoners and prison staff involved. However, the majority were in favour and it remains one of the main forms of prisoner rehabilitation in Russia. After release, the integration of the prisoner into the local community is established as part of a continuous process based on the communication and exchange of needs during imprisonment. The 'barter' system is significantly different from other countries and provides a model of inclusivity whereby the prisoner's skills are exchanged for clothing amongst other material or nutritional needs. It is an example of an attempt to modernise prisons in countries that recently changed from highly repressive prison systems to regimes that in some respects conform to international human rights. It also demonstrates the way in which clothing improvements can be integral to this type of transition.[27]

However, this is just one example of changes in Russian penal establishments. The Russian prison system also retains remnants of the Gulag whereby prisoners are still forced to work in meaningless occupations and there are also examples of Western practices such as the use of prisoners as cheap labour for privatised companies.

Many Russian prisons suffer from severe overcrowding and an overly bureaucratic system. As a result prisoners experience privations such as the lack of appropriate clothing or the enforced wearing of humiliating prison clothing. For example, in the early 1990s, in Perm Women's Obligatory Work Camp, inmates worked to pay for their time in prison. They sewed the uniforms of Russian firemen and had to wear 'uniforms of thick tights, heavy knee-high leather boots, and short fitted skirts . . . and a white kerchief covered each woman's head'.[28] This uniform draws on a mix of dress traditions. The thick tights and kerchiefs derive from elderly female attire reminiscent of the peasantry and traditional Russian dress, and the tight short skirt and knee-high boots originate from a former USSR interpretation of 1960s Western fashionability. Male prison guards in this female prison wore military uniforms. Punishment for these 1990s women resided in the sartorial embodiment of a past redolent with imposed notions of fashionability. They are reminders of aspects of fashion strictures that had dominated the cold war era when the Soviet Union was suspicious of the luxury Western fashion system. This did not go unnoticed by the women, many of whom felt humiliated in this attire and refused to be photographed by the Western photographer who visited the prison.[29] In many instances in Russia and globally, imprisonment has increasingly relied on the privatisation of prisons, corporate solutions and the large-scale containment of inmates. Since the Russian barter system is a local initiative, prison regimes have largely overlooked it in favour of short-term market-led policies.

contemporary prison clothing in South Africa

South Africa provides a different model of transition from Russia, since the African National Congress (ANC) victory over the Apartheid regime in the elections of 1994. From 1966 Nelson Mandela (b. 1918) and other ANC members had fought for improved clothing conditions alongside 'political status' in South African jails. During this period the Apartheid regime issued prison clothing to Africans that was deliberately humiliating. White inmates were exempt from this imposition. 'Only Africans are given short trousers, for only African men are deemed "boys" by the authorities'[30] (see Fig. 6.2). Mandela insisted that not only political prisoners but also all African prisoners should be able to wear long trousers. 'From the first day I had protested about being forced to wear short trousers...I insisted that all African prisoners must have long trousers.'[31] Prison clothing demonstrated the deliberate discriminatory control exercised by the Apartheid regime. Mandela and other ANC prisoners saw the fight against this prison uniform as integral to the fight against Apartheid. Additionally, Apartheid discrimination extended to African family members associated with prison inmates. Sartorial dress codes were controlled when family members appeared at the courts where their male relatives were tried. Winnie Mandela, Mandela's wife (b. 1936) was only allowed to attend the court where he was being tried 'on condition that she did not wear traditional dress,...a Xhosa gown'.[32] In 1969 prisoners won the right to wear long trousers and their own set of prison uniform clothing that they could wash themselves as political prisoners. Throughout Nelson Mandela's imprisonment in numerous prisons, in particular in Robben Island from 1966 to 1994, the fight against Apartheid was both a national struggle and an everyday fight against injustices within and outside the prison walls. On every level these were practices that 'robbed you of your freedom...an attempt to take away your identity'.[33]

Immediately after the elections in 1994 the ANC and National Unity Government challenged conventional forms of law and order through the establishment of legal innovations such as the Truth and Reconciliation Commission (TRC) in 1995. This was a court-like body whereby victims and perpetrators of violence gave evidence and requested amnesty from prosecution. The Commission was integral to South Africa's transition to full and free democracy. The TRC ended in 1998 and although there were criticisms from members of the Apartheid regime and victims of Apartheid it was a serious attempt to consider an alternative to punishment as incarceration.

Just after the elections in 1994 the colonial prison uniform was also abolished in South African prisons, but since then conditions have reflected the transitional nature of the South African political State. The resultant mixture of clothing practices in South African prisons resembles those in a number of other countries in the world, most importantly in South America. Although many prisoners are permitted to wear their own clothing, male gangs that have existed 'for more

Figure 6.2 Nelson Mandela in Pretoria Prison before being sent to Robben Island, 1960s.

than 100 years'[34] and those with access to financial gain outside prison retain status and control over more impoverished inmates. Gang members relate how when prisoners are transferred from one prison to another their regalia and rank is communicated through voicing an 'imaginary uniform...from the colour of socks to the insignia stamped on the inside of a helmet'.[35] In reality inmates in

Pollsmoor Maximum Security Prison wear blue prison issue trousers and sport bare tattooed torsos. However, transvestite prostitutes appear in see-through tops and black leather jackets with elaborate make-up and dyed hair. They wield power over others as the gang generals' 'molls' and receive their clothing by means of purchases on the outside through relatives or other contacts. South African prison gangs are similar to those in other parts of the world. Their control of prison cultures is reinforced by subcultural sartorial codes, even if, in the case above, it is an oral rather than a visual embodiment of their allegiance. Gang dress codes act as resistance to imposed identity constructs by prison authorities whether this be in the form of a uniform or constraints in the purchase or acquisition of clothing. However, the majority of prisoners in South Africa suffer inadequate clothing and impoverishment in overcrowded prisons. A mixture of prison clothing practices in South Africa reflects the mix of prison policies that combine a heritage of the colonial prison regime and a criminal justice system that is market-led, dependent on outside funding from Europe and local reform agencies. There is a lack of communication between these bodies in order to politically affect radical change in the prison system or in the fairer distribution and provision of clothing. Increasingly, since 1998, the prerogative has been to develop a system whereby more criminals are caught and imprisonment is perceived as an effective form of punishment.[36] Initiatives such as 'bartering' that occurred in Russia have not been implemented in South Africa. As a result the lack of adequate clothing is just one of the conditions prevalent in overcrowded prisons in South Africa as is the case in Asia, South America and the rest of Africa.

prison clothing in Africa, South America, Asia and the Middle East

In Africa, Asia and South America, for the most part, overcrowding and lack of funding have led to prison conditions reminiscent of eighteenth-century European 'malign neglect'. For inmates, survival is the predominant ethos. For example, a woman who was in Malawi prisons for 12 years and who has since then toured a number of African prisons mentions that 'conditions in Malawi, South Africa, in Mozambique are almost the same in every country...there is a lack of soap, clothes, food, beds...and they are dressed in torn clothing in which they arrived in prison.'[37] As a result any improvement in clothing conditions, as in the provision of other everyday staple requisites, is dependent on an inmate's financial resources. Economic distinctions between prisoners prevail within the prison as they do outside in regions of rural or urban poverty.

This situation occurs in many South American prisons, such as in Mexico, Guatemala and El Salvador. In these countries overcrowding is due to the length of time that those arrested spend in prison before they are charged with a crime and eventually sentenced. In Guatemala, a prison that started as 'one of Latin America's most progressive penal institutions based on rehabilitation', has been run for the last decade by druglords who rule through corruption. The prison authorities have ceded power to gangs. Inmates pay the committee that runs the prison for everything from clothing to prison visits. In return the gangs retain order and those who are unable to pay are put to work in drug laboratories or beaten by those in power. Although human rights reformers are active in attempting to change these conditions, their lack of success is largely due to the Government's failure to support these initiatives.[38]

In Brazil a similar situation exists whereby the corruption and brutality of the police outside the prison walls are matched by the rough treatment by prison guards and the powerful gangs who preside over the prisons. The gangs operate in a similar manner to the gangs in Guatemala, in 'massively overcrowded, under-funded and under-staffed prisons'[39] whereby the acquisition of everyday items such as clothing is dependent on an inmate's financial situation.

In contrast, in Argentina and Chile[40] prison conditions are considerably better since court proceedings are faster and overcrowding is less of a problem. However, in Venezuela, prison authorities are firmly in control of the prisons. They are over-crowded and there exists a spontaneous culture of corruption amongst prisoners, where the only way to survive is through 'money. Its all about money',[41] as one inmate commented. Clothing as well as other daily necessities are only acquired through consumption. Although Hugo Chavez' Government has introduced reforms in an attempt to redistribute wealth in other parts of Venezuelan society, prison regimes have been exempt from such measures. Although women's prisons are less violent, inmates are still dependent on their outside financial resources to acquire clothing and other requisites.

In Cuba there is a semblance of equality amongst prisoners as opposed to the differential clothing based on wealth that operates in South and Central American prisons. Prison uniforms as a visible embodiment of punishment prevail from the era when Castro's Cuba was influenced by the Soviet Union. Clothing in Cuban prisons is in grey and blue and lacks 'individualisation or aesthetics...and when inmates appear in public to work in the streets their clothing is stamped with a "P" on the back'.[42]

In India similar rates of imprisonment and overcrowding exist, as in the major-ity of South American prisons. However, conditions differ from prison to prison. A lack of adequate clothing exists in a prison such as in Bihar, where the majority of inmates await trial and are not provided with prison issue clothing. However, in one of the largest prisons in India, Central Prison Yerawada, rehabilitation and training are considered a prerequisite and a white prison uniform is provided that is made in the prison workshops.

In the years prior to Independence in 1947, when India was under British colo-nial rule, prisoners wore a uniform similar to British prison uniforms. This apparel consisted of blue-and-white stripes, and was abandoned by most states after 1947.[43] Although prison uniforms in India vary in detail from State to State, in the main they are based on the clothing Gandhi wore in prison under the colonial rule of the British in the 1920s and 1930s (see Chapter 3). He considered that the clothing he wore identified him with Nationalist political resistance in the struggle for independence. The clothing worn by inmates today in Rajasthan, for example, consists of 'half-sleeve kurtas on the upper part of the body and pyjama-type shorts on the lower part...male inmates wear a Gandhi cap to cover the head...and women convicted prisoners are provided with two sets of saree–kurti–petticoats per year. The colour of the uniforms is white and only when a prisoner is promoted to be an overseer is he or she allowed to wear colour in the garments – which is a yellow or black cap for men and the same colour border of the sari for women'. The cloth for the clothing is 'woven on handlooms and powerlooms in prisons and the entire work of tailoring is also done at respective prison factories by prisoners as part of their labour'.[44] Prisoners perform cheap labour for India's mass production of clothing; although, in the production of khadi cloth, there is still the memory of anti-colonial struggle. In prisons where the majority of prisoners await trial, overcrowding is rife and inmates wear their own inadequate clothing.

In China most inmates wear uniforms that differ from region to region. For example, men in Chongqing prison[45] wear a mix of traditional blue shirts with stripes covering the shoulders and tracksuit bottoms with a stripe down the leg. As in many Western prisons, male and female inmates refuse to wear prison clothing in order to assert their innocence or 'political status'.[46] Despite issues of human rights in Chinese prisons, there are attempts to reform prison clothing in line with rehabilitation. For example, in Nanjing women's prison summer uniforms were specifically redesigned in 2007 to allow for the heat. This clothing included a 'white polo shirt and creamy calf length baggy pants...women looked little different from women on the streets outside the prison'.[47] The report mentions female rehabilitation as feminisation and, as in Europe and America, prison authorities' attitude to female inmates is to provide facials and body massages in order to improve self-esteem.

As in most prisons globally, in the Middle East prison clothing is based on the comparative wealth of individual prisoners. Prison institutions encourage competition between prisoners and distinction between prison staff and inmates. But rather than financial distinctions resting on the ability of inmates to buy in clothing, as in many Western countries, in Iran, for example, women prisoners in Evin Prison are also permitted to buy services from other inmates. They could 'hire five or six other inmates for varieties of services: one for doing their laundry, one for manicure and pedicure...one for waxing their shoes or doing their make-up'.[48] The privileges of wealth point up a hierarchy that is demonstrated throughout the system and specifically in the way the prison guards and inmates with financial means treat less well off women and political prisoners punitively. Although this account was written from her experiences in Evin prison in the late 1990s and early 2000s, at the end of Azadeh Azad's account there is an additional comment stating that conditions have not changed in recent years.

prison clothing in North America, New Zealand and Australia

A variety of innovatory and traditional prison systems co-exist in North America. As in many other countries, overcrowding has resulted in primitive conditions. In a jail in Toronto, for example, in the late 1990s, the prison clothing consisted of coveralls that retained the smell of the previous occupant even when they had been cleaned. Prisoners were 'trapped in the threads of the coveralls so that even when you put on clean ones the smells clamp onto your skin, seizing hold of the pores in your nostrils and embedding themselves in your memory'.[49] Additionally, during court appearances prisoners were shackled at the ankles as they often are in America. However, in Kwikwexwlhp minimum security prison in British Columbia[50] where the majority of prisoners are Native American, the prisoners run the prison and wear whatever they choose. Prison staff do not wear uniforms so there is no distinction between staff and prisoners, much in the same way that was the case in the Special Unit in Barlinnie Prison in Scotland in the 1970s and 1980s.

In Australia the rate of imprisonment is less than in Britain, the USA, South America and Russia.[51] Nevertheless, it is still high and the majority of inmates are Aborigines. They have famously been called 'the most imprisoned race in the world'.[52] Overcrowding exists as it does in prison regimes in other countries. Prison issue clothing is provided for inmates in most Australian prisons but in some State prisons, as opposed to Federal prisons, inmates are permitted to wear their own clothing. The rules for clothing are much the same as exist in Britain and although it is specifically stipulated that prison issue clothing 'shall in no manner be degrading or humiliating'[53] there are punitive traditional forms of prison uniform. For example, Aborigine women in one Australian prison wear blue-and-white striped garments reaching to the ankles that are shapeless, ungainly and overtly degrading.[54] Workwear clothing brands such as King Gee[55] utility menswear are contracted by State prisons to provide prison issue clothing, rather than being produced and distributed within the prison as in Britain.

Despite New Zealand's more neo-liberal political and cultural traditions than Australia, the rate of imprisonment has been consistently high. Prisoners suffer from the same overcrowded conditions as elsewhere globally and prison clothing regulations are similar to those in Australia. Branding has also appeared as prisoner-made clothing. In New Zealand's Wellington prison, for example, a range of T shirts, branded 'Convict Gear' with a logo of a muscled man breaking out of a prison cell, was designed in 2006 by an inmate named Justin Rys.[56] Contemporary fashion shifts traverse the prison wall in both directions. Fashion brands that proliferate on global high streets have entered the prison signifying the inclusion of inmates in the commercialisation of dress. And prisoners themselves start their own brands to sell online outside the prison. In New Zealand prisoners' branded clothing represents macho subcultural gangs with which inmates identify.

In many ways the Australian and New Zealand provision of prison clothing mirrors the commercial market-driven prison economy that exists in America. The system simultaneously permits prisoners to engage with the branded fashion system outside prisons at the same time as centrally issuing prison clothing that embodies punishment in its design.

prison clothing in America

America has the highest incarceration numbers in the world per percentage of population, with huge rates of overcrowding and a vast prison building expansion policy. Additionally the majority of inmates are black and hispanic.[57] Prison clothing in America varies from State to State and between Federal and State prisons. In State prisons the classification of prisoners is largely through colour coding of the clothing. Individual Governors or Sheriffs control the design and colour of the garments. For example, in Rikers Island in Manhatten, inmates are dressed in ' "greens" '.[58] 'Greens' consist of 'khaki' clothing. In one instance, a prisoner wears 'a yankee cap, khaki pants, and a dirty denim jacket'.[59] The khaki-coloured prison uniform is significant in its similarity, in colour, to military wear. Militarisation is an aspect of American jails that is unlike prison clothing in most other countries and corresponds to the harsh conditions of some US prisons. Prison uniforms are frequently customised by the prisoner through their alteration or maintenance in a variety of ways. For example, one inmate appears 'in his pressed greens and polished shoes'.[60] This is similar to the situation in England where an ex-inmate saw survival as retaining a smart appearance compared to the prison guards' expectation of inmates as 'scruffy'. In Indiana State prison for Women, the implementation of 'greens' also takes the form of 'a khaki uniform'. The militaristic uniform for women is justified by the prison authorities as a replacement for 'street dress'. Inmates habitually wore clothing that distinguished them as members of gangs. Although 'prisoners claimed this to be untrue,'[61] prison authorities reinstated prison uniform in order to reduce gang status and as blatant social control. The design of the uniform, unlike in Rikers, did not approximate to everyday clothing outside the prison. Instead its design is not dissimilar to the jumpsuit. Although not an all-in-one design, since it consists of a top and pants, it is a uniform and therefore not part of a rehabilitative process. Despite the restrictions in clothing practices in American State prisons, some inmates find ways in which to express individuation or collective identity. A couple of transvestites, for example, in a maximum security prison in Pittsburgh, 'attempted to look as feminine as possible – within the range of what it was possible to do with state issued clothing'.[62] One man had acquired rhinestone sandals and was tolerated by the guards. Another 'would tie his white t-shirt in a knot at the bottom and roll the sleeves up slightly in a feminine way'.[63] But, universally, strict clothing restrictions pertain, and as in the case of the prohibition of alleged women's gangs in Indiana prisons, gang identification through clothing is prevented by sartorial prison rules.

For example, since 'red and blue are common gang colours many prisons do not allow you to buy red or blue striped socks for an inmate'.[64] But gangs proliferate despite attempts at containment. In San Quentin State prison, for example, inmates are divided along racial lines. White supremacist gangs vie against black gangs despite the imposition of a casual prison uniform. It consists of jeans or track suit bottoms and different coloured T-shirts – orange, blue or white according to the inmate's sentence. Gang membership continues, however, and is identified by discrete sartorial codes such as the colour of socks. To a large extent gangs control the day-to-day working of the prison and the ethos is about punishment whether inflicted by prison officers or between gang members. One inmate commented, 'we live in a hostile environment. We react hostilely'.[65]

California Valley State Prison is considered one of the harshest women's prisons. Here women adopt 'families' rather than become members of gangs. The prison issue clothing is called 'State Blues' and consists of T-shirts, jeans and flip flop sandals. However, when the women exercise in the yard they are dressed in orange Tshirts and track suits. Although all women wear prison issue clothing, different 'families' identify themselves through the procurement of small items of clothing that they receive in exchange for drugs. This is a sort of informal barter system that takes place within the prison walls. Officers wear military-style dark green overalls and baseball caps that visually differentiate them from the inmates.[66]

Similar to British prisons, ill-fitting prison issue clothing means that inmates need to have inside knowledge as to how to procure clothing that is both sanitary and comfortable. As in other countries, inmates find ways in which to improve the heavily regulated provision of clothing. However, the prevailing ethos is one whereby the prisoner's dependency on the system to meet their most basic needs, infantilises them in the process. 'They tell you what to wear; but they supply the uniform.'[67] In two states in America, Arizona and Texas, the punishment of male inmates is expressly through the imposition of prison uniforms. It is taken to the extreme of providing all pink clothing. Sheriff Clint Low in Mason County, Texas claims that inmates 'don't want to wear them'[68] and thus the practice is a gendered normalisation penal policy whereby the feminisation of men is sartorially imposed as a deterrent. In 2005 Sheriff Joe Arpaio introduced pink handcuffs as well as pink boxer shorts for male prisoners in Phoenix Arizona. These were to be worn under 'black and white striped inmate uniforms'[69] that he had introduced in 1997. Ostensibly, this iconic clothing was re-introduced as punishment for both male and female inmates in order to identify those who worked on traditional chain gangs outside the prison walls. However, it becomes apparent, in his explanation for its reintroduction, that it was a Right-wing reaction against the public perception of the 'molly-coddling' of inmates.[70] Underwear was also dyed pink for male inmates in order to deter them from 'walking off with the white trunks' on release. 'Most men, especially those in jail, do not like the colour pink'.[71]

The visual embodied humiliation of inmates as public punishment has returned in the first decade of the twenty-first century. Men convicted for drunken driving, for example, who were put to work cleaning rubbish in the streets of Phoenix in 2008 wear pink T-shirts emblazoned with 'Clean(ing) and Sober' and black-and-white striped track suit bottoms.[72] Prison uniform as a visible embodiment of punishment, reminiscent of Auburn prison practices in the nineteenth century, is seen as a deterrent in itself and additionally based on gendered sartorial codes of humiliation. It is hardly surprising that reminders of former punishment clothing practices occur in line with shifts in the politics of incarceration. The return of the overtly visible nineteenth-century black-and-white stripes as embodiment of punishment takes on an even more stigmatised meaning than it did originally. Comic representations of the iconic uniform in film have meant that audiences have questioned this type of visible embodied punishment. Yet, Right-wing prison authorities depend precisely on these historical associations in order to make inmates ridiculous to the outside world. Shaming instead of rehabilitation is embodied in the return of the iconic black-and-white stripes. But not only is punishment inscribed on the body for all to see as it was historically. Additionally, prescribed underwear, as publicly invisible punishment, is felt, seen and touched only by the inmate and the prison authorities. Thus, the whole body of the inmate is the property of the prison and the invisible clothing acts as a self-regulating mechanism of control. This is a deliberately punitive form of incarceration. And inmates voice their doubts as to its effectiveness. An American inmate commented that he couldn't see that a prison system based on the principle, voiced by Arpaio, that 'prisoners should be damned to hell' could possibly work.[73] Local regulations, such as those in Arizona and Texas reflect neo-conservative policies of specific Sheriffs in Republican strongholds.

A slightly different system operates in Federal jails. These are prisons that are centrally controlled by the American legislature yet retain limited local powers. The Code of Federal Regulations stipulates that in Federal prisons, 'civilian clothing ordinarily is not authorised for retention by the inmate'.[74] Thus the onus is on the inmate to buy in clothing from approved vendors that advertise on the internet. These companies provide Inmate Catalogs[75] advertising men's and women's prison clothing such as 'sweats', 'shoes' (trainers) and jeans. Alternatively, if inmates cannot afford to buy clothes they are forced to wear prison issue clothing. Inmates are also employed by companies to produce clothing. They produce ordinary lines of clothing the company distributes outside or clothing under their own trademark that is owned by the State in which the prison is located. For example, 'Prison Blues'[76] was set up by inmates to design and market jailhouse clothing and became an established company under the auspices of an alternative clothing corporation outside the prison. Some of the items of clothing produced by the company have 'Prison' stamped on them and blue baseball caps have 'PRISN BLU' in the form of a car registration plate sewn on the rim. The status of American prison clothing has become both visible and desirable in the international fashion market. This has occurred since the company is now expanding into Europe and Asia in order to export the subversion of stigmatised prison clothing outside the walls, while the prisoner-producer remains invisible in their incarceration.

Despite inmate enterprises, the provision of prison issue clothing and the code of Federal Regulations, in overcrowded American prisons many inmates find themselves without adequate clothing in conditions not dissimilar to other countries around the world. A visitor to a Woman's Federal prison in Illinois, for example, mentions that 'no one comes to visit them; no one sends them clothes. I met a woman with shoes that had been glued and re-glued, who was sentenced for 7 years for each gram of cocaine on her – she had three.'[77]

There is also the iconic orange jumpsuit that is worn particularly when the prisoner is a maximum security prisoner or on Death Row, whether female or male. This is particularly the case when inmates have a visit. In this publicly visible situation not only is the orange jumpsuit worn but inmates are handcuffed. 'And then there were the jumpsuits, invented by a man who hadn't considered that a woman handcuffed and dressed in one of them would be unable to go to the bathroom.'[78] The orange jumpsuit not only embodies punishment as did the black-and-white stripes, but as an androgynous item of clothing it doubly discriminates against women in its gendered design. Concurrent with the expansion of the female prison population over the past decade up to the end of 2008, has been the disproportionate increase in the incarceration of black women.[79] The very design of the orange jumpsuit raises issues of gender and race discrimination as much as issues concerning the embodied punishment of assumed criminality. For many women of religion, particularly Muslim women, it is against their faith to wear trousers and the jumpsuit thus becomes an additional assault on their identity as Muslim women.

Although the visibility of American prison clothing is apparent as a national sign of punishment, vast numbers of imprisoned people in America remain hidden. 'Like most prisons and jails in America, Rikers Island performs an expert magic trick: It makes people vanish. It not only hides prisoners from public view, but in a double sleight of hand it keeps *in* those who want to get out and keeps *out* those who want to get in'.[80] For example, Robert King, a former Black Panther, was 'hidden' for twenty-nine years in solitary confinement in Louisiana State penitentiary (also known as Angola prison). He was charged with killing a prison officer. He was released in 2001 when his conviction was overturned.[81] Two other inmates accused at the same time remain in solitary. 'King' talks of the American prison system as 'the immoralism of prison as slavery' – a system informed by racist ideology – and resisted on a daily basis by those inside. The visibility of inmates in iconic prison clothing outside on the streets of Phoenix conceals thousands of incarcerated prisoners. Despite attempts at reform, this is a prison system that has progressively become 'deformed' since the 1970s. King's answer is that people internationally need to be 'dispossessed as to the immorality of prison that may lead to its abolition'.[82] It is no coincidence that with King's awareness of the history of prisons, he reiterates Kropotkin's mantra for the abolition of prisons made a century before in Russia.

The harshness of punishment regimes in America's internal penal system was, up to the end of 2008, extended to include global injustice. For, the logic of justice did not prevail in prisons of rendition globally and in Guantánamo Bay. The reiteration by George Bush, post-9/11, of a 'state of exception',[83] apparently justified the contradictions implicit in American global justice. Due to America's superpower status it took seven years before the injustices embodied in innocent men wearing hoods and orange jumpsuits were challenged.

penal clothing as global pre-eminence

As we have seen, prison clothing has historically vacillated between discrete invisibility and overt public shaming. Prison clothing as public humiliation of the prisoner who wears it, particularly emerges at politically expedient moments. The 'War against Terror' is one such moment. Until 2001 sentencing policies of Nation States and the clothing of prisoners, whether innocent or guilty, were revealed or concealed according to the degree of publicity considered politically strategic in the advertisement of a specific Government's punishment policies. Conversely, the excess of visibility of the unidentified international enemy of the USA, between 2001 and 2008 before Barack Obama's inauguration as President, stood in for our lack of knowledge of the sentencing and punishment procedures that were set in motion by America in geographical non-places. These places ranged from specific sites such as Guantánamo Bay to secret prisons around the world fabricated under the 'rendition' programme. The sites were deliberately invisible judicial geographies outside of international penal jurisdiction. Yet, people around the world who had access to the media of any description, knew that inmates at these sites wore hoods or the orange jumpsuit (see book cover and Fig. 6.3).

The hood is an item of apparel indicative of power as bodily torture, not publicly used since the fourteenth century. Although hoods were used in early nineteenth-century American prisons they were hidden away as were masks used in Benthamite British prisons in the mid-nineteenth century. Additionally, these masks were designed with holes cut for the eyes and mouth. Hoods used to disorientate 'enemy combatants', picked up around the world after 2001, had no such breathing openings. They were more like the hoods used in fourteenth-century Europe to cover the heads of those condemned to execution. In the lack of design of the twenty-first-century hood and in their very fabric that varied from black or white plastic to crudely woven hessian sacking, there was a visible denial of humane practices.

America and its Allies considered themselves the ambassadors of civilisation. Yet, these methods of punishment were a throwback to an era that lacked civilisation. 'Under the hood I felt I couldn't breathe properly, it pulled in and out against my mouth and nose with every breath. Not being able to see made me feel unbearably vulnerable; I thought I was going to be struck in the face, or worse, at any moment...The perpetual darkness was frightening.'[84] Not only were hoods a method of physical torture for those confined, but also through the removal of facial

Figure 6.3 Soldiers detain Afghan men in hoods.

identity the hooded suspect became an embodiment of menace of the unknown 'other'. This image of the captured enemy was mediated to the public of the world as a frightening warning.[85]

It was not merely the US military that used hoods as visually degrading prison clothing in order to punish captured 'enemies' in Afghanistan or Iraq. British soldiers, court martialed for offences against Iraqi prisoners, were acquitted for mistreating detainees who were 'handcuffed, hooded with sacks, deprived of sleep and forced to maintain a "stress position"'. Their acquittal was due to blame being attributed to US commanders who had 'criticised British forces in 2003 for failing to extract sufficient intelligence from detainees'.[86]

Although these practices were unlawful under the Geneva Convention, Brigadier Euan Duncan, director of the British army's Intelligence Corps, said that 'he believed the use of hooding was acceptable, since it protected prisoners from being identified as potential informers by other detainees'.[87] Along with the flouting of the Geneva Convention, the British and Americans demonstrated flagrant disregard for the UN Agreement of 1955 whereby prison clothing was not to be inhumane. The iconography of old-fashioned modes of branding as punishment, reminiscent of the nineteenth century, returned as signs of the essence of the prisoner in a trans-national lawless context. The prison clothing adopted by coalition forces in the supposed global war against terror was just one element of this most recent visual display of unrestrained power.[88] Global 'pre-eminence'[89] allowed America and its Allies to get away with flagrant indifference to international law. Contempt for global and local norms of justice extended the erosion of liberties both within America and the world.

Additional to the use of hoods was the global appearance of the orange jumpsuit. As we have seen, this uniform is used internally within American prisons. When foreign inmates in the legal no-man's land of Guantánamo Bay wore it, it became symbolic of American global power. The richness of the visible signification of the orange jumpsuit as non-individualised bodily punishment was not lost on those who, in turn, in asserting their power subverted its use for their own political ends. Insurgents in Iraq transmitted video recordings of executions of American or English captives dressed in orange jumpsuit-like clothing. This was a knowing refashioning of their own power in the mould of American political dominance.

One specific item of penal clothing demonstrated the political significance of embodied punishment within a global 'war', dominated by images of real brutality against untried captives on both sides. Inmates in Guantánamo demonstrated another form of subversion of iconic prison clothing. After eighteen months torture in a secret prison in Morocco and two years in Guantánamo Bay, Binyam Ahmed Mohammed faced his first military commission in 2006.[90] These commissions were held as simulations of justice and were considered by campaigners and lawyers as 'kangaroo courts.'[91] Guantánamo inmates were aware of the media sham of the trials. Binyam Mohammed's technique of demonstrating the masquerade of the trial was to subvert the orange jumpsuit during his appearance in court. He wore a 'traditional Muslim shirt dyed prisoner orange.'[92] His reasoning was that since he had spent years shackled and in the orange jumpsuit he was not going to comply with the American military ruling that he should appear in civilian clothing, in their attempt to show the world's press a 'humane' side to their prison regime.

A system of privileges according to prisoners' behaviour operated in Guantánamo as it does in American jails. Jumpsuits in the same fabric[93] and design came in white for those who complied with the rules, orange for those who did not and brown for those who were segregated in solitary confinement. This was another instance of the lack of observance of the Geneva Convention and the UN agreement of 1955, whereby not only should untried and convicted prisoners not wear humiliating clothing but also there should not be a system of clothing implemented that regulates inmates according to behaviour. After hunger strikes against these practices in Guanatánamo Bay, a minor victory was achieved in 2005 when a 'level system' was implemented.[94]

The politics of humiliation embodied by prison clothing re-emerged in the early years of the twenty-first century.

> The same humiliation that had greeted me when I arrived in Kandahar bade me farewell when I left Afghanistan. It was the harsh reminder that no matter how well I got on with the guards, I, and everyone else in orange, was still the enemy.[95]

The orange jumpsuit symbolised global American post-colonial power and the punishment of its subjects. It replaced the MacDonalds logo suggesting, after 9/11, both the superiority and weakness of American power. The sign of the materialist American Dream was no longer merely the shape of a burger. The export of both real and imagined punishment in the form of the orange jumpsuit, gave visible and punitive materiality to America's power. At the same time it signified the recognition of its own weakness. There *was* a threat to its power – both real and imagined. There was thus a perceived need by the George Bush administration to punish the opposition of the 'Other' in both hidden and visible corners of the world. Post colonialist war-mongering was materialised in the orange jumpsuit as a symbolic embodiment of late capitalism. It was a garment that was imposed on anyone considered to be in opposition to the apparent pre-eminence of US political and economic power. Prison clothing was the ideal object with which to convey visual messages of supremacy. From 2001 with the aid of technological global networks, American prison clothing was made deliberately visible. Images of the punished whether culpable or not and dressed in US prison garb were transmitted across the world. Yet, precisely because of its visual significance, the orange jumpsuit also became an object of resistance for those who were forced to wear it. In an age when human rights issues are of global concern, prison clothing, when used indiscriminately against an ill-defined 'enemy', provided a message of global power and brutal inhumanity.

conclusion

What was true in the historical past is still true in the early twenty-first century. Just as in Newgate and the Bastille in the eighteenth century, many countries continue to imprison people in the clothes in which they were arrested. They are denied access to clothing from outside, and to replacement clothing from the institution. And this global state of overcrowding and rags continues to reflect the inmates' pre-prison experience of life. Just as was the case two centuries ago, lack of money and thus lack of access to the outside world denies prisoners the chance to improve their dress and their wellbeing. There have been reforms in the condition of prison clothing in countries around the world and yet in many cases the increasing rates of imprisonment have led to overcrowding that militates against improved provision.

Early twenty first-century penal systems also include harsh regimes of punishment and saw the return of iconic prison clothing such as the orange jumpsuit. Hoods worn by captives in the 'war against terror' were more brutal even than masks worn by prisoners in the harsh penitentiaries of Victorian England. Prison clothing played a visual role in the media stigmatisation of global terrorists-cum-insurgent suspects. The invisible 'enemy' played a similar media game, with captives hooded before their beheading. Thus these public spectacles of punishment were reminiscent of pre-reform practices in eighteenth-century Europe.

The eighteenth and nineteenth centuries still speak to us because we are still using the same language of bodily humiliation as punishment of criminality regardless of culpability. This chapter has focused on prison clothing practices internationally, reinforced by the perceptions of inmates. The next chapter turns to the wearer of prison clothing and his or her own construction of identity through imagined and real representations of prison garb.

CHAPTER 7

the view from outside/visions behind the bars

Convicts' garb is striped pink and white.

Jean Genet, *The Thief's Journal* (New York, 1964/1949)

I have been classified, collated and rated
fingerprinted photoed and filed
I am an examined, inspected cut of meat
dressed in khaki garb and set in concrete.

Nolan Gelman, Fair Hill Prison, in Bell Gale Chevigny (ed.),
Doing Time: 25 Years of Prison Writing (New York, 1999)

bright shiny bracelets
    jangling on my arm
wide leather belt
    snug about my waist
chains dangling seductively
                between my legs.
I am captured
    But not subdued.

Judee Norton, 'Arrival', Arizona State Prison Complex – Perryville, in
Bell Gale Chevigny (ed.), *Doing Time: 25 Years of Prison Writing* (New York, 1999)

Is this punishment for mistakes I've made
Inside becomes outside I fade.

Anon, 'Excrement King' , Ashen Hill Maximum Security Unit, Arthur Koestler Award
winner, *Annual Competition of Arts from UK Prisons* (London, 2005)

introduction

The regulation of clothing has prevailed for more than two hundred years as a repressive instrument of punishment. The history of prison clothing is partly about the social construction of the wrong doer by the State and according to prevalent penal policies. Its significance also lies in the intricate interweaving of politics and the construction of self in confinement. Prison authorities globally employ a variety of techniques of normalisation in the attempt to control the reconstruction of the prisoner's identity through clothes. Prison clothing practices also deprive the body of inclusion in a world where those with the means to buy into physical care through the acquisition of adequate, appropriate, fashionable, sensual or collectively different sartorial covering are considered normal.

Thus, there is an ideological implication, on the part of penal authorities, that the inmate identity is fixed, unalterable and needful of further shaming during their time of incarceration.

Yet, representations of the incarcerated and their clothing challenge this fixity and move over, under and through the walls. Mediated images of the clothed prisoner appear in film, TV documentaries and docu-dramas, and photography. Prison clothing styles influence fashions on the street just as fashions outside affect the way inmates wear and consume clothing inside the prison walls. The images that appear outside prison are based on this fragmented knowledge and in part are mythical constructions of the condemned identity filtered through the lens of the 'normative' world outside.

In opposition to the construction of inmate identity in the outside world is the way in which inmates themselves imagine the clothed self. As the poems above indicate, there are a number of ways in which prisoners imagine themselves as both institutionally condemned by and resistant to imposed dress regulations. Sometimes these depictions resonate with the images of inmates we receive outside. More often they challenge those perceptions. In the previous chapters the voices of prisoners have punctuated and informed the tracing of the garments' histories. The final section focuses on the inmate's construction of identity in institutional dress as agency and self-discovery through the process of writing and art.

Jean Genet (1910–1986) was a self-dramatised thief who was in and out of innumerable prisons in France after the Second World War. The first sentence of his autobiography (see above), *The Thief's Journal*, transforms the grim convict reality around him of men bowed by indignity and clothed in 'brown homespun', berets of the same rough fabric and 'wooden shoes' into a homo-erotic imagined world inhabited by inmates in 'pink and white stripes'. He describes 'an inner prison that I discover within me after going through the region of myself'.[1] Through writing he transforms his experience of incarceration into a colourful world where the inmate's inner self becomes clothed in beauty. Genet sees the prison as a metaphor for the grim, impoverished world outside. To protect himself from its terror, he envelopes himself in an erotic myth of his own construction.[2]

Also quoted above, Nolan Gelman writes of the process of de-humanisation when stripped of his clothing and identity on entry to prison. Through writing he discovers control of his feelings in words. Judee Norton imagines restrictive prison chains as erotic jewellery and thus imaginatively escapes the grim reality of prison clothing, much in the same way as Genet. The anonymous writer in an English prison in 2005 writes of his fading identity both inside and outside prison. He resists imprisonment through naming his awareness of the ineffectiveness of the process.

Inside comes outside in the reconstruction of the fragmented clothed inmate self.

prison clothing – the view from outside

The public are drip-fed images of how the imprisoned are dressed in printed and photographic media and documentary and feature films. This section looks at the image of the inmate in prison clothing that is available to the public through representations on television, in film and in the world of fashion.

The printed media, as a source of public knowledge about the dress of prisoners, is used politically to flaunt punishment to the public. This is evident in the transmission of extreme forms of prison dress, such as the American orange jumpsuit between 9/11 and the end of 2008 and pink clothing for male inmates in Arizona and Texas. Exposé journalism of prison conditions features photographs of gang identity in clothing, scant apparel or uniformed inmates. These images have been used as evidence for the contemporary documentation and analysis of clothing in prisons in previous chapters. News items on television and prison documentaries have entered prisons in the past fifty years and broadened public awareness of the apparel that is worn by inmates in prison institutions around the world. However, prisons are secret places and the visual information we receive is selective. These documentaries and prison feature films have been referred to in tracing the history of prisoners' clothing. But in a broader sense, prison feature films, docu-dramas and sitcoms have a popular hold on the imagination. This form of representation of the clothed inmate accounts, to a great extent, for the way the public gain knowledge of conditions inside. The prison film genre[3] is a subject in its own right. Its consideration here serves the specific purpose of juxtaposing public knowledge with inmates' representations of identity construction in prison clothing in their writing and art.

prison clothing in film and television

Prison recurs as a setting for feature films throughout the twentieth century and has also proved attractive to the makers of television serial drama, sitcoms and documentaries. Together they chart a variety of glimpses into a secret world of enduring friendships, survival against adversity, brutality, redemption and dreams of escape. The conventions of the prison film genre, at certain periods, fuel protest against prison conditions and aid outside prison reform. At other times they dramatise prevailing concerns about sexuality, double dealing and victimisation that reaffirm the legitimacy of prison.

As far as prison clothing is concerned, sub-genres of prison film rely partially on an accurate portrayal of the changes in prison dress, according to the geographical location of the prison and historical period in which the film is set, and partly on cinematic visual shorthand in the dramatisation and characterisation of 'types'.

For example, the retro prison film *Shawshank Redemption* (1994) is set in America between the 1940s and 1960s and prison clothing hardly changes. As Red, the black American prisoner-protagonist says, 'prison is slow time'. Male inmate workwear changes in 20 years from denim jackets, shirts with a prison number emblazoned on them and jeans to braces and dungarees. The significance of clothing lies in the way, at the beginning of the film, the black inmates wear a version of the flat cap and white prisoners wear baseball caps. There is an explicit racial divide and yet at a point in the middle of the film, after the cross-race friendship of Andy and Red has been established as the focus of the film, the iconography of prison clothing as characterisation is visually represented by both characters wearing the same hat. There is a tendency for film makers to rely on clearly defined uniforms whether historically accurate or not. This serves to identify bodily control of the inmate by the prison institution and, in any particular image, economically reminds the viewer of the setting. Thus, in *The Birdman of Alcatraz* (1962), the protagonist/inmate, Robert Stroud, is imprisoned in 1912 in iconic black-and-white striped clothing. He continues to wear this uniform well into the 1920s despite its abolition in America in 1914. The clothing symbolises his life-long struggle to retain individual identity in a prison system dominated by imposed rules. To retain his identity inside he teaches himself about the care of birds in his cell, for the most part in solitary confinement. Despite his apparent 'good behaviour,' he is denied parole on a number of occasions throughout 23 years. The prison clothing reinforces Stroud's comment about imprisonment. 'You rob prisoners of the most important thing in their lives – their individuality – so they take it out on society.' The film appeals to the audience's sympathy for Stroud that is justified in the film when 50,000 signatures on a public petition save his birds from extermination by the prison authorities. He is allowed to keep the birds but Stroud's experience of inhumane prison regulations are imprinted on him forever, even when he is released and can wear civilian clothing at the end of the film. He is bowed and old beyond his years after 53 years of imprisonment. He says,

> you want your prisoners to dance out the gates like puppets on a string with rubber stamp values impressed by you with your sense of conformity, your sense of behaviour...You rob prisoners of the most important thing in their lives – their individuality. When they're outside they're lost – automatons just going through the motions of living, but underneath there's a deep hatred for what you did to them.

Differences in the way inmates wear prison clothing not only signify dramatic characterisation to the audience outside, but they also resonate with the audience inside prisons. For example, in a serial British docu-drama, *Criminal Justice* (BBC, July 2008), an innocent young man, Ben Coulter, is wrongly imprisoned for the murder of a girl. Corrupt prison officers and inmates alike dominate his life inside until he is eventually proved innocent. Inmates wear a variety of grey prison issue clothing and self-styled tattoos. Ben's scheming but seemingly kindly cell-mate, Hooch, wears a T-shirt branded with his apparent insider identity: 'Listener'. Power hungry inmates and gang leaders, such as Freddy Graham, modify prison clothing to express individuality. More vulnerable and new prisoners, such as Ben Coulter, concede to the all-grey prison regulation clothing as a statement that they do not know where they fit in the prison hierarchy. This is a realistic character-isation of the role clothing plays in the construction of inmates' identity inside,[4] and yet it is stylised for dramatic effect as it is also Ben's innocence which is symbolised by his inability to customise this uniform. This cross-over between film iconography and the realistic portrayal of prison life applies to women's prison docu-dramas and sitcoms.

In *Bad Girls,* a TV series that was located in a fictional prison called HMP Larkhall and ran in Britain for more than five series in the late 1990s and early 2000s, the clothing the women wore represented their awareness of the inmate hierarchy and demonstrated their places within it. Although the women in *Bad Girls* were considered by some inmates and outside critics as over-glamorised, there were aspects of dramatic characterisation that hold true to the distinctions in prison between the corrupt and the downtrodden, whether staff or prisoners. For exa-mple, Natalie Buxton's immaculate appearance in fashionable clothing belied her evil ways and her intimidation of more vulnerable women such as Rachel Hicks. Rachel dressed, in contrast, soberly with little care for her appearance.

Prison films and television present a microscopic vision of the prison to an audi-ence mystified as to the reality of imprisonment. But it can also send a message, through the use of exaggerated dress styles as characterisation, that prison too read-ily labels inmates and that the closed prison environment often encourages prison-ers to live up to these stigmatisations rather than helping them to overcome them. Prison uniforms and restrictive dress codes distinguish authorities from inmates. It is through the minutiae of difference in the way clothing is worn or omitted that we know an inmate is worthy of our approval or repulsion, whether a prison officer has overstepped the mark in his or her exertion of power or demonstrates considered fairness in the execution of their duties. For example, in the popular British sitcom *Porridge* (BBC, 1973–1977), there were two main prison officers.

Barrowclough is kind-hearted and soft-natured compared with the eagle eye of the harsh and suspicious McKay. They wear their military peaked hats distinctively. McKay wears it as a Major in the army, perched on his head with the peak threaten-ingly worn over his eyes. Barrowclough wears it pulled further down over the back of his head with the peak easily clearing his eyebrows so that his eyes are visible and honestly meet the public and inmate gaze. Of course, this is a prison version of the sartorial stereotype of 'good cop bad cop', but many prison sitcoms rely on dress in this way to convey details of characterisation to the audience.

The prison is a real space of confinement at the same time as it is a dramatic setting where the inmate everyman or everywoman and more humane prison officer have to overcome adversity and the apparel of power. It is an enclosed space where the condemned and their guards play out the real and dramatised conditions of imprisonment. The audience is entertained by the prison film in their knowledge of popular sitcom, feature film and docu-drama conventions. Where these films differ from other genres is in the glimpse they offer of an unknown world that is above all set in same-sex institutions and normally concealed from the public gaze. The way gender and sexuality are represented in an environment supposedly free of intimate relationships is through the knowing manipulation of the restricted dress codes offered by the iconography of prison clothing on the part of film-maker, staff and inmates. Same-sex friendships, antagonism amongst inmates and the exploration of the nature of femininity and masculinity are a staple of all prison genre films.

Carandiru (Brazil, 2003) is an exposé prison film directed by Hector Babenco and based on a prison riot in Brazil's largest correctional facility in 1992. The riot was brutally put down by 300 policemen who stormed the prison and killed 111 unarmed inmates. The gang leaders rule the prison with a variety of codes and laws. They exhibit a hierarchy of sexual 'types'. Outwardly gay 'femme' inmates wear silk tops and transvestites dress in figure-hugging dresses. At a prison wedding, men dressed in a white wedding dress and sober suit perform normative male and female identities. But this is prison and it is small privations such as the lack of provision of underpants that unites inmates, causes dissension and the first stirrings of revolt. In *Carandiru* there is a problematisation of male sexuality and friendships that proclaim homo-erotic sensuality reminiscent of Jean Genet's only film *Un Chant d'Amour* (1950). Genet's film is set in a French prison. A prison guard takes voyeuristic pleasure observing two inmates dressed in tight-fitting prison clothing and eventually scantily clad who perform masturbatory sexual acts. The guard's power over them is diminished by the intensity of attraction between the inmates in their two adjacent cells, while the sensuality of the cinematography emphasises the men's bodies rather than their uniforms.

In contrast to the overt homo-erotic nature of men's prison films, sexuality in women's prison films often crosses over into a stereotype of 'chicks-in-cells' pornography. This has little to do with the experience of women in prison and more to do with the conventions of dress and undress in pornography. Some women's prison series, however, such as the Australian *Prisoner Cell Block H* (1979–1987), tackled serious issues of rape, homosexuality and violence in prison and at the same time became cult programmes. The hierarchies of inmates and their sexual identity were identified in the way different women wore their prison issue check shirts, dungarees or jeans in a loose- or tight-fitting manner. Similarly, the British women's prison series *Bad Girls* (ITV, 1999–2003) addressed issues of sexuality in prison but inmates were identified in a dramatic exaggeration of dress styles. The series commented on the power relations that prison institutions foster. The screen writer[5] herself commented on how dress served to characterise inmates and staff as dominatrix or submissive not for ostensibly pornographic but reform ends. Yet, a global audience outside the prison identified with the women in the series according to their own sexual persuasion. Thus, cults around prison films and television are cultivated regardless of the intentions of the writers and film-makers. But in many prison films the reason that characters are deliberately dress coded is in order to illicit empathy and understanding from the audience.

Documentary, popular and art house films and other media images enhance our knowledge of the possibility of bridging the gap between those with a history of imprisonment and those without. We think we know prisoners through their dress and representation in film. Prisoners and ex-prisoners see this public demystification of their insider identity as an important potential development in their social inclusion on release. Yet, the dramatic iconography of film may also contribute to our distorted knowledge of the reality of incarceration. When a prison inmate started working in the outside world as a transition to release after 20 years of imprisonment, he said,

> it was unsettling that prison life was such a mystery to society. There seemed an assumption among many on the outside that people in prison were inherently different. Prisoners were seen not as individuals, but as a collective, with the same crude standards, values and culture – a sub-race almost.[6]

Film and television, then, provide the public with a plethora of visual images of the prisoner. The conditions in which a hitherto hidden and excluded group are held are both exposed and controlled. The outside world sees the criminal in film as constructs and types familiar to specific genres that reveal the contradictory politics of imprisonment in the society in which they are produced.

the fashion of prison clothing

The fashion industry's ephemerality, at times, provides modernity with the excitement of the fleeting moment of utopia in its dreaming of a future that counters the standardisation of a moribund global homogeneity. At other times it bows to the boredom of its own making and turns to the artificial replication of the broader visually induced dynamics of a political dystopia epitomised in images of death and punishment in an increasingly surveillant world. Despite the concealment of prison clothing from the public eye, contemporary fashionability has always affected the changes in prison clothing historically. Prison dress and inmate styles of wearing have also influenced outside fashions. The fashion media, the press, TV and electronic media traverse the walls of incarceration in their greedy dissemination of the visual influences on fashionability from all corners of the world. The appropriation of prison clothing culture by the fashion industry takes a number of forms.

First, there is the redistribution of actual prison clothing. For example, in 1998, blue-and-white striped prisoners' shirts became collectors' items in Britain. Prisoners in prison workshops had made them. The initials of the prison stamped on the shirt in indelible ink were the signs of fashionable authenticity. The value of the shirt increased according to the prison it came from. For example, a shirt from a central London men's prison in Wandsworth, stamped with WW, retailed at a higher price than one from KHM (a local prison named Kirkham Wood Prison in Lancashire) (see Fig. 7.1). The shirts sold at 'anything up to £250'. Inmates, recognising the value of these garments, would 'stuff 25 shirts in two plastic bags' on release and 'sell them to London street markets' where they retailed 'at £50 each or more'.[7] The seasonal catwalk fashion shows in Milan, New York, Paris and London at this time featured menswear that combined utility and tailored functionality that fitted with the iconic blue-and-white striped shirt. Subsequently, an ex-con was re-imprisoned for stealing prison clothing from an HMP establishment. The fashionable hierarchical elevation in the value of prison clothing provides the previously concealed garment with an element of inclusivity in the fashionable world outside. This exchange increases outside knowledge of the make of prison clothing. Yet, through inflating the value of clothing, the fashion industry further excludes the subject of imprisonment – the inmate themselves. Ex-prisoners return to incarceration when they attempt to profit from the products of their own labour. In Fig. 7.1, the shirt takes prominence and the prisoner's gaze is directed to the garment. Although

Figure 7.1   An inmate displaying a shirt from Kirkham Wood Prison, Lancashire, UK.

the shirt has entered the fashion market, the prisoner remains behind prison walls, forever branded as 'inmate' in the grounds of the prison. The inmate's value and future rehabilitation has no place in the reified world of consumption. As Friedrich Engels (1820–1895) observed about crime in the mid-nineteenth century, 'society creates a *demand* for crime which is met by a corresponding *supply*'.[8]

The way clothing is fetishised within capitalist economies that exchange prison clothing and their former wearers' bodies for money has not changed significantly for more than a century. The fashion industry is irrevocably integral to 'a society that consumes ever more concrete human bodies'.[9]

The manner in which prisoners wear clothing, rather than the garment itself, has also traversed the prison walls. In the early years of the twenty-first century, for example, low-slung jeans that revealed the bum became fashionable for young men and women in Europe and America. The style took as its inspiration the way prisoners were not allowed belts. Similarly shoe laces, forbidden in prisons, disappeared from view on the street. These youth styles signified their wearers' distinction from elitist fashionable circles. They also revealed an ironic disreputable allegiance to the hierarchical fashion system through the exposure of designer underwear labels such as Calvin Klein. These styles emulated prisoner status as inclusive within subversive youth cultures and in turn became appropriated by the all-pervasive fashion system.

The fashion industry at the same time appropriates the imagery of prison clothing that resonates with current political visual narratives disseminated by the press. The fashion photographer, Steven Meisel, presented a fashion shoot entitled 'State of Emergency' in *Vogue Italia's* 'Fashion Power' issue in September 2006. This shoot turned the real suffering of terror suspects at the hands of the military and police into artificially air-brushed and perfected images. Meisel is considered 'subversive'[10] in the field of fashion photography, yet these images dangerously play with the spectacle of violence in the promotion of expensive fashionability. The fashion shoot professionalises the hand-held photographic images of the American torture of Iraqi prisoners at Abu Ghraib prison in 2004. Although the model does not wear a hood over her head, she is photographed stepping into the hood-like construction of a skirt. Her half-nakedness is juxtaposed with images, in our memory, of piles of completely naked and humiliated Iraqi prisoners who were photographed and jeered at by American soldiers. In the *Vogue* shoot male and female soldiers impassively look on as the model steps into her 'hood' that neither masks her perfected, glamorous face nor near suffocates her in her déshabillement. Security scanners and dogs feature in the shoot and the police are armed and wear visors. The violence of these images and their association with images of imprisonment are not accidental. Prison clothing is referred to in another image[11] in this shoot in which the model is dressed in an orange Valentino satin and georgette dress that refers to the orange jumpsuit. A policeman wearing boots stamps on his model victim. Rather than providing social commentary or satire, these fashion photographs[12] were complicit in the global game of the 'War Against Terror' that was instigated by the regime of George Bush. These images appeared in 2006 as an antidote to the boredom of Paris Fashion Week. The fashion collections of October 2006 were characterised by 'a languor born more out of boredom with the shows themselves than the endurance they require'.[13]

In playing on the real images of violent torture and punishment of unsentenced prisoners that took place between 2001 and 2008, the fashion shot replaced the iconic prison clothing with the fashion garment. The fashion model's fake fear replaced the real suffering of terror suspects. Rather than being asked 'not to forget' the inhumanity of the treatment of prisoners, these violent images draw the specta-tor into a world of de-sensitised titillation. One of the messages of fashion photog-raphy is to encourage us to acquire power in the consumption and the wearing of new clothes. In the process of viewing these images, we buy into the 'suffering of others' since, in this context, they contain none of the 'nuances of political reflec-tion' that such 'atrocious images'[14] should invoke.

Whether prison clothing becomes fashionable on the streets around the world or is replicated in images in the fashion media it has become more visible in the late twentieth and early twenty-first centuries than in previous periods of its his-tory. But prison dress is filtered to the outside world through the distorting lens of fashionability and has little to do with the reality of clothing experienced by the prison inmate.

writing prison clothing

People in prison become aware of themselves as reconstituted in their own image through writing. The act of writing about clothing and how the regulations around clothing affect them inside makes the incarcerated visible to the world outside. Inmates' writing counters the prison authorities inside and the media and legal systems outside that speak for the inmate and rob people of their identity. Through writing, prisoners reclaim agency in the way they represent how it feels to wear the limited clothing prescribed by the establishment. Language is one of the few forms of expression left to those inside and even this is often denied. 'To rob a man of his language in the very name of his language: this is the first step in all legal murders.'[15] Despite these restrictions, inmate literature has burgeoned and much of it is about clothing. The forms of prison clothing writing are varied. Some prisoners, such as Jean Genet above, imagine themselves transcending the harsh reality of institu-tional clothing regulations. I have called this writing the imagined self. Others write about the lack of sensuality of prison clothes and their loss of identity. This writing, that I term descriptive autobiography, evokes either humiliation or resistance. The following sections trace the everyday writing of the inmate's experience of clothing from the induction process to the return to the world outside. The serving of time is measured by the perceptions of the clothed inmate between these two events.

Prison clothes are also written about with reference to the gendered ambiguity of cross-dressing, gang identity and as journalistic observation for the gaze of the outside world.

descriptive autobiography: initiation into prison clothing

Robert L. Johnson, on entering San Quentin prison in America in the 1990s, writes of the process of induction objectively as though looking down on himself,

> once off the bus, we all lined up in our bright orange jumpsuits as a guard with a hand-held metal detector perused body parts for hidden weapons. Inside, we stripped so more guards could look into more body spaces for more weapons...I was given a new jumpsuit.[16]

The abruptness of the words he uses to describe the reception of a new uniform reinforces the inhumane bodily search that he talks about in the previous sentences.

Nawal El Saadawi, imprisoned as an unsentenced socialist feminist in 1970s Egypt in the Barrages Women's Prison, writes, 'I no longer had my first or last name, or my own personality. I became "Detainee No. 1536"',[17] and she was left for days in the same clothes she had hastily grabbed when arrested. The women in Egypt, whether imprisoned for political reasons or on the grounds of poverty or prostitution, had no access to a change of clothing. ' "We want clothes from home," said one of the young women. "I came here in this one dress which I have been wearing day and night. Whenever I wash it, I sit beside it until it is dry and then put it on again" '.[18] The same process of stripping the individual of a previous identity affects prisoners across class and gender and in different prisons geographically. Through the process of writing, the inmate and reader become aware of the extent of the suffering through the replacement of the historical self with anonymity and degradation.

Prison clothing regulations either stigmatise the inmate in minimal clothing or impose a prison uniform of public humiliation. Moazzam Begg writes of his treatment by Americans in Kandahar in 2001:

> I was standing there, with no clothes on, shivering. The guards mocked me for what they assumed was fear...but I was shaking from the cold. I was then dressed in a thin pale-blue cotton jumpsuit and old shoes. They also gave me some underclothes and a far too big Afghani cap.

As in Egypt and in nineteenth-century prisons, Moazzam Begg's identity was substituted by a number: 'I was given the number "558", handed to me on an Enemy Prisoner of War (EPOW) card, and the number was also written on my back.'[19]

On the journey to Guantánamo, he writes,

> we were kitted out for the journey with a jacket and an orange hat as well as the orange clothes we already had...We were all shackled, with a chain around the waist that was attached to the handcuffs and reclassified. 'Hey, one-eight-zero', said one of the MPs, 'you're gonna be five-five-eight again in Gitmo, so I'm gonna write it on your shirt'.[20]

The penal construct of identity does not allow the prisoner to recognise individual difference in the history of the self. But through writing, the inmate asserts knowledge of self, despite the humiliating ways in which the authorities operate.

descriptive autobiography:
prison clothing collective resistance

Through their writing, inmates acknowledge collective resistance to prison clothing as well as self-knowledge.

John McVicar, who was sentenced to 23 years imprisonment in the late 1960s and was held in Durham maximum security prison, describes the collective response of inmates to the imposition of stringent dress regulations that resulted in a riot:

> Now we should have to wear shoes instead of the basket-ball boots that everyone wore all the time, and instead of wearing overalls all the time, which we also did, they were only to be worn at work, and there was a new rule that on association grey flannel trousers were to be worn. Prison shirts were also to be worn, and there were to be no more T-shirts, vests or other eccentricities...The cause of the uproar wasn't so much the discomfort of prison shoes and flannel trousers as the increased regimentation they represented...and the threat of having even these trivial freedoms taken away amounted to an attack on our identity...The general feeling was in favour of a complete refusal to cooperate.[21]

McVicar writes of the agency of the group in resisting the imposition of increased bodily and clothing regulations that denied individuation. After the inmates had erected barricades and taken over the prison records office, they won the right to wear plimsolls. McVicar's writing exposes the lengths to which prisoners are collectively prepared to go in asserting their identity through choice of clothing. He also highlights that, despite minor concessions, prison institutions contribute to the spiral of disruption through the prevention of the inmate's reconstruction of identity through the restriction of clothing.

In Egypt, women's families were not allowed to bring clothes into the prison. In response prisoners collectively demanded permission from the male Internal Security official who replied, '"whoever needs clothes will write a request to that effect, listing the clothes she wants and submitting the request to the Internal Security policeman in charge"'. Nawal El Saadawi replied that '"the problem is that we do not know how to write these requests without having access to pens and paper". He turned in my direction, his eyes darkening in sudden anger. "You have a point", he replied. "The lady warden will bring you a pen and some paper to write these requests" '.[22] Through her writing Nawal El Saadawi reveals the official's lack of knowledge of the conditions in which his authority holds prisoners. She expresses the women's collective knowledge in contrast to the ignorance of the bureaucrat. Inmates' writing exposes the lack of credibility of the power of institutional knowledge. There is, however, resistance in the spoken collective knowledge of deprivation that is the prisoner's identity. Inmates' writing also exposes their awareness of the falsity of the sartorial distinction between the guarded and the guards. Walter Probyn, who served more than 30 years between 1941 and 1974 in British prisons, observes that 'many screws are ex-forces and seem to require a uniform to give them identity. It is incredible how their confidence and self-assurance seems to ebb when they appear (on rare occasions) in civilian clothes'.[23]

descriptive autobiography: writing cross dressing

Inmates' experience of the way others dress contributes to their ability to fit into prison culture or retain independence from it. Sometimes the close proximity to others is confusing. Robert L. Johnson writes of his initiation into the ambiguity of cross-dressing identity constructs common in male and female prisons:

> I jumped down and looked out the bars for a minute. I thought for a second that I had seen a girl in here. After my cellie had stopped laughing, he informed me that what I had seen was known as a "he-she" – a man who dresses and acts like a woman ... (they use Kool-Aid in the lunches to make lip-stick).[24]

Prison language accepts sartorial difference and is not tainted with the dramatisation that characterises tabloid reports of cross dressing outside. A woman in Holloway prison in Britain similarly wrote in an accepting manner about a fellow prisoner who was taking sex change hormonal pills and growing a beard.[25] Inmates' writing displays interest rather than judgement in the differences in appearance of those who surround them in gender segregated institutions.

descriptive autobiography: writing gang clothing

Inside, particularly in American and South American jails, there are gangs in both men's and women's prisons, as there are on the city street. Gangs express collective sartorial identity against some of the more violent and oppressive aspects of prison regimes and their appearance often intimidates other inmates, ' "ghetto thugs" ... doo-rags, low-slung pants, tattoos on muscle – I've seen it all day, I've seen it in every borough. I've seen it on men in prison yards upstate'.[26] The writer uses prison language to describe the reality inside. He describes the universality of imposed prison dress that is transformed into styles of gang allegiance as unruly resistance.

descriptive autobiography: prison clothing journalism

Prisoners' writing is also deliberately journalistic. A long-term inmate was contracted to write a column for an English newspaper when he was still in prison. His writing describes prison clothing and inmate identity as inside knowledge revealed to the reader outside. Inmates flaunt their imagined or actual material status through clothing in order to resist distinctions imposed by prison clothing regulations and prison officers' expectations of inmates as unkempt. Rather, inmates preserve their dignity through the scrupulous maintenance of clothing. He writes,

> a stream of denim-clad men in identical blue-and-white striped shirts are shuffling past my door…With his athletic form draped in designer sportswear, gold chains and hundred-pound-plus trainers, Kyte presented an impressive image…Mickey was a short, dapper man and, though he was tiring under the weight of his sentence, even in prison clothes he was always immaculately turned out.[27]

He writes of the self-knowledge of the inmate's resistance through their retention of individuality in the minutiae of everyday clothing preferences.

descriptive autobiography: release from prison clothing

However long the prison sentence, the inmate's release into the outside world of sartorial fashions can mean the return to the self-expression of identity. But after the restrictions imposed by the prison, this depends on the availability of clothing. In their writing of the experience of release, the ex-prisoner often describes himself or herself as 'other' in an unfamiliar world. This sense of difference often makes it difficult to renegotiate their identity as socially inclusive human beings.

However, privileged prisoners have no such difficulties. An upper middle-class English inmate writes of donning blue-and-white shirts and prison garb that made him look 'like a refugee dressed by Oxfam'[28] that was common to male inmates in English prisons. On release, however, even if they left the prison with one black bag of possessions and in casual clothing, wealthy inmates have the material means whereby they can return to the previous sartorial apparel appropriate to their social status.

This was not the case for a newspaper reporter-inmate who writes of his lack of ease on release. He devised a technique in order not to feel out of place in the

outside world after years inside. He deliberately recalled his inmate sartorial identity with which he had become accustomed in order to negotiate the strangeness
of the unfamiliar. In order to get over his initial fear and lack of experience in talking
to people on the phone, for example, he writes that 'a good technique…was to
imagine that the estate agents I talked to were wearing blue and white striped convict shirts…it helped to negate my status anxiety'.[29]

For many, release from prison represents a continuity of humiliation and exclusion in inadequate clothing. When an inmate has been imprisoned wrongly and
is innocent this experience of exclusion is felt even more poignantly. When a
Guantánamo inmate was notified of his eventual release after 4 years with no charge
or conviction, he wrote movingly of his preparation for release,

> shortly after that, guards came to take my measurements again. In a moment
> of madness I thought they were going to make me some tailor-made clothes.
> But they came back with a horrible, thin, white made-in-Bangladesh T-shirt,
> and jeans and a denim jacket that I wouldn't be caught dead in. There were
> some shoes too. I tried them on, and of course they were too big. In fact
> everything was too big.[30]

The writing expresses self-knowledge in the recognition that his sartorial choices
are still intact after 4 years of punishment and torture. During all those years he
had worn the orange jumpsuit, hoods and all the paraphernalia of prison clothing
imposed by the USA in Guantánamo Bay until the end of 2008. Yet, the language
indicates individual agency against the extremities of power signified by imposed
prison uniformity. He exposes the attitude of the authorities who still see him, on
release, as a 'criminal' in shaming and shabby clothing.

There is another type of writing than the autobiographical description. Some
inmates, such as Jean Genet, use writing creatively as a way of transforming their
present conditions of abjection.

imagined selves:
stories of prison clothing as transcendence

In this form of writing the inmate reconstructs the deprived sartorial 'self' in imagined
clothing. Jean Genet wrote his entire first novel, *Our Lady of the Flowers*, based
on homo-erotic imaginative reverie when he was sentenced to life imprisonment in
France. The authorities and the daily conditions of imprisonment have no place in his
writing. In Genet's world it is the sensation of extreme bodily abjection from which he
forms an imagined self and a sense of identity that wins through. Whether based on
masturbatory fantasy or self-knowledge, his writing enables him to enter 'further into
abjection' in order to 'have the knowledge – strength or weakness – to take advantage
of such a fate'.[31] He can then figuratively share the experience with his fellow inmates.
Thus, they are all dressed in pink and white stripes.

A woman inmate, imprisoned in America for 20 years to life, writes about a skirt her mother wears on a visit. The writing prompts her to recognise a positive shared history and future with her mother that is materialised in a fashionable skirt, distinctive from prison clothing.

> You were forty-five and I was fourteen
> when you gave me the skirt.
> 'Its from Paris!' you said
> as if that would impress me
> who at best had mixed feelings
> about skirts.
>
> But I was drawn by that summer cotton
> with splashes of black and white – like paint
> dabbed by an eager artist.
> I borrowed your skirt
> and it moved like waves
> as I danced at a ninth-grade party...
>
> Now you are eighty and I almost fifty.
> We sit across from each other
> in the prison visiting room.
> Your soft gray-thin hair twirls into style.
> I follow the lines on your face, paths lit by your eyes
> until my gaze comes to rest
> on the black and white,
> on the years
> that our skirt has endured.[32]

Another woman, Judith Clarke, also imprisoned in Bedford Hills Correctional Facility, similarly sees her previous 'self' resurrected in a shirt saved and worn by a friend on a visit. The shirt had been abandoned as she had been in the process of imprisonment:

> among the everyday
> pieces lost
> a bright pink Indian cotton shirt...
>
> set adrift among the debris
> of police searches, overturned lives
> tossed into a pile of orphaned clothes
> and taken to a tag sale
>
>> where my friend,
>> recognizing it,
>> bought it
>> to keep me close
>
> and wore it one day
> to bring my daughter for a visit...

when I stood at that great divide,
the visitor's exit gate,
and watched my shirt and my child
leave
with my friend.[33]

The writer expresses strong emotions of loss and departure that are symbolised in the image of the shirt. Like her friend and daughter, the shirt inhabits a world in which she is no longer a part. Yet, the shirt is recognised as hers and kept close by her friend. The shirt represents an imagined future of her own return to the outside world with her friend and daughter.

In America and much of Europe the majority of prison inmates are black or Hispanic. Racial distinction between officers and prisoners and between inmates varies between regions and types of establishment. As we have seen, clothing plays an important part in the retention of individual and collective identity. The ability on the part of the prisoner to reconstruct sartorial cultural self-esteem within the confines of the prison walls cuts across racial distinctions. When prisoners are divested of personal items of clothing or jewellery, the formulation of self-identity is as much to do with what is unseen as to do with outward appearance.

In 'The African Child,' an inmate in an English prison writes that the charm he brought to England from Africa 'was confiscated'.

'They could only impound what they saw, how about what they could never see, the oracles of the triple rabbits, the more you look, the less you see, that's what I call magic.'[34] In writing his own cultural stories that are part of the charm that has been confiscated, the inmate understands the meaning invested in it and transforms the loss into self-knowledge. Writing of their own or imagined clothing provides confirmation of self-identity as continuity and the transcendence of imposed prison clothing conditions.

imagined selves:
stories of prison clothing as shame

Inmate writing also expresses the process of self-knowledge that results from the internalisation of shame inculcated by prison authorities and the exclusion from wider society. Prison clothing regulations stress the permanence of criminal identity and do not account either for the inmate's self-determined sense of shame or individual changes that occur inside. In placing the onus of rehabilitation on remorse felt through bodily punishment, prison institutions perpetuate an ethos of a division between the body and mind. At the same time as prescribing the punishment of the body in the everyday practice of clothing, some institutions provide discursive, practical or therapeutic services. These take the form of education, training, drug rehabilitation, creative writing, art and craft sessions. The process in some institutions of continuing to bodily shame inmates at the same time as nurturing the mind through the provision of therapeutic help can result in confusion, self-harm and suicide. In times of overcrowding and a lack of resources, the very needed therapeutic services are cut and the inmate is left with the embodiment of shame.

A female inmate in an English prison in 2005 writes of the violated look of the women around her:

> Now as I stood on the exercise yard doing nothing except breathe and look around, I saw scars on the bodies of almost all my fellow prisoners...As we started to look at the imprinted gash, Jess looked ashamed...They are stories that I thought society could learn a great deal from. What I heard from each of these women on the exercise yard that day showed me how each of them sought refuge in their denial...Don't we all say that we are tough bitches out here on the exercise yard? This prison defines us as such...But there would be much greater power in what you and I can see out here if we could all see ourselves as human beings first.[35]

Prison regimes tend to discourage prisoners from the reconstitution of 'self' as an intricate process of the acknowledgement of the past, interwoven with the possibilities, both material and emotional, of the future. As the writer above mentions, prisons foster a culture of dependency in all manner of everyday practices including that of clothing preferences. Another inmate writes, 'you can dress only one way; you can only adjust your uniform so far'.[36] Although the incarcerated find small ways of holding onto individual identity,[37] prison is coercive in its control of people's lives. The prison regime is 'synonymous with that used during infancy'.[38]

As Eddie Ellis, a prison activist who spent over two decades on the inside in Rikers Island prison in New York, commented, 'they tell you what to wear but they supply the uniform'. Thus, prisoners often emerge with outdated skills, antisocial tendencies, hatred for authority, and sagging self-esteem. Much of prisoners' writing reflects the degrading appearance of people inside. The negative effects of incarceration can embed the prisoner further into levels of criminality.[39]

Although prisoners do find ways in which to preserve or reconstruct identities through writing of their clothing, many express the loss of sartorial dignity and disempowerment. This aspect of prison writing identifies the lack of encouragement given to inmates in making everyday choices about clothes that contribute to a spiral of exclusion on release. Individuals have few possessions or the material means and confidence with which to regain or renew their sartorial identity outside. They return to the same situation of exclusion from which they came and the possibility of recidivism and despair.

The public are denied knowledge of the way in which inmates construct their identity through the clothing they wear. It is largely through their own writing and image-making that we comprehend processes of elation and despair that make up the way prisoners imagine and see themselves in prison garb. And prisoners' writing is not widely publicised.[40] 'We have indirectly constituted ourselves through the exclusion of some others: criminals, mad people, and so on.'[41] Yet, inmates themselves recognise the power of creative communication as inclusion in the world outside and a way to explore the self within the confines of the prison walls. 'I write because I can't fly'[42] writes an American inmate and 'writing is my way of sledgehammering these walls',[43] writes another.

the art and design of prison clothing

In prisoners' art and design, as much as their writing, there are connections made between the historically constituted self as clothed and the present self dressed in the apparel of the punished. As in the writing, there are images of the idealisation of self or the reinvention of self and the de-moralised self. There is a vast array of prisoner art and design that visualises prison clothing in relation to the incarcerated self. I have selected four types of image and a design that demonstrates the depth of feeling with which prison clothing is imbued. Within the disparate and globally uncurated archives of prisoners' work, self-portraits are often conventional. Yet, there are also pieces that express the process whereby they have come to a recognition of a new self through painting, sculpting and the design of clothing in prison. These works depict a succession of emotions and experiences inmates have felt prior to imprisonment, interwoven with present interactions with the world from their prison perspective. Jimmy Boyle painted a work entitled 'Social Outcast' in 1979 when he was in the maximum security Special Unit in Barlinnie Prison in Scotland. The imprisoned subject crouches in the foreground, hands to his head. He is separated from the group of individuals surrounding him both by the cell space in which he is positioned and by the striped blue-and-white clothing he wears. The surrounding group comprises professionals such as doctors in white coats, the police in uniforms, male bureaucrats and priests and individuals on the outside such as entertainers, punks, hippies, and criminals. They are juxtaposed on pieces of jigsaw puzzle that are superimposed on the machine that is the prison unit. The blue-and-white striped jumpsuit garment that Boyle wears was not part of the Barlinnie Prison clothing at the time. The iconic garment represents the entrapment of the convict 'other' on display to the public and professionals and yet excluded from them. Jimmy Boyle explains in a caption to the painting: 'During this period I felt there was something happening inside. I was losing part of myself and yet gaining more. The Unit is like a machine, remaking the model.'[44]

The Barlinnie Special Unit was a progressive regime at this time (see Chapter 5). Prisoners could wear their own clothing and prison officers wore civilian clothing in order to break down the distinctions between the guarded and the guards. Despite this, Jimmy Boyle sees himself as entrapped by the institutional identity construction imposed by the therapeutic helpers in the prison. The realisation of himself in prison uniform refers to his present sense of confinement and his history in conventional prison clothing in more brutal prisons.

In the unit he is surrounded by institutionalised facilitators into a 'normalised' world that is eccentrically frightening in his exclusion from it. The striped prison clothing defines and identifies him publicly in his self-acknowledged difference from and continuity with the prisoner he was when held in a conventional prison. He is wary of professional 'treatment' in so far as it can lead to the obliteration of his individual identity. The striped uniform is a visual metaphor for the internalised sense of branded public and private shame that the inmate feels even when the stripes are no longer worn.

Prison art in America and Europe is liberally scattered with portraits of the inmate self in horizontally striped prison clothing. Spatially the inmate is excluded from the outside world. But they are also excluded in the internalised self-knowledge of the fixity of public recrimination through the physical branding of criminality that is represented in the image of the prison uniform.

In contrast to the internalised scrutiny of self as other in prison clothing, much prisoners' art idealises the self. These images create a utopian world beyond the immediacy of the prison walls. For example, Faruq Shabazz, a black American who confronted racism inside[45] during a 50-year sentence in the 1980s, drew a range of 'designer' fashion jeans. They were emblazoned with a brightly coloured logo of birds' tail-feathers in red, green, blue and black. He named them 'Universal Tail-feathers'.[46]

These jeans were not designed for himself, but for women. He explains that the erotic image of the design came to him in a dream. 'The curve in the wing of a bird and then a rooster appeared with flowing tailfeathers.' He translated this image into the recognition of a purpose as a Muslim. 'It was the perfect creation to express God's will, with practical and spiritual applications . . . the message of a better world, loving and unified, would be borne on trousers and tops, gowns, robes, dresses, pyjamas, earrings and boots.'[47] He did not paint the punished self. Rather, Faruq Shabazz designed apparel for those outside the prison. They represent his imagined freedom from incarceration. The eroticised image acts as agency in uniting the imprisoned with the outside world and in transcending the excluded self in the present. The piece represents a type of idealisation of self through design. Inmates also daily alter, customise and redesign prison issue clothing in order to individualise their apparel. Additionally, Reform organisations, groups of artists, designers, literary figures and film-makers actively encourage inmates to express themselves creatively in the arts and design. In some prisons sewing, embroidery and dress design classes are held and the clothing is sold or exhibited.[48]

Prisoners also creatively devise equipment in order to circumnavigate the deliberate and inadequate deficiencies in the maintenance of prison clothing. This type of adaptation is demonstrated by an inmate's designs in a Los Angeles prison. Angelo describes how inmates invent methods for washing and drying clothing in their cells. He talks of the deficiencies in prison laundry services that only wash prison issue clothing and not personal clothes. Clothing is not returned to inmates so that there are problems with fit and the condition of clothing. Inmates working the laundry often steal personal items. He says, 'like it or not, washing of clothes by inmates in their cells is occasionally necessary'. He explains that 'the cell sink can be used for washing and the toilet for rinsing. Or the toilet can be purged of cold water and filled with hot water from the sink'. Washing lines are forbidden so they have to be made from available materials:

> Most clotheslines are devised from strips torn from bed sheets...The most ingenious method, devised by my cellie Randy, used a system of paperclip hooks embedded in wooden dominoes, which he glued to the cell walls with contact cement to provide mounts for his specially made nylon lines (spun from superstrong thread smuggled from the shops).[49]

This inmate's designs and observations are confirmation of prisoners' creativity and resourcefulness in the struggle for the assertion of self-identity in the alleviation of clothing privation.

There are also pieces of art that are complex images of punishment that refer to prison clothing in the reconstruction of identity as a process of pain.

An inmate called 'Nadia' (see Fig. 7.2) made a sculpture of herself out of waste prison materials. The piece exhibited is a series of photographs of the sculpture. The shirt she wears is an 'inmate's shirt (covered in modroc and painted)'. 'The skirt and belt use damaged F2055 Training Record cards' and cardboard packaging has

Figure 7.2 Photographs of sculpture of Nadia. Her Majesty's Youth Offender's Institution, Koestler Trust for Arts Inside Exhibition, London, September 2005.

Figure 7.3 The Puppet Master by P. Thomas, HMP Dumfries, Scotland. Koestler Trust Third Prize for Sculpture, 2007.'

been used to strengthen the torso and legs. A piece of blue-and-white prison shirt fabric is attached to one of the models and a blank 'Inmate Personal Record' form is fixed over the back view of the sculpture with the skirt lifted to reveal knickers.

The abused self is punished by the prison system and self-censored by the placement of the prison record form over her body. The sculpture is photographed in a number of corridors in anonymous institutional spaces that could be a school, hospital or prison. These settings are the places she has known in her history. The girl's prison shirt is tied provocatively over her breasts and the bobby socks she wears imply she is a young girl. The image is both seductive and infantile in the knowingness of a past imbued with the contradictions of being a girl in the outside world. The sexual predator is expected, as one hand is placed over the genital area of the skirt, and abhorred, and the other hand is raised in dismay to the forehead. The sculpture is made from discarded prison material. Prison clothing and ephemera represent a number of conflicting identities re-configured in the re-invention of self. The swatch of prison clothing, for example, is from a male prison shirt. There is ambiguity in the artist/inmate's shame in her identification with the imprisoned male perpetrator of the encounter. The images are of pain but not simply of self as victim.

There is uncertainty in where this knowledge might lead her once released back to the outside world of seductive clothing and its gender expectations.

In an overtly political sculpture, entitled 'The Puppet Master' (see Fig. 7.3), P. Thomas exposes the hierarchy of the Criminal Justice System. The judge controls the police, lawyers and prison officers. The justice system is a lottery in which the fate of the judged is determined by a game of cards played by the police and lawyers. The prisoners at the bottom of the heap hold up the shaky system, clothed in uniforms emblazoned with the broad arrow. The sculpture reveals the inmate's recognition of the history of the stigmatisation of the prisoner in the iconic uniform and its continued currency in the eyes of the world. The prisoner's position and identity in the hierarchy is fixed and culpable in the outdated public gaze, yet the system is toppling, balanced precariously on the prisoners' shoulders. Prison clothing historically and contemporaneously extends the politics and power of the institution in its visibly shaky subjection of the prisoner's identity. In written and visual language the inmate redefines his or her historical, sartorial, political and self-identity.

conclusion

In the ebbs and flows of late modernity lies apocalyptic instability. This is metaphorically demonstrated in the toppling 'Criminal Justice' system balanced precariously on the shoulders of broad arrowed prisoners and the faked brutality unleashed on models as 'terror suspects' in the fashion media.

Prison clothing and the imprisoned are no longer locked away from public sight. In the writing and visual images created by inmates, prisoners express their re-invention of self through sartorial identity. The writing, art and design of the clothing of the prisoner make connection with the outside world. Yet, the prisoner's creativity reaches a small audience. The Film and Fashion industries, the press and electronic media transmit information and images of the inmate. But we are surrounded by the continued invisibility of the subject in the very public visibility of the raiment of punishment.

Despite periods of reform that established the right of the punished to clothing that was less humiliating, the cycle of the history of prison clothing has come full circle. Global penal practices still pertain to pre-nineteenth-century European and American models of malign neglect or the nineteenth-century visibility of the iconic uniform. Rather than imprisonment losing value in line with the criticisms that have been voiced since its inception, the population of the incarcerated increases.

Political power manifests itself with fundamentalist zeal in labelling its opponents as criminal. The voices of humanistic reform and more radical change are treated with disdain.[50] Yet, precisely because of the very visibility of illegality, materialised in the return of the iconic prison uniform between 2001 and 2008, we are not inured to the plight of prisoners who are not, for the most part, inhumane miscreants. We do not passively imbibe information and images of prison atrocities and inequalities that are represented in prison clothing. We politically, aesthetically and morally position ourselves in the way in which we choose to view, empathise with and act to change the political prerogatives upon which are based the continued stigmatisation of the imprisoned.

notes

introduction: unravelling prison clothing

1. Wilfred McCartney, *Walls Have Mouths* (London, 1936), p. 66.
2. John Steele, *The Bird that Never Flew*, cited in Julian Broadhead, *Unlocking the Prison Muse: The Inspirations and Effects of Prisoners' Writing in Britain* (Cambridge, 2006), p. 104.
3. See Michel Foucault, *Discipline and Punish: The Birth of the Prison* (London, 1991).
4. The regulated formation of prisoners who were marched in line close together in early nineteenth-century American prisons.
5. See Erving Goffman, *Asylums: Essays on the Social Situation of Mental Patients and Other Inmates* (London, 1968).
6. Ann Owers, HMP Inspector of Prisons, UK, *The Guardian*, 11 July 2006.
7. Jane E. Atwood, *Too Much Time: Women in Prison* (London, 2000), p. 158.
8. See Giorgio Agamben, *State of Exception* (Chicago, 2005).
9. Giorgio Agamben, *Homo Sacer: Sovereign Power and Bare Life* (Stanford, 1998), p. 125.
10. Ibid., p. 20.
11. See Moazzam Begg, *Enemy Combatant: A British Muslim's Journey to Guantánamo and Back* (London, 2006).
12. This was a term reformers used to characterise the disorder of prisons before they were 'modernised' in the early nineteenth century. See Norval Morris and David. J. Rothman (eds.), *The Oxford History of the Prison: The Practice of Punishment in Western Society* (Oxford, 1995), p. 71.
13. See Margaret Maynard, *Fashioned from Penury: Dress as Cultural Practice in Colonial Australia* (Cambridge, 1994); Clare Anderson, ch. 4, 'The Question of Convict Dress', in *Legible Bodies: Race, Criminality and Colonialism in South East Asia* (Oxford, 2004).
14. See Nathan Joseph, *Uniforms and Non-uniforms: Communication through Clothing* (New York, 1986); Paul Fussell, *Uniforms: Why We Are What We Wear* (Boston, 2002); Jennifer Craik, *Uniforms Exposed: From Conformity to Transgression* (Oxford, 2005).
15. See Brian McVeigh, *Wearing Ideology: State, Schooling and Self-presentation in Japan* (Oxford, 2000).
16. See Narmala Halstead, 'Branding "Perfection": Foreign as Self, Self as "Foreign-Foreign", *Journal of Material Culture*, 7:3 (2002), pp. 273–293.
17. Jock Young, *The Vertigo of Late Modernity* (London, 2007), pp. 9–16.
18. Interviews were carried out with male and female ex-prisoners and women in Holloway prison, London. Questionnaires were distributed in Holloway prison and to 40 European and American prisons. Correspondence was

conducted with inmates in American prisons and a number of international contacts.

19. See Morris and Rothman, *The Oxford History of the Prison.*
20. See John Lea, *Crime and Modernity* (London, 2002); Roger Matthews, *Doing Time: An Introduction to the Sociology of Imprisonment* (London, 1999).
21. See Douglas K. Hall (ed.), *Prison Tattoos* (New York, 1997).

1   from near naked to uniforms, pre-1800 to 1830s

1. Elizabeth Fry cited in Rosamund Morris, *Prisons* (London, 1976), p. 43.
2. Lucia Zedner, 'Wayward Sisters: The Prison for Women', in Norval Morris and David J. Rothman (eds.), *The Oxford History of the Prison,* p. 300.
3. Edward P. Thompson, *The Making of the English Working Class* (London, 1968), p. 66.
4. Ibid.
5. Sean McConville, 'Local Justice: The Jail', in Norval Morris and David J. Rothman (eds.), *The Oxford History of the Prison,* p. 272.
6. A Bill for the Better Regulation of Prisons and Houses of Correction within the Kingdom of England and Wales, 10th March 1779, p. 76 (House of Lords Records Office, London).
7. John Howard, 'Advertisement', introducing *Historical Remarks and Anecdotes on the Castle of the Bastille* (London, 1784), p. 15.
8. Simon Schama, *Citizens: A Chronicle of the French Revolution* (London, 1989), pp. 391–392.
9. John Howard, 'Introduction', *An Account of the Present State of the Prisons and Houses of Correction*, p. xii.
10. Ibid.
11. Ibid., pp. vi–x.
12. Matthews, *Doing Time,* p. 18.
13. Ibid.
14. John Howard, *An Account of the Present State of the Prisons and Houses of Correction,* in *the Western Circuit* (1789), p. xiii.
15. John Howard, *An Account of the Present State of the Prisons and Houses of Correction,* in *the Midland Circuit* (1789), p. 3.
16. John Howard, *An Account of the Present State of the Prisons and Houses of Correction and Hospitals* in *London and Westminster* (1789), p. 2.
17. Ibid., p. 7.
18. Ibid., p. 11.
19. *Liverpool Courier,* March 1826, cited in Steven King and Christiana Payne, 'Introduction', *Textile History Journal*, 33:1 (2002), p. 2.
20. Ibid.
21. Ibid., p. 5.
22. Lucia Zedner, 'Wayward Sisters: The Prison for Women', in Norval Morris and David. J. Rothman (eds.), *The Oxford History of the Prison,* p. 298.
23. See John Styles, 'Involuntary Consumers? Servants and Their Clothes in Eighteenth Century England', *Textile History Journal*, 33:1 (2002), 9–21.

24. John Tagg, *The Burden of Representation: Essays on Photographies and Histories* (London, 1988), p. 11.
25. Ibid.
26. See Joanna Innes, 'The King's Bench Prison in the Later Eighteenth Century: Law, Authority and Order in the Debtor's Prison', in John Brewer and John Styles (eds.), *An Ungovernable People: The English and Their Law in the Seventeenth and Eighteenth Centuries* (London, 1980).
27. National Archives, London, HO 44/44 ('Letters 1801').
28. Ibid., HO 44/6 ('Letters 1820').
29. Henry Mayhew and John Binney, *The Criminal Prisons of London* (London, 1971/1867), p. 235.
30. 9 March 1819, Rules and Regulations for the General Penitentiary, Milbank, ordered by the House of Commons, House of Lords Records Office, London, pp. 22–23.
31. Foucault, *Discipline and Punish,* p. 26.
32. 1823, 'Gaol Act', House of Lords, London, 4° Geo. IV, p. 373.
33. Rules and Regulations for the Government, House of Lords, London, Microfiche 38.90, p. 381
34. See Michael Ignatieff, *A Just Measure of Pain: The Penitentiary in the Industrial Revolution, 1750–1850* (London, 1978).
35. Goffman, *Asylums*, pp. 269–270.
36. Transportation to America had ended in the wake of US independence in 1776.
37. These disciplinary procedures in relation to dress will be looked at in chapter 2.
38. See Maynard, *Fashioned from Penury.*
39. Ibid., p. 10
40. Ibid., p. 23.
41. See Thorstein Veblen, *The Theory of the Leisure Class* (London, 1970/1899).
42. Collections of 'parti-coloured' clothing marked with the broad arrow are kept in the Queen Victoria Museum and Art Gallery, Tasmania; the Powerhouse Museum Sydney and the National Library of Australia.
43. See Maynard, *Fashioned from Penury,* pp. 9–26.
44. Ibid., p. 24.
45. Clare Anderson, 'Fashioning Identities: Convict Dress in Colonial South and Southeast Asia', *History Workshop Journal,* 52 (Autumn 2001), 156.
46. Ibid.
47. Dhotis are traditional Indian male clothing consisting of fabric wrapped around the lower half of the body.
48. Anderson, 'Fashioning Identities', p. 157.
49. Robert Hughes, *The Fatal Shore: A History of the Transportation of Convicts to Australia 1787–1868* (London, 1988), p. 454.
50. Thomas Watling, 'Letters of an Exile', p. 18, cited in Robert Hughes, *The Fatal Shore*, p. 104.
51. 'Parti-dress' is mentioned in the 1823 Parliamentary Act in Britain, House of Lords Records Office, London, p. 373.

52. 'Convict Uniform', National Library of Australia information sheet, http://www.gov.au/convicts, last accessed 14 September 2006, p. 1.

53. See the National Library of Australia, nla.pic-an6393471 and the Beattie Collection at Queen Victoria Museum and Art Gallery, Tasmania, QVM.2003.H.0584.

54. Bev Baker, Curator of the NCCL Galleries of Justice Prison Photography Archive.

55. Maynard, *Fashioned from Penury,* p. 21.

56. David Rothman, 'Perfecting the Prison: United States, 1789–1865', in Norval Morris and David Rothman (eds.), *The Oxford History of the Prison*, p. 102.

57. Norman Johnston, *Prison Reform in Pennsylvania* (2004), Pennsylvania Prison Society, http://www.prisonsociety.org/about/history.shtml, last accessed 20 September 2006, p. 1.

58. Ibid., p. 2.

59. Robert J. Turnbull, 'A Visit to the Philadelphia Prison' *Charleston Daily Gazette* (1796/1797), 16–17.

60. Ibid., p. 4.

61. Ibid., p. 25.

62. See Matthews, *Doing Time*, pp. 26–49.

63. 'New York's First Prison', http://www.newgate.html, last accessed 20 September 2006, p. 2.

64. See particularly Oscar Wilde's *De Profundis* (London, 1911), p. 130.

65. 'New York's First Prison', http://www.newgate.html, p. 5.

66. Michel Pastoureau, *The Devil's Cloth: A History of Stripes and Striped Fabric* (Columbia, 2001), p. 58.

67. 'New York's First Prison', http://www.newgate.html, p. 4.

68. Tom McCarthy, General Secretary of the New York Correction History Society, e-mail 20 April 2006.

69. Foucault, *Discipline and Punish,* pp. 135–170.

70. Alexis de Tocqueville, 'Journey to America 1831–1832', trans. George Lawrence, J. P. Mayer (ed.) (New York 1960), pp. 209–211.

71. Charles Dickens, *American Notes* (London, 1898), p. 119.

2   uniforms: stripes, broad arrows and aprons, 1830s to 1900

1. See Foucault's *Discipline and Punish*.

2. See Pastoureau, *The Devil's Cloth,* p. 56.

3. Ibid.

4. See amongst others, Craik, *Uniforms Exposed.*

5. Michel Foucault, 'The Eye of Power: A Conversation with Jean-Pierre Barou and Michelle Perrot' in T.V. Lewin, Ursula Frohe and Peter Weibel (eds.), *CTRL and Space* (New York, 2002), p. 95.

6. Ibid.

7. Ibid.

8. Tony Bennett, *Culture: A Reformer's Science* (London, 1998), p. 137.
9. Robin Evans, *The Fabrication of Virtue: English Prison Architecture: 1750–1840* (Cambridge, 1982), pp. 171, 189–194.
10. Ibid., p. 171.
11. Ibid., p. 190.
12. Peter Ackroyd, *London: A Biography*, (London, 2000), p. 290.
13. The introduction of masks will be looked at in greater detail later in this chapter.
14. Evans, *The Fabrication of Virtue,* p. 196.
15. Ibid.
16. Phillip Priestley, *Victorian Prison Lives: English Prison Biography, 1830–1914* (London, 1999), p. 13.
17. Charles Dickens, *Little Dorrit* (London, 1967), p. 131.
18. Thomas Carlyle, 'The World in Clothes', ch. 5, in *Sartor Resartus,* in Julian Symons (ed.), *Carlyle: Selected Works, Reminiscences and Letters* (London, 1955/1831), p. 90. See also Michael Carter, *Fashion Classics: From Carlyle to Barthes* (Oxford, 2003).
19. Tagg, *The Burden of Representation,* p. 74.
20. See Peter Hamilton and Roger Hargreaves, *The Beautiful and the Damned: The Creation of Identity in Nineteenth Century Photography* (London, 2001).
21. Ian Mortimer of I.M. Imprint for information regarding methods of wood engraving.
22. Tagg, *The Burden of Representation,* p. 76.
23. Dickens, *American Notes,* p. 119.
24. Mayhew and Binney, *The Criminal Prisons of London*, p. 141.
25. Ibid., p. 125.
26. Ibid., p. 141.
27. *Report on the Discipline and Management of Convict Prisons for the Year 1853.* Cited in Mayhew and Binney, *The Criminal Prisons of London*, p. 142.
28. H. Mayhew and J. Binney, *The Criminal Prisons of London*, p. 116.
29. Ibid., p. 155.
30. Ibid., p. 147.
31. Pastoureau, *The Devil's Cloth,* p. 57.
32. Ibid., p. 56.
33. Ibid., p. 54.
34. Ibid.
35. Mayhew and Binney, *The Criminal Prisons of London*, p. 146.
36. Craik, *Uniforms Exposed,* p. 15.
37. Dartmoor prison website, Legendary Dartmoor Research, Dartmoor Prison Escapes', p. 2.
38. Christopher Breward, *The Hidden Consumer: Masculinities, Fashion and City Life 1860–1914* (Manchester, 1999), p. 90.
39. Mayhew and Binney, *The Criminal Prisons of London*, p. 151.
40. Ibid.
41. See Leonore Davidoff and Catherine Hall, *Family Fortunes: Men and Women of the English Middle Class* (London, 1987).

42. Lucia Zedner, 'Wayward Sisters: The Prison for Women', in Norval Morris and David J. Rothman (eds.), *The Oxford History of the Prison*, p. 298.
43. Ibid., p. 301.
44. E-mail, Eilleen McHughes, Curator at the Cayuga Museum, New York State.
45. Catherine Prade, Curator of Musée National des Prisons, Fontainebleu, France.
46. Steven King and Christiana Payne, 'Introduction: The Dress of the Poor', *Textile History*, 33:1 (2002), 5. In the same issue, John Styles, 'Involuntary Consumers? Servants and Their Clothes in Eighteenth Century England'.
47. Mayhew and Binney, *The Criminal Prisons of London*, p. 269.
48. Ibid., p. 272.
49. See Joanne Entwistle, 'The Dressed Body', in Joanne Entwistle and Elizabeth Wilson (eds.), *Body Dressing* (Oxford, 2001).
50. Mayhew and Binney, *The Criminal Prisons of London,* pp. 272–273.
51. Jeremy Bentham, 'Circumstances and Sensibility', ch. 4, *The Principles of Morals and Legislation,* in J.H. Burns and H.L.A. Hart (eds.), *Collected Works of Jeremy Bentham* (New York, 1988), p. 64.
52. Lea, *Crime and Modernity*, p. 31.
53. See Veblen, *The Theory of the Leisure Class.*
54. Raphael Samuel, *Theatres of Memory: Vol. II: Island Stories: Unravelling Britain* (London, 1998), p. 80.
55. Ibid., p. 81.
56. Bennett, *Culture*, pp. 110, 137.
57. *Report from the Select Committee of the House of Lords* (1863), House of Lords Archive, London, microfiche 69.58 p. 163.
58. Ibid., microfiche 69.59, pp. 328–329.
59. Ibid., microfiche 69.60, p. 427.
60. D_S_, *Eighteen Months Imprisonment* (London, 1883), p. 22.
61. Ibid., p. 140.
62. See Ben Fine, *The World of Consumption: The Material and Cultural Revisited* (London, 2002), for a detailed account of 'systems of provision (sops)' economically, socially and historically.
63. D_S_, *Eighteen Months Imprisonment*, p. 140.
64. National Archives, Kew, London, PRIS 9/31.
65. Sarah Waters, *Affinity* (London, 2000), p. 39.
66. D_S_, *Eighteen Months Imprisonment*, p. 142.
67. Fine, *The World of Consumption*, p. 83.
68. E. Sylvia Pankhurst, *The Suffragette Movement: An Intimate Account of Persons and Ideals* (London, 1931), p. 231.
69. Jeremiah O'Donovan Rossa, *Irish Rebels in English Prisons* (New York, 1967/1882), p. 127.
70. See Havelock Ellis, *The Criminal* (Boston, 1977/1890).
71. See Peter Kropotkin, *In Russian and French Prisons* (Montreal, 1991/1905).
72. Laurence McKeown, *Out of Time: Irish Republican Prisoners Long Kesh 1972–2000* (Belfast, 2001), p. 12.

73. Ibid.
74. Ibid., p. 13.
75. See O'Donovan Rossa, *Irish Rebels in English Prisons*.
76. Wilfrid Blunt, *The Land War in Ireland* (London, 1912), pp. 380–385.
77. Ibid., p. 385.
78. Fyodor Dostoyevsky, *The House of the Dead* (London, 2003), p. 36.
79. Ibid., p. 29.
80. Ibid., p. 32.
81. Ibid., p. 39.
82. Fyodor Dostoyevsky, *Crime and Punishment* (Oxford, 1998), pp. 519–520.
83. Kropotkin, *In Russian and French Prisons*, pp. 50–55.
84. Ibid., p. 143.
85. Ibid., p. 266.
86. Ibid., pp. 328–334.
87. Ibid., p. 346.

3 seams of change: the abolition of iconic uniforms, 1900s to 1930s

1. See Mica Nava, *Visceral Cosmopolitanism: Gender, Culture and the Normalisation of Difference* (Oxford, 2007) and TV programme, 'Shopping for England', BBC 4.
2. Gavin Weightman and Steve Humphries, *The Making of Modern London 1815–1914* (London, 1983), pp. 63–64.
3. Charles Baudelaire, *Paris Spleen* (trans. Louise Varese), (New York, 1970), pp. 52–53.
4. Ibid., p. 26.
5. See Craik, *Uniforms Exposed.*
6. See Fine, *The World of Consumption.*
7. See Lea, *Crime and Modernity.*
8. McKeown, *Out of Time,* p. 13.
9. John Maclean cited in Nan Milton, *John MacClean* (London, 1973), p. 126.
10. Ibid.
11. See Susan Bean, 'Gandhi and Khadi: The Fabric of Independence', in A. Weiner and J. Schneider (eds.), *Cloth and Human Experience* (1989) and Dipesh Chakrabarty, 'Khadi and the Political Man', in Dipesh Chakrabarty (ed.), *Habitations of Modernity: Essays in the Wake of Subaltern Studies* (Chicago, 2002), pp. 51–64.
12. Mahatma Gandhi, 'Civility', in Dennis Dalton (ed.), *Mahatma Gandhi: Selected Political Writings* (Indiana, 1996), p. 48.
13. Constance Lytton and Jane Warton, *Prisons and Prisoners: Some Personal Experiences* (London, 1914), p. 1.
14. Pankhurst, *The Suffragette Movement,* p. 232.
15. Catalogue of the 'The Women's Exhibition', London, 1909, and Glasgow, 1910, The Women's Press, London, pp. 38–39 (Museum of London Archive).

16. Patricia Heatley and Mike Tomlinson, 'The Politics of Imprisonment in Ireland: Some Historical Notes', cited in Laurence McKeown, *Out of Time: Irish Republican Prisoners Long Kesh 1972–2000* (Belfast, 2001), p. 12.

17. Ibid., p. 13.

18. Lucia Zedner, 'Wayward Sisters: The Prison for Women', in Norval Morris and David J. Rothman (eds.), *The Oxford History of the Prison*, p. 319.

19. Ibid., p. 320.

20. In *Technologies of the Self,* Michel Foucault revised his earlier denial in *Discipline and Punish* that the prisoner had agency in bodily or spoken resistance against the prison system. See Luther H. Martin, Huck Gutman and Patrick H. Hutton (eds.), *Technologies of the Self: A Seminar with Michel Foucault* (Massachusetts, 1988), p. 20.

21. Pankhurst, *The Suffragette Movement,* p. 232.

22. Ibid.

23. Carolyn Steedman, *Landscape for a Good Woman: A Story of Two Lives* (London, 1989), p. 89.

24. Pankhurst, *The Suffragette Movement,* p. 236.

25. Ibid., p. 238.

26. Steedman, *Landscape for a Good Woman,* p. 89.

27. Daniel Guerin, *100 Years of Labour in the USA* (trans. Alan Adler) (London, 1979), p. 81.

28. Sheila Rowbotham, *A Century of Women: The History of Women in Britain and the United States* (London, 1997), p. 100.

29. Emma Goldman, *Living My Life*, vol. 1 (New York, 1970), pp. 133–134.

30. James P. Cannon, *Notebook of an Agitator* (New York, 1958), p. 37.

31. A Life Prisoner, *The Kansas Inferno: A Study of the Criminal Problem; A Description of the Kansas Prison as it Is and as it Should Be* (1906), cited in Larry E. Sullivan (ed.), *Bandits and Bibles: Convict Literature in Nineteenth Century America* (New York, 2003), p. 180.

32. Adolph Edwards, *Marcus Garvey: 1887–1940,* (London, 1967), p. 22.

33. Ronald Segal, cited in Carol Tulloch, ' "Out of Many One People": The Relativity of Dress, Race and Ethnicity to Jamaica, 1880–1907', in *Fashion Theory*, 2:4 (1998) 372.

34. Patricia O'Brien, 'The Prison on the Continent: Europe, 1865–1965', in Norval Morris and David J. Rothman (eds.), *The Oxford History of the Prison,* pp. 190–191.

35. Anderson, *Legible Bodies,* pp. 88–89.

36. Catherine Prade, Curator of the Musée National des Prisons, France.

37. See Elizabeth Wilson, *Adorned in Dreams: Fashion and Modernity* (London, 1985).

38. Ellis, *The Criminal* (1914 edition), p. xxvi.

39. Havelock Ellis, *Views and Reviews: A Selection of Uncollected Articles (1884–1932),* First Series 1884–1919 (London, 1932) and Edward Carpenter, *Prisons, Police and Punishment* (London, 1905), p. 322.

40. Ellis, *The Criminal,* p. 373.

41. Raphael Samuel, *Island Stories: Unravelling Britain: Theatres of Memory,* vol. 2 (London, 1998), p. 305.

42. Larry E. Sullivan, *Forlorn Hope: The Prison Reform Movement* (New York, 2002), p. 30.

43. Ibid.

44. Ibid., p. 34.

45. Eileen McHughes, Curator of the Cayuga Museum at Auburn, New York State.

46. Phillipe Mazuet et Catherine Prade, *Henri Manuel: Photographies de Prisons 1928–1932,* CD-ROM, (Musée National de Prisons, Ministerre de la Justice, France, 2000).

47. Erwin James, 'Among the Ghosts', *The Guardian: G2,* 4 December 2006, p. 13.

48. Sally Alexander, *Becoming a Woman and Other Essays in 19th and 20th Century Feminist History* (London, 1995), p. 215.

49. Steven Schlossman, 'Delinquent Children: The Juvenile Reform School', in Norval Morris and David J. Rothman (eds.), *The Oxford History of the Prison,* p. 330.

50. Ibid., p. 335.

51. Ibid.

52. National Archives, Kew, London, PCOM 7/546.

53. Ross McKibbin, *Classes and Cultures: England 1918–1951* (Oxford, 1998), p. 340.

54. National Archives, Kew, London, PCOM 7/546.

55. Ibid.

56. Morris, *Prisons*, p. 53.

57. McCartney, *Walls Have Mouths*, p. 66.

58. National Archives, Kew, London, PCOM 7/314.

59. National Archives, Kew, London, PCOM 7/667.

60. National Archives, Kew, London, PCOM 7/314.

61. See Fine, *The World of Consumption.*

62. Interview with George Kirby, *Forbidden Britain*, British Library Sound Archives, C590/02/28–31.

63. Fenner Brockway and Stephen Hobhouse (eds.), *English Prisons Today: Being the Report of the Prison System Enquiry Committee* (London, 1922), p. 131.

64. Ibid., pp. 131–132.

65. Ibid., pp. 132–133.

66. Ibid., p. 139.

67. Ibid., p. 133.

68. Ibid., p. 653.

69. Thomas McCarthy, New York Corrections History Society.

70. Burdette G. Lewis, 'The Offender', p. 242, cited in Fenner Brockway and Stephen Hobhouse (eds.), *English Prisons Today,* p. 660.

71. Ibid.

72. Anderson, *Legible Bodies,* p. 128.

73. Ibid., p. 130.
74. Beatrice and Sidney Webb, *English Prisons under Local Government* (London, 1927), p. 235.
75. Ibid., p. lxii.
76. Ibid., p. lxvii.
77. Victor Serge, *The Case of Comrade Tulayev* (1948 in French; London, 1968), p. 362.

4 inside out: from extremes to reform, resistance and back, 1930s to 1990s

1. Agamben, *Homo Sacer*, p. 12.
2. See Patricia O'Brien, 'The Prison on the Continent: Europe, 1865–1965', in Norval Morris and David J. Rothman (eds.), *The Oxford History of the Prison*, pp. 178–201.
3. Agamben, *State of Exception*, p. 4.
4. Fernando Claudin, *The Communist Movement: From Comintern to Cominform* (London, 1975), p. 255.
5. Ibid., p. 259.
6. See Radu Stern, *Against Fashion: Clothing as Art 1850–1930* (New York, 2004); Tatiana Strizhenova, *Soviet Costumes and Textiles: 1917–1945*, (London, 1991); Ol'ga Vainshtein, 'Female Fashion, Soviet Style, Bodies of Ideology', in Helena Goscilo and Beth Holmgren (eds.), *Russia, Women, Culture* (Indiana, 1996).
7. Serge, *The Case of Comrade Tulayev*, p. 234.
8. See Peter Sedgewick's Introduction to his translation of Victor Serge, *Memoirs of a Revolutionary 1901–1941*, (Oxford, 1963) for a full account of Victor Serge's life.
9. Serge, *'The Case of Comrade Tulayev'*, p. 184.
10. Ibid., p. 189.
11. Arthur Koestler, *Darkness at Noon* (New York, 1994/1940), p. 171.
12. Ibid., p. 140.
13. Ibid., p. 209.
14. Foucault, *Discipline and Punish*, p. 25.
15. Serge, *Men in Prison*, p. 111.
16. Ibid., p. 24.
17. Aryeh Neier, 'Confining Dissent: The Political Prison', in Norval Morris and David J. Rothman (eds.), *The Oxford History of the Prison*, p. 362.
18. Aleksandr Solzhenitsyn, *The Gulag Archipelago* (1918–1956) (London, 1974), p. 575.
19. Marian Mark Bilewicz, *I Escaped the Dark*, cited in Riszard Kapuscinski, *Imperium* (London, 1998), p. 160.
20. Ibid., p. 202.
21. Edith Bone, *Seven Years of Solitary* (London, 1957), p. 168.
22. Ibid., p. 171.

23. Ibid., p. 176.
24. Patricia O'Brien, 'The Prison on the Continent', p. 194.
25. See www.archive.org/details/nazi_concentration_camps and the documentary film, *Shoah*, directed by Claude Lanzmann that includes detailed accounts of concentration camp survivors.
26. Claude Lanzmann, film *Shoah*, Era Two/Part Two. Memoir of a survivor of Auschwitz.
27. After 1941, the 'Final Solution' policy of the Nazis meant that the rate of extermination of 'undesirables' increased and systems of classification in the camps were largely dispensed with.
28. Pastoureau, *The Devil's Cloth,* p. 56.
29. Ibid., p. 61.
30. Claude Lanzmann film, *Shoah*, Era One/Part Two. Memoir of a survivor of Auschwitz.
31. See Agamben, *Homo Sacer.*
32. Raul Hilberg, Historian, in Claude Lanzmann film, *Shoah*, Era One/Part Two.
33. Agamben, *Homo Sacer*, p. 37.
34. Evelyn Le Chene, *Mauthausen: The History of a Death Camp* (London, 1971), p. 39.
35. Agamben, *Homo Sacer*, p. 123.
36. Louise Rinser, *Prison Journal* (London, 1987), p. 112.
37. William Ash, *Under the Wire: The Wartime Memoir of a Spitfire Pilot, Legendary Escape Artist and 'Cooler King'*, (London, 2005), p. 235.
38. Ibid., p. 173.
39. Sir Alexander Paterson and S. Ruck (eds.), *Paterson on Prisons*, (London, 1951), p. 83.
40. Ibid., p. 85.
41. Helen Bryan, *Inside* (New York, 1953), p. 27.
42. Elizabeth Gurley Flynn, *The Alderson Story: My Life as a Political Prisoner* (New York, 1963), p. 34.
43. See Susannah Handley, *Nylon: The Story of a Fashion Revolution* (Baltimore, 1999).
44. See Rebecca Arnold, *The American Look: Fashion, Sportswear and the Image of Women in 1930s and 1940s New York* (London, 2008).
45. Bryan, *Inside*, p. 27.
46. See Chapter 7 for more analysis of this film.
47. Erwin James, in conversation with author, 2005.
48. See Joanne Entwistle, 'The Dressed Body', in Joanne Entwistle and Elizabeth Wilson (eds.), *Body Dressing* (Oxford, 2001); Martin Luther, Huck Gutman and Patrick Hutton, *Technologies of the Self: A Seminar with Michel Foucault'* (Massachusetts, 1988), p. 107; Goffman, *Asylums,* p. 279.
49. 'United Nations Standard Minimum Rules for the Treatment of Prisoners', adopted by the Economic and Social Council of the United Nations, 31 July, 1957, cited in Leonard Orland, *Prisons: Houses of Darkness* (New York, 1978), p. 169.

50. Michael Cavadino and James Dignan, *Penal Systems: A Comparative Approach* (London, 2006), pp. 50–51.

51. Young, *The Vertigo of Late Modernity*, p. 10.

52. Cavadino and Dignan, *Penal Systems,* p. 52.

53. Jessica Mitford, 'Kind and Usual Punishment' in Angela Davis, *If They Come in the Morning: Voices of Resistance* (London, 1971), p. 70.

54. George Jackson, *Blood in My Eye* (New York, 1972), p. 84.

55. Ibid.

56. Angela Davis, *If They Come in the Morning: Voices of Resistance* (London, 1971), p. 89.

57. Caroline Cox, *Good Hair Days: A History of British Hairstyling* (London, 1999) p. 205.

58. Davis, *If They Come in the Morning*, p. 121.

59. Ibid., p. 132.

60. See Carol Tulloch, 'My Man, Let Me Pull Your Coat to Something: Malcolm X', in Stella Bruzzi and Pamela Church-Gibson (eds.), *Fashion Cultures* (London, 2000).

61. Davis, *If They Come in the Morning*, p. 63.

62. Sullivan, *Forlorn Hope*, p. 101.

63. Ibid., p. 106.

64. Ibid., p. 108.

65. David Ward, 'Sweden: The Middle Way to Prison Reform', in Marvin. E. Wolfgang (ed.), *Prisons Present and Possible* (New York, 1979), p. 122.

66. Sullivan, *Forlorn Hope*, p. 109.

67. Watterson, *Women in Prison*, p. 72.

68. Norman Mailer, *The Executioner's Song* (New York, 1979), p. 472.

69. Ibid., p. 673.

70. Ibid., p. 840.

71. Ibid., p. 987.

72. Watterson, *Women in Prison*, pp. 73–74.

73. Ibid., p. 80.

74. The Stanford experiment conducted by Phillip Zimbardo and Craig Haney, cited in Jennifer Wynn, *Inside Rikers Island: Stories from the World's Largest Penal Colony* (New York, 2002), p. 92.

75. Artur Zmijewski restaged the 'Stanford experiment' in Poland in a video piece entitled 'Repetition' (2005), where the guards and inmates negotiated a reasonable humane way out of a situation they could not tolerate. *Prison* Exhibition, Bloomberg Space, London, April 2007.

76. Sullivan, *Forlorn Hope*, p. 142.

5 consumption as redemption? Britain, 1950s to 1990s

1. In conversation with Erwin James, Hastings, December 2005.

2. See Christopher Sladen, *The Conscription of Fashion: Utility Cloth, Clothing and Footwear 1941–1952* (London, 1995); *Make Do and Mend* [Board of

Trade Pamphlet. Reprinted by the Imperial War Museum, 2002], (London, 1943); Judy Attfield (ed.), *Utility Reassessed: The Role of Ethics in the Practice of Design* (Manchester, 1999).

3. See Lou Taylor, 'Paris Couture 1940–1944', in Juliet Ash and Elizabeth Wilson (eds.), *Chic Thrills: A Fashion Reader* (London, 1992).

4. See Marjorie Beckett, 'Paris Forgets this is 1947', *Picture Post*, 27 September 1947, p. 220.

5. See Hilary Fawcett, 'Doon the Toon: Young Women, Fashion and Sexuality', in Cheryl Buckley and Hilary Fawcett, *Fashioning the Feminine: Representation and Women's Fashion from the Fin de Siecle to the Present* (London, 2002) and Christopher Breward, *Fashioning London: Clothing and the Modern Metropolis* (Oxford, 2004).

6. Matthews, *Doing Time,* pp. 83–128.

7. Ibid., p. 121.

8. See Jock Young, *The Exclusive Society* (London, 1999).

9. See Pat Carlen and Anne Worrall, *Analysing Women's Imprisonment* (Devon, 2004); Chris Hale and Steve Box, 'Liberation, Emancipation, Economic Marginalisation or Less Chivalry: The Relevance of Three Theoretical Arguments to Female Crime Patterns in England and Wales 1951–1980', *Criminology Journal,* 22 (1984), 473–498 and 'Economic Crisis and the Rising Prison Population in England and Wales, *Crime and Social Justice Journal,* 17 (1982), pp. 20–35.

10. Matthews, *Doing Time,* p. 117.

11. Prison Clothing Committee minutes, 1955–1959, National Archives, London, PCOM/1879.

12. Kitty Hauser, 'The Fingerprint of the Second Skin', in Christopher Breward and Caroline Evans (eds.), *Fashion and Modernity* (Oxford, 2005), p. 156.

13. In conversation with Ronan Bennett, September 2005, London.

14. In conversation with Erwin James, Hastings, December 2005.

15. National Archives, London, PCOM 9/1980.

16. Alan Sillitoe, *The Loneliness of the Long Distance Runner* (London, 1972), pp. 9–10.

17. In conversation with Erwin James, Hastings, December 2005.

18. Prison clothing from a number of British prisons has been collected centrally in the NCCL Galleries of Justice prison archive.

19. Anya Cronberg, MA History of Design RCA/V&A unpublished course essay on 'Prison Clothing', March 2005.

20. Goffman, *Asylums,* p. 271.

21. *Evening Standard,* 28 April 1972.

22. In one of the blouses in the Prison Clothing Archive is a 'Derita' label. Derita was a 1970s cheap high street outlet with a mail order component.

23. The 1970s saw some increase in the imprisonment of women, but progressively during the 1980s, 1990s and 2000s, the female prison population doubled year on year. Correspondingly, women's self-harm began to increase from the 1970s. See Carlen and Worrall, *Analysing Women's Imprisonment.*

24.   Helena Kennedy, *Eve Was Framed: Women and British Justice* (London, 1992), p. 19.

25.   In conversation with Erwin James, Hastings, December 2005.

26.   See Pastoureau, *The Devil's Cloth.*

27.   OZ magazine was part of the Underground press and the subject of an obscenity trial in 1971. The editors were acquitted on appeal after initially being found guilty and sentenced to harsh jail sentences.

28.   Richard Neville, *Hippie Hippie Shake: The Dreams, the Trips, the Trials, the Love-ins, the Screw-Ups: The Sixties* (London, 1995), p. 335.

29.   This shirt is in the NCCL Galleries of Justice Prison Clothing Archive.

30.   Buzz Aldrin was an American astronaut who piloted Apollo 11 for the first lunar landing in 1969. He was the second man to walk on the moon.

31.   In conversation with Erwin James, Hastings, December 2005.

32.   Stanley Cohen and Laurie Taylor, *Psychological Survival: The Experience of Long-term Imprisonment* (London, 1972), pp. 134–136.

33.   In conversation with Tom Clulee, London, July 2003.

34.   In conversation with Ronan Bennet, London, September 2005.

35.   Margaretta D'Arcy, *Tell Them Everything: Women in Armagh* (London, 1981), pp. 44–45.

36.   In conversation with Ronan Bennet, London, September 2005.

37.   Ibid.

38.   Louise Purbrick, 'The Architecture of Containment', in Donovan Wylie (ed.), *The Maze* (London, 2004), p. 101.

39.   In conversation with Ronan Bennet, London, September 2005.

40.   Email from Laura McAtackney, Researcher in the Archaeology Department of Bristol University who is doing research into the Maze prison, Ireland.

41.   D'Arcy, *Tell Them Everything*, p. 64.

42.   McKeown, *Out of Time,* p. 81.

43.   Questionnaire returned from the Northern Ireland Prison Service, 22 July 2005.

44.   Jimmy Boyle, *The Pain of Confinement: Prison Diaries* (Edinburgh, 1984), p. 5.

45.   Ibid., p. 35.

46.   Ibid., p. 272.

47.   Ibid., p. 280.

48.   Questionnaire, returned from Dr. Jim Carnie at the Scottish Prison Service, July 2005.

49.   Letter from Brian Quail to Barlinnie Prison Governor, April 2001, Trident Ploughshares website.

50.   Keith Hayward and Majid Yar, 'The Chav Phenomenon: Consumption, Media and the Construction of a New Underclass', *Crime, Media, Culture: An International Journal,* 2:1 (April 2006), 11.

51.   Facilities List, HMP Holloway Prison, Autumn 2006.

52.   Questionnaire and discussion with women prisoners in Holloway prison, London, December 2006.

53. Interview with the Head of Textiles and a designer at Prison Enterprises, London, 14 October 2005.

54. Ibid.

55. Ibid.

56. Ibid.

57. ANSA news agency report, UPI, 31 October 2006, http://web.lexis-nexis.com

58. Interview with the Head of Textiles and a designer at Prison Enterprises, London, 14 October 2005.

59. Ibid.

60. See Fine, 'Consumption through Systems of Provision', ch. 5, in *The World of Consumption*, for a detailed account of the historical complexity of 'systems of provision' and p. 98 specifically.

61. Interview with the Head of Textiles and a designer at Prison Enterprises, London, 14 October 2005.

62. Ibid.

63. Ibid.

64. In conversation with Erwin James, Hastings, December 2005.

65. In conversation with Jennifer Wolfenden, Holloway prison counsellor, 1994–2000, London, 13 January 2006.

66. 'Life in the Shadows: Women Lifers', Briefing paper, *The Howard League for Penal Reform* (1999), p. 13.

67. In conversation with the Resettlement Officer, Holloway prison, 3 August 2006.

68. In conversation with Holloway prison inmate, London, December 2006.

69. Questionnaire, followed by interviews in December 2006 in Holloway prison, London.

70. Ibid.

71. In conversation with Erwin James, Hastings, December 2005.

72. *Designs from Inside* is one of the organisations that runs art and design courses and projects inside and outside prisons for prisoners and ex-prisoners.

73. Syd Shelton brought a pair of these socks from America in 2007.

74. For example, an illustration of prisoners in broad arrow clothing, *The Guardian*, 7 December 2007, p. 41.

75. Julian Borger and Joe Jacobs, *The Guardian G2*, 17 June 2008, p. 2.

76. Mark Serwotka, General Secretary, Public and Commercial Services Union, in a Letter to *The Guardian*, 24 April 2007.

77. http://www.hmprisonservice.gov.uk/prisoninformation/privateprison. Sourced 1 January 2004.

78. Mark Serwotka, General Secretary, Public and Commercial Services Union, in a Letter to *The Guardian*, 24 April 2007.

79. Ann Owers, HM Chief Inspector of Prisons in a Report on Rye Hill Private Prison, cited in Nick Cohen, 'Drugs and Corruption Rife in Our Prisons', *The Observer*, 20 August 2006, p. 11.

80. Questionnaire response from Director, HMP Bronzefield Women's Private Prison, 23 April 2007; and Director, HMP Altcourse Men's Private Prison, 24 April 2007.

81. Matthews, *Doing Time,* p. 255.

82. See the Howard League for Penal Reform, 'Life in the Shadows: Women Lifers', Briefing Paper, 2006, p. 17. Also reports on prison conditions in Britain produced by Amnesty International, the Prison Reform Trust and the Government commissioned report on women in prison in Britain led by Baroness Corston (2007) that called for an end to women's imprisonment apart from the few women who were serious offenders.

6   contemporary prison clothing: inside turns out

1. Raphael Samuel, *Theatres of Memory:* vol. 1 *Past and Present in Contemporary Culture* (London, 1994), p. 8.

2. Cavadino and Dignan, *Penal Systems,* p. 4.

3. Brendan O'Friel, Governor Strangeways Prison, 1990, 'Strangeways Riot 1990', *BBC Radio Four,* 9.0 am, 2 May 2008.

4. Paul Taylor, 'Strangeways Riot 1990', BBC Radio 4, 9.0 am, 2 May 2008.

5. See Phillipe Sands, *Torture Team: Deception, Cruelty and the Compromise of Law* (London, 2008).

6. Clive Stafford Smith, *Bad Men: Guantánamo Bay and the Secret Prisons* (London, 2007), p. 37.

7. Dayna Curry and Heather Mercer, *Prisoners of Hope: The Story of Our Captivity and Freedom in Afghanistan* (London, 2002) p. 153.

8. Cavadino and Dignan, *Penal Systems,* p. 4.

9. See Lea's *Crime and Modernity,* and in conversation, 27 February 2007.

10. Questionnaire response from the Bundesministerium der Justiz, Berlin, 3 August 2005.

11. Swatches of the fabric for prison clothing were received from the Bundesministerium der Justiz.

12. Questionnaire response from the Bundesministerium der Justiz, Berlin, 3 August 2005.

13. Questionnaire response from Catherine Prade, Curator of La Musée National des Prisons, Fontainebleau, France, August 2005.

14. In 2008, France declared these titan prisons a failure and has stopped building them. http://prisons.free.fr/statistiques.htm, last accessed 10 January 2007.

15. Cavadino and Dignan, *Penal Systems,* p. 149.

16. Atwood, *Too Much Time,* 113.

17. 'Dutch Open Big Brother-style Prison', *The Guardian,* 19 January 2006, p. 19.

18. Foucault, *Discipline and Punish,* p. 217. See also Ursula Frohne, Thomas Lewin, and Peter Weibel (eds.), *Ctrl: State Rhetorics of Surveillance from Bentham to Big Brother* (New York, 2002).

19. Questionaire response from Michael Petras, Czech Prison Service, Department of Detention and Imprisonment, August 2005.

20. Paul M. Klenowski, 'Winds of Change: Democratic Reform in the Polish Prison System', *CT Journal* (December 2004), 4.

21. Michal Petras, Department of Detention and Imprisonment, Czech Prison Service, in questionnaire response, August 2005.

22. Laura Piacentini, *Surviving Russian Prisons: Punishment, Economy and Politics in Transition* (Portland, 2004), p. 147.

23. Ibid., p. 152.

24. Ibid., p. 136.

25. Ibid., p. 138.

26. Ibid., p. 137.

27. Ibid., p. 178.

28. Atwood, *Too Much Time*, p. 74.

29. Ibid.

30. Nelson Mandela, *Long Walk to Freedom*, Vol. 2, p. 3.

31. Ibid., p. 82.

32. Ibid., p. 32.

33. Ibid., p.4.

34. Geraldine Bedell, 'Sharp Focus: Feature on "Ghetto", a Book on Prison Cultures Around the World', *The Observer Magazine*, 27 July 2003, p. 38.

35. Ibid.

36. Piacentini, *Surviving Russian Prisons*, p. 154.

37. *New York Times* report on 'African Prisons', November 2005.

38. Rory Carroll, 'Bars, Brothels and a Regime of Terror – Inside the Jail run by its Inmates', *The Guardian*, 30 September 2006, p. 19.

39. Tom Phillips, 'Report on Sao Paulo Riots and Prisons', *The Observer* 17 September 2006, p. 27.

40. BBC News online, 29 June 2006.

41. Rory Carroll, 'Inside Story of a Regime of Terror', *The Guardian*, 28 December 2006, p. 23.

42. Email from a Cuban Professor of Design History, Lucila Fernandez, January 2007.

43. Email from Saxena, who works in prisons in Rajasthan forwarded by Lola Chatterji, who worked on a CHRI (Commonwealth Human Rights Initiative) manual for prison visitors in Delhi.

44. Ibid.

45. China Photos/Getty Images, http://images.google.co.uk (viewed 28 August 2008).

46. 'Mao Hengfeng Protests Abusive Confinement', 19 September 2007, http://www.hrichina.org (viewed 28 August 2008).

47. 'Women Start Life Anew in prison', Autumn in Huizhou, http://russian.china.org.cn (viewed 28 August 2008).

48. Azadeh Azad, 'Evin Prison: Female Inmates' Abysmal Conditions' in *Prisoners of 'Love'*, part 4, p. 3, www.iranian.com, visited 5 March 2007.

49. Eva E. Hanks, *Test of Faith: Hope, Courage and the Prison Experience (Toronto, 2002)*, p. 12.

50. Hugh Brodie, film director, *The Meaning of Life*, 2008.

51. See the International Centre for Prison Studies (Kings College London) at www.prisonstudies.org, last accessed 11 February 2007.

52. D. Brown, 'Penalty and Imprisonment in Australia', cited in Michael Cavadino and James Dignan, *Penal Systems*, p. 81.
53. See the 'Revised Standard Guidelines for Corrections in Australia' (2004).
54. Ibid.
55. King Gee 'utility pants' are produced by an Australian workwear company called Sears Workwear that has existed since 1926.
56. 'New Zealand Prisoner Markets "Convict" Clothing Line', Agence France Press – English, 29 September 2006.
57. A breakdown of American incarceration statistics shows that out of a prison population of 737 per 100,000 residents in 2005 there were 2531 blacks imprisoned per 100,000 residents; 393 whites and 957 Latinos. Statistics as of 30 June 2005 taken from 'Prison and Jail Inmates at Mid-year 2005, www.prisonsucks.com. Visited 4 March 2007.
58. Wynn, *Inside Rikers Island*, p. xiii.
59. Ibid., p. 2.
60. Ibid., p. 37.
61. Email correspondence with Michelle Brown, Criminologist researching into women's prisons at Ohio University, 2007.
62. Email from Marc Fischer, who had worked as a volunteer in a Maximum Security prison in Pittsburgh, 1 May 2006.
63. Ibid.
64. Ibid.
65. San Quentin inmate in Louis Theroux documentary, *Behind Bars*, BBC 2 TV, 13 January 2008.
66. Channel 5 UK TV documentary 'Lockdown', 3 February 2008.
67. Wynn, *Inside Rikers Island*, p. 46.
68. *London Lite*, Friday 13 October 2006, p. 6.
69. The Maricopa Sheriff's Office website, www.mcso.org. Visited 2 October 2005.
70. Sullivan, *Forlorn Hope*, p. 143.
71. The Maricopa Sheriff's Office website, www.mcso.org. Visited 2 October 2005.
72. Julian Borger and Joe Jackson, *The Guardian G2*, 17 June 2008, p. 2.
73. 'Arpaio Visits Wormwood Scrubs Prison', 'Today' programme, *Radio 4*, 2 September 2005.
74. 'Limitations on Inmate Personal Property', 553.11, *Code of Federal Regulations* (CFR), ch. 5 (7–1-05 Edition), p. 668.
75. See for example, 'California Inmate Catalog', www.jmarcuscatalog.com, last accessed 15 February 2007.
76. See www.prisonblues.com.
77. Linda White, 'Battered Women', *Concrete Garden: Women and the Criminal Justice System*, vol. 4 (1996), p. 203.
78. Atwood, *Too Much Time*, p. 108.
79. Earl Ofari Hutchinson, 'Why So Many Black Women Are Behind Bars', www.alternet.org/story/45149, accessed 5 December 2006.
80. Wynn, *Inside Rikers Island*, p. 4.

81. Robert 'King' Wilkerson in conversation, Royal College of Art, London, 20 June 2008.
82. Ibid.
83. See Agamben, *State of Exception*.
84. Begg, *Enemy Combatant*, p. 108.
85. Although not designed to look grotesque, the effect of the hood on the viewer is similar to that of the deliberately science-fiction-like design of the US Stealth fighter, Dr. Mark Dorrian, lecture on 'The Grotesque' at the Royal College of Art, February 2008.
86. Steven Morris and Audrey Gillan, 'Soldiers Cleared over ill-treatment of Iraqi Prisoners', *Guardian Newspaper*, 14 March 2007, p. 4.
87. Richard Norton, 'Officers in Quandary over legality of orders to 'condition' detainees', *Guardian Newspaper,* 14 March 2007, p. 4.
88. Gary Younge, *The Guardian*, 23 June 2008, p. 25.
89. Ken Kennard, 'A Contemporary Re-articulation of Power: United States Policy, 1776–1941', Paper given at the Society for Historians of American Foreign Relations (Shafr) Conference in Washington, June 2005.
90. See Clive Stafford Smith, *Bad Men.*
91. Ibid., p. 95.
92. Ibid., p. 101.
93. In the early days of Guantánamo it was said that the jumpsuits were made of heat-retaining polyester. Since then most jumpsuits are made of light weight cotton/synthetic mix fabric.
94. Clive Stafford Smith, *Bad Men,* p. 195.
95. Begg, *Enemy Combatant*, p. 191.

7 the view from outside/visions behind the bars

1. Jean Genet, *The Thief's Journal* (New York, 1964/1949), p. 244.
2. Jean Paul Sartre, Foreword, Jean Genet, *The Thief's Journal* (New York, 1964/1949), p. 2.
3. See Sean O'Sullivan and David Wilson, *Images of Incarceration: Representations of Prison in Film and Television Drama* (Winchester, 2004).
4. Erwin James, e-mail, 10 August 2008.
5. Maureen Chadwick, National Film Theatre series of prison film viewings, South Bank, London, March 2004.
6. Erwin James, *A Life Inside: A Prisoner's Notebook* (London, 2003), p. 74.
7. Amelia Gentleman, 'Shirts that Turn a Sentence into a Statement', *The Guardian,* 13 August 1998, p. 11.
8. Frederick Engels, 'Outlines of a Critique of Political Economy,' in *Karl Marx, Frederick Engels Collected Works,* vol. 3 (London, 1975), p. 442.
9. Peter Stallybrass, 'Marx's Coat', in Patricia Spyer (ed.), *Border Fetishisms: Material Objects in Unstable Spaces* (New York, 1998), p. 183.
10. Raphael Stopin and Michel Mallard, 'Fashion in the Mirror: Self Reflection in Fashion Photography', catalogue for an exhibition of fashion photography of this name, the Photographers' Gallery, 18 July–14 September 2008, p. 4.

11.   See *Vogue Italia*, no. 673, September 2006, pp. 525–554. I was not permitted to reproduce this fashion shoot. The reason given was that '*Vogue* did not want fashion to be associated with criminality', e-mail response to my request for picture permission from *Vogue Italia*, 11 July 2008.

12.   See Adrian Searle, Review of 'Fashion in the Mirror: Self Reflection in Fashion Photography', at the Photographers' Gallery, London, *The Guardian G2*, 22 July 2008, p. 25.

13.   Hadley Freeman, Report on the Autumn Fashion Shows 2006, *The Guardian*, 10 October 2006, p. 17.

14.   Susan Sontag, *Regarding the Pain of Others* (London, 2003), pp. 98–99, 102.

15.   Roland Barthes, 'Dominici, or The Triumph of Literature,' *Mythologies* (London, 1972) p. 46.

16.   Robert L. Johnson, 'Revolving Door', San Quentin, California, in Jeff Evans (ed.), *Undoing Time: American Prisoners in Their Own Words*, p. 88.

17.   Nawal El Saadawi, *Memoirs from the Women's Prison* (Berkeley, 1994), p. 24.

18.   Ibid., p. 50.

19.   Begg, *Enemy Combatant*, pp. 113–114.

20.   Ibid., pp. 190–191.

21.   John McVicar, *McVicar by Himself* (London, 1977), p. 39.

22.   El Saadawi, *Memoirs from the Women's Prison*, p. 51.

23.   Walter Probyn, *Angel Face: The Making of a Criminal* (London, 1977), p. 76.

24.   Evans, *Undoing Time*, p. 92.

25.   Questionnaire, Holloway prison, London, August 2006.

26.   Wynn, *Inside Rikers Island*, p. 143. For a more detailed account of gangs inside and outside American prisons, see Dave Brotherton, Luis Barrios and Louis Kontos (eds.), *Latin King and Queen Nation: Street Politics and the Social Transformation of a New York Gang*, (New York, 2006).

27.   James, *A Life Inside*, pp. 49, 74, 132

28.   Jonathan Aitken, *Porridge and Passion: An Autobiography* (London, 2005), p. 23 and Jeffrey Archer, *A Prison Diary* (London, 2004).

29.   James, 'A Life Inside', column, *The Guardian*, G2, 8 April 2004, p. 5.

30.   Begg, *Enemy Combatant*, p. 348.

31.   Genet, *The Thief's Journal*, p. 20.

32.   Kathy Boudin, 'Our Skirt', Bedford Hills Correctional Facility, New York, in Bell Gail Chevigny, *Doing Time: 25 Years of Prison Writing*, pp. 225–226.

33.   Judith Clarke, 'After My Arrest', Bedford Hills Correctional Facility, New York, Ibid., pp. 237–238.

34.   'The African Child', HMP Highpoint, 2005 Arthur Koestler Award winner, annual competition of Arts from UK prisons, 'Prose', (London, 2005), pp. 13–14.

35.   'Indelible Marks', HMP Cookham Wood, England, 2005 Arthur Koestler Award winner, annual competition of Arts from UK prisons, 'Prose' (London, 2005), pp. 27–30.

36.   Waterson, *Women in Prison*, p. 79.

37. See Goffman, *Asylums*.

38. Waterson, *Women in Prison,* p. 79.

39. Wynn, *Inside Rikers Island*, p. 46.

40. There are organisations around the world that give inmates the opportunity and skills to write and yet their work is not widely published. See the Koestler Trust in Britain and Temporary Services, Chicago, USA.

41. Michel Foucault, 'The Political Technology of Individuals', in Luther H. Martin, Huck Gutman and Patrick H. Hutton (eds.), *Technologies of the Self*, p. 146.

42. Jackie Ruzas, Sawangunk Correctional Facility, Wallkill, New York, in Bell Gail Chevigny, *Doing Time: 25 Years of Prison Writing*, p. xiii.

43. Alejo Dao'ud Rodriguez, Sing Sing Correctional Facility, Ossining, New York, Ibid.

44. Christopher Carrell and Joyce Laing (eds.), *The Special Unit: Barlinnie Prison: Its Evolution Through its Art* (Glasgow, 1982), p. 84.

45. Phyllis Kornfeld, *Cellblock Visions: Prison Art in America* (Princeton, 1997), p. 45.

46. Ibid. I was unable to obtain permission to reproduce this image since Phyllis Kornfeld wrote that Faruq Shabazz wishes to retain his own patent on his images, e-mail, 24 July 2008.

47. Ibid.

48. Art and Design organisations work in prisons on a non-profit-making basis. They teach creative skills and encourage prisoners to exhibit or publish work. See *Designs from Inside,* UK; *The Prisons Foundation* in America and the *Koestler Trust* in Britain. In America, Marc Fischer and Brett Bloom set up *Temporary Services*. They exhibit prisoners' work and published *Prisoners' Inventions* in conjunction with Whitewalls Press: see www.temporaryservices.org.

49. Angelo in *Prisoners' Inventions* (Chicago, 2005), pp. 57–58.

50. Dick Hebdige, 'Unimagining Utopia', Paper given at *The Second International Conference on Cultural Criminology*, the Goodenough College, London, 12 May 2006, elaborated on some of these themes.

select bibliography

5 Years Penal Solitude (By One Who Has Endured it) (London, 1878)

25 Years in 17 Prisons by No. 7 (The Life Story of an Ex-convict) (London, 1903)

Agamben, Giorgio, *Homo Sacer: Sovereign Power and Bare Life* (Stanford, 1998)

Agamben, Giorgio, *State of Exception* (Chicago, 2005)

Alexander, Sally, *Becoming a Woman: And Other Essays in 19th and 20th Century Feminist History* (London, 1995)

Anderson, Clare, *Legible Bodies: Race, Criminality and Colonialism in South East Asia* (Oxford, 2004)

Arendt, Hannah, *Eichmann and the Holocaust* (London, 2005)

Attfield, Judy (ed.), *Utility Reassessed: The Role of Ethics in the Practice of Design* (Manchester, 1999)

Atwood, Jane Evelyn, *Too Much Time: Women in Prison* (London, 2000)

Babington, Anthony, *The English Bastille: The History of Newgate Prison* (London, 1971)

Barrios, Luis, Dave Brotherton and Louis Kontos (eds.), *Latin King and Queen Nation: Street Politics and the Social Transformation of a New York Gang* (New York, 2006)

Barthes, Roland, *The Fashion System* (New York, 1983/1967)

Basset, Elizabeth, *Each in His Prison: An Anthology of Prison Writing* (Norwich, 1978)

Baxandall, Rosalyn, Linda Gordon and Susan Reverby (eds.), *America's Working Women: A Documentary History: 1600 to the Present* (New York, 1976)

Begg, Moazzam, *Enemy Combatant: A British Muslim's Journey to Guantánamo and Back* (London, 2006)

Benjamin, Walter, *The Arcades Project (*Harvard, 1999*)*

Bennett, Tony, *Culture: A Reformer's Science* (London, 1998)

Bentham, Jeremy, *The Principles of Morals and Legislation* in J.H. Burns and H.L.A Hart (eds.), 'Collected Works of Jeremy Bentham' (New York, 1988/1781)

Blank, Jessica and Erik Jensen, *The Exonerated (the Script)* (London, 2006)

Bone, Edith, *Seven Years of Solitary* (London, 1957)

Boyle, Jimmy, *The Pain of Confinement: Prison Diaries* (Edinburgh, 1984)

Bozovic, Miran (ed.), *Jeremy Bentham's Panopticon Writings* (London, 1995)

Brandon, David and Alan Brooke, *Bound for Botany Bay: British Convict Voyages to Australia* (National Archives, London, 2005)

Breward, Christopher, *The Hidden Consumer: Masculinities, Fashion and City Life 1860–1914* (Manchester, 1999)

Breward, Christopher and Caroline Evans, *Fashion and Modernity* (Oxford, 2005)

Brewer, John and John Styles (eds.), *An Ungovernable People: The English and Their Law in the Seventeenth and Eighteenth Centuries* (London, 1980)

Bright, Charles, *The Powers that Punish: Prison and Politics in the Era of the 'Big House' 1920–1952* (Michigan, 1996)

Britain, Victoria and Gillian Slovo, *Guantánamo: Honour Bound to Defend Freedom* (London, 2004)

Broadhead, Julian, *Unlocking the Prison Muse: The Inspirations and Effects of Prisoners' Writing in Britain* (Cambridge, 2006)

Brockway, Fenner and Stephen Hobhouse (eds.), *English Prisons Today: Being the Report of the Prison System Enquiry Committee* (London, 1922)

Bryan, Helen, *Inside* (New York, 1953)

Buckley, Cheryl and Hilary Fawcett, *Fashioning the Feminine: Representation and Women's Fashion from the Fin de Siecle to the Present* (London, 2002)

Burman, Barbara, *The Culture of Sewing: Gender, Consumption and Home Dressmaking* (Oxford, 2002)

Butler, Judith, *Precarious Life: The Powers of Mourning and Violence* (London, 2004)

Cannon, James P., *Notebook of an Agitator* (New York, 1958)

Carlen, Pat and Anne Worrall, *Analysing Women's Imprisonment* (Devon, 2004)

Carlyle, Thomas, 'The World in Clothes' in *Sartor Resartus* (1838) in Julian Symons (ed.), *Carlyle: Selected Works Reminiscences and Letters* (London, 1955/1838)

Carrell, Christopher and Joyce Laing, *The Special Unit: Barlinnie Prison: Its Evolution Through its Art* (Glasgow, 1982)

Cavadino, Michael and James Dignan, *Penal Systems: A Comparative Approach* (London, 2006)

Chevigny, Bell Gale (ed.), *Doing Time: 25 Years of Prison Writing* (New York, 1999)

Chomsky, Noam, *Failed States: The Abuse of Power and the Assault on Democracy* (New York, 2006)

Claudin, Fernando, *The Communist Movement: From Comintern to Cominform* (London, 1975)

Cleaver, Eldridge, *Post-prison Writings and Speeches* (London, 1971)

Cohen, Stanley and Laurie Taylor, *Psychological Survival: The Experience of Long-term Imprisonment* (London, 1972)

Cohen, Stanley and Laurie Taylor, *Prison Secrets* (London, 1976)

Concrete Garden Journal, 'Writings from Women in American Prisons and Criminal Justice Educators', vol. IV (Buffalo, Buffalo Group on Justice and Democracy, 1996)

Craik, Jennifer, *Uniforms Exposed: From Conformity to Transgression* (Oxford, 2005)

Curry, Dayna and Heather Mercer, *Prisoners of Hope: The Story of Our Captivity and Freedom in Afghanistan* (London, 2002)

Danner, Mark, *Torture and Truth: America, Abu Ghraib, and the War on Terror* (London, 2004)

D'Arcy, Margaretta, *Tell Them Everything: Women in Armagh* (London, 1981)

Davis, Angela, *If They Come in the Morning: Voices of Resistance* (London, 1971)

Dickens, Charles, *American Notes* (London, 1898)

Dickens, Charles, *Little Dorrit* (London, 1967)

Dostoevsky, Fyodor, *Crime and Punishment* (Oxford, 1998)

Dostoevsky, Fyodor, *The House of the Dead* (London, 2003)

D-S- Eighteen Months Imprisonment (London, 1883)

Ellis, Havelock, *The Criminal* (Boston, 1977/1890/1914)

Entwistle, Joanne and Elizabeth Wilson, *Body Dressing* (Oxford, 2001)

Evans, Robin, *The Fabrication of Virtue: English Prison Architecture: 1750–1840* (Cambridge, 1982)

Faith, Karlene (ed.), *Soledad Prison University of the Poor* (California, 1971)

Faubion, James D. (ed.), *Power: Essential Works of Michel Foucault 1954–1984*, vol. 3 (London, 2002)

Fine, Ben, *The World of Consumption: The Material and Cultural Revisited* (London, 2002)

Finzsch, Norbert and Robert Jutte (eds.), *Institutions of Confinement, Hospitals, Asylums and Prisons in Western Europe and North America 1500–1950* (Cambridge, 2003)

Fishman, William J., *East End 1888* (London, 1988)

Flynn, Elizabeth Gurley, *The Alderson Story: My Life as a Political Prisoner* (New York, 1963)

Foucault, Michel, *Discipline and Punish: The Birth of the Prison* (London, 1991)

Frohne, Ursula, Thomas Lewin and Peter Weibel (eds.), *Ctrl: State Rhetorics of Surveillance from Bentham to Big Brother* (New York, 2002)

Fry, Elizabeth, *Observations on Visiting, Superintending and Government of Female Prisons* (London, 1827)

Fussell, Paul, *Uniforms: Why We Are What We Wear* (Boston, 2002)

Gandhi, Mahatma, *Selected Political Writings* (Indiana, 1996)

Genet, Jean, *Our Lady of the Flowers* (London, 1966)

Genet, Jean, *The Thief's Journal* (New York, 1964)

Goffman, Erving, *Asylums: Essays on the Social Situation of Mental Patients and Other Inmates* (London, 1968)

Goffman, Erving, *The Presentation of Self in Everyday Life* (London, 1969)

Gonthier, David, *American Prison Film since 1930* (New Hampshire, 2006)

Gramsci, Antonio, *Selections from the Prison Notebooks* (London, 1971)

Gregory, Sandra, *Forget You Had a Daughter: Doing Time in the 'Bangkok Hilton'* (London, 2003)

Guerin, Daniel, *100 Years of Labor in the USA* (trans. Alan Adler) (London, 1979)

Hamilton, Peter and Roger Hargreaves, *The Beautiful and the Damned: The Creation of Identity in Nineteenth Century Photography* (London, 2001)

Hanks, Eva Evelyn, *Test of Faith: Hope, Courage and the Prison Experience* (Toronto, 2002)

Hayward-Burns, W., *The Voices of Negro Protest in America* (Oxford, 1963)

Hibbert, Christopher, *The Roots of Evil: A Social History of Crime and Punishment* (London, 1966)

Hobsbaum, Eric and Terence Ranger (eds.), *The Invention of Tradition* (Cambridge, 1992)

Howard, John, *Historical Remarks and Anecdotes on the Castle of the Bastille* (London, 1784)

Howard, John, 'An Account of the Present State of the Prisons and Houses of Correction',: *Introduction* (to all the following) *The Western Circuit* (1789); *The Midland Circuit* (1789); *London and Westminster* (1789); *Home Circuit* (1789); *The Midland Circuit* (1789)

Howard, John, 'A Visit to the Philadelphia Prison', *Charleston Daily Gazette* (Charleston, 1796)

Hughes, Robert, *The Fatal Shore: A History of the Transportation of Convicts to Australia 1787–1868* (London, 1988)

Humphries, Steve and Gavin Weightman, *The Making of Modern London 1815–1914* (London, 1983)

Ignatieff, Michael, *A Just Measure of Pain: The Penitentiary in the Industrial Revolution 1750–1850* (London, 1978)

Jackson, George, *Blood in My Eye* (New York, 1972)

Jacobs, Sunny, *Stolen Time: One Woman's Inspiring Story as an Innocent Condemned to Death* (London, 2007)

Jacobson, Michael, *Downsizing Prisons: How to Reduce Crime and End Mass Incarceration* (New York, 2005)

James, Cyril L.R., *The Black Jacobins: Toussaint L'Ouverture and the San Domingo Revolution* (London, 1963)

James, Erwin, *A Life Inside: A Prisoner's Notebook* (London, 2003)

James, Erwin, *The Home Stretch: From Prison to Parole* (London, 2005)

Jones, Steve, *Capital Punishments: Crime and Prison Conditions in Victorian Times* (Nottingham, 2003)

Joseph, Nathan, *Uniforms and Non-uniforms: Communication through Clothing* (New York, 1986)

Kennedy, Helena, *Eve Was Framed: Women and British Justice* (London, 1992)

Klungness, Elizabeth J., *Prisoners in Petticoats: The Yuma Territorial Prison and Its Women* (Arizona, 1993)

Knight, Etheridge, *Black Voices from Prison* (New York, 1970)

Koestler, Arthur, *Darkness at Noon* (New York, 1994/1940)

Kornfeld, Phyllis, *Cellblock Visions: Prison Art in America* (Princeton, 1997)

Kray, Reg, *Born Fighter* (London, 1990)

Kropotkin, Peter, *In Russian and French Prisons* [1905] (Montreal, 1991/1905)

Le Chene, Evelyn, *Mauthausen: The History of a Death Camp* (London, 1971)

Lea, John, *Crime and Modernity* (London, 2002)

Levi, Primo, *If This Is a Man* (London, 1987)

Lipovetsky, Gilles, *The Empire of Fashion: Dressing Modern Democracy* (Princeton, 1994)

Lyons, Lewis, *The History of Punishment* (London, 2003)

Mailer, Norman, *The Executioner's Song* (New York, 1979)

Mandela, Nelson, *The Road to Freedom* (London, 2006)

Martin, Luther, Huck Gutman and Patrick Hutton (eds.), *Technologies of the Self: A Seminar with Michel Foucault* (Massachusetts, 1988)

Marwick, Arthur, *Class: Image and Reality in Britain, France and the USA since 1930* (London, 1981)

Matthews, Roger, *Doing Time: An Introduction to the Sociology of Imprisonment* (London, 1999)

Mayhew, Henry and John Binney, *The Criminal Prisons of London* (London, 1971/1867)

Maynard, Margaret, *Fashioned from Penury: Dress as Cultural Practice in Colonial Australia* (Cambridge, 1994)

McCartney, Wilfred, *Walls Have Mouths* (London, 1936)

McKelvey, Blake, *American Prisons: A History of Good Intention* (New Jersey, 1977)

McKeown, Laurence, *Out of Time: Irish Republican Prisoners Long Kesh 1972–2000* (Belfast, 2001)

McKibbin, Ross, *Classes and Cultures: England 1918–1951* (Oxford, 1998)

McVeigh, Brian, *Wearing Ideology: State, Schooling and Self-presentation in Japan* (Oxford, 2000)

McVicar, John, *McVicar by Himself*, (London, 1979)

Milton, Nan, *John Maclean* (London, 1973)

Morash, Merry, *Understanding Gender, Crime and Justice* (London, 2006)

Morris, Norval and David J. Rothman (eds.), *The Oxford History of the Prison: The Practice of Punishment in Western Society* (Oxford, 1995)

Morris, Rosamund, *Prisons* (London, 1976)

Norfolk Prison Bothers (eds.), *Who Took the Weight: Black Voices from Norfolk Prison* (Elma Lewis School of Fine Arts, USA, 1972)

Norman, Frank, *Bang to Rights: An Account of Prison Life* (London, 1958)

Orland, Leonard, *Prisons: Houses of Darkness* (New York, 1978)

O'Sullivan, Sean and David Wilson, *Images of Incarceration: Representations of Prison in Film and Television Drama* (Winchester, 2004)

Pallasmaa, Juhani, *The Eyes of the Skin: Architecture and the Senses* (Chichester, 2005)

Pankhurst, E. Sylvia, *The Suffragette Movement: An Intimate Account of Persons and Ideals* (London, 1931)

Parkins, Wendy, *Fashioning the Body Politic* (Oxford, 2002)

Pastoureau, Michel, *The Devil's Cloth: A History of Stripes and Striped Fabric* (Columbia, 2001)

Pearson, John, *The Profession of Violence: The Rise and Fall of the Kray Twins* (St. Albans, 1973)

Piacentini, Laura, *Surviving Russian Prisons: Punishment, Economy and Politics in Transition* (Portland, 2004)

Pountain, Dick and David Robins, *Cool Rules: Anatomy of an Attitude* (London, 2000)

Priestley, Philip, *Victorian Prison Lives: English Prison Biography, 1830-1914* (London, 1999)

Probyn, Walter, *Angel Face: The Making of a Criminal* (London, 1977)

Reeve, Alan, *Notes from a Waiting Room: Anatomy of a Political Prisoner* (London, 1983)

Richards, Stephen C. and Ross, Jeffrey I., *Behind Bars: Surviving Prison* (Indianapolis, 2002)

Rinser, Louise, *Prison Journal* (London, 1987)

Rose, David, *Guantánamo: America's War on Human Rights* (London, 2004)

Rossa, Jeremiah O'Donovan, *Irish Rebels in English Prisons* (New York, 1967/1882)

Rowbotham, Sheila, *A Century of Women: The History of Women in Britain and the United States* (London, 1997)

Ruck, S.K. (ed.), *Paterson on Prisons* (London, 1951)

Sacco, Vincent F., *When Crime Waves* (London, 2005)

Samuel, Raphael, *Theatres of Memory: Past and Present in Contemporary Culture*, vol. 1 (London, 1994) and *Theatres of Memory: Island Stories Unravelling Britain*, vol. 2 (London, 1998)

Sanderson, Mary, *Journal* (London, 1817)

Sands, Phillipe, *Torture Team: Deception, Cruelty and the Compromise of Law* (London, 2008)

Schama, Simon, *Citizens: A Chronicle of the French Revolution* (London, 1989)

Schulberg, Budd (ed.), *From the Ashes: Voices of Watts* (The New American Library, 1967)

Seale, Bobby, *Seize the Time: The Story of the Black Panther Party* (London, 1970)

Serge, Victor, *The Case of Comrade Tulayev* (1948 in French; London, 1968)

Serge, Victor, *Men in Prison* (London, 1972)

Settle, Mary, *Prisons* (New York, 1987)

Sillitoe, Alan, *The Loneliness of the Long Distance Runner* (London, 1972)

Simmel, Georg, 'Fashion', *American Journal of Sociology,* Vol. 62.6: 541 (1957)

Sladen, Christopher, *The Conscription of Fashion: Utility Cloth, Clothing and Footwear 1941–1952* (London, 1995)

Smith, M. Hamblin, *Prisons and a Changing Civilisation* (London, 1934)

Solzhenitsyn, Aleksandr, *The Gulag Archipelago (1918–1956)* (London, 1974)

Sontag, Susan, *On Photography* (London, 1979)

Sontag, Susan, *Regarding the Pain of Others* (London, 2003)

Stafford-Smith, Clive, *Bad Men: Guantánamo Bay and the Secret Prisons* (London, 2007)

Stallybrass, Peter, 'Marx's Coat', in Patricia Spyer (ed.), *Border Fetishisms: Material Objects in Unstable Spaces* (New York, 1998)

Steedman, Carolyn, *Landscape for a Good Woman: A Story of Two Lives* (London, 1989)

Sullivan, Larry E., *Forlorn Hope: The Prison Reform Movement* (New York, 2002)

Sullivan, Larry E. (ed.), *Bandits and Bibles: Convict Literature in Nineteenth Century America* (New York, 2003)

Tagg, John, *The Burden of Representation: Essays on Photographies and Histories* (London, 1988)

Taylor, Lou, *The Study of Dress History* (Manchester, 2002)

Taylor, Lou, *Establishing Dress History* (Manchester, 2004)

Thompson, Edward P., *The Making of the English Working Class* (London, 1968)

Timilty, Joseph, *Prison Journal: An Irreverent Look at Life on the Inside* (Boston, 1997)

Veblen, Thorstein, *The Theory of the Leisure Class* (London, 1970/1899)

Voices for Freedom: An Amnesty International Anthology (London, 1986)

Wander, Fred, *The Seventh Well* (Berlin, 1976)

Waters, Sarah, *Affinity* (London, 2000)

Watterson, Kathryn, *Women in Prison* (Boston, 1996)

Webb, Sidney and Beatrice Webb, *English Prisons Under Local Government,* (special subscription edition, printed by the authors for subscribers, London, 1927)

Welch, Michael, *Ironies of Imprisonment* (London, 2005)

Wilde, Oscar, *De Profundis* (London, 1911/1905)

Wildeblood, Peter, *Against the Law* (London, 1957)

Wilson, Elizabeth, *Adorned in Dreams: Fashion and Modernity* (London, 1985)

Wolfgang, Marvin E. (ed.), *Prisons Present and Possible* (Pennsylvania, 1979)

Wylie, Donovan (ed.), *The Maze* (London, 2004)

Wynn, Jennifer, *Inside Rikers Island: Stories from the World's Largest Penal Colony* (New York, 2002)

Young, Jock, *The Exclusive Society* (London, 1999)

Young, Jock, *The Vertigo of Late Modernity* (London, 2007)

index